# SICILY FROM AENEAS TO AUGUSTUS

NEW PERSPECTIVES ON THE ANCIENT WORLD

General Editors
Roger Green, *University of Glasgow*
Christopher Smith, *University of St Andrews*
Karen Stears, *University of Edinburgh*

*Published*
1
*Sicily from Aeneas to Augustus*
*New Approaches in Archaeology and History*
edited by Christopher Smith and John Serrati

2
*Religion in Archaic and Republican Rome and Italy*
*Evidence and Experience*
edited by Edward Bispham and Christopher Smith

# SICILY FROM AENEAS TO AUGUSTUS

## New Approaches in Archaeology and History

Edited by
Christopher Smith and John Serrati

Edinburgh University Press

930.1
Sic

Edinburgh University Press Ltd
22 George Square, Edinburgh

Typeset in Times
by Norman Tilley Graphics, Northampton
and printed and bound in Great Britain
by The University Press, Cambridge

A CIP record for this book is available from the British Library

ISBN 0 7486 1367 6 (hardback)
ISBN 0 7486 1366 8 (paperback)

# CONTENTS

# PREFACE

This volume reflects the proceedings of a conference held in St Andrews in June 1998. The editors wish to thank the Classical Association of Scotland and the School of Greek, Latin and Ancient History for generous financial support. Mrs B. Fleming provided the lunches with customary efficiency and good humour. Many colleagues were generous with their hospitality, and also helped by chairing sessions. We owe a particular debt of gratitude to Jennifer Barringer for assistance with the bibliography, and to Professor H. M. Hine for generously supporting the conference, and for providing a computer during the editing process.

The editors also wish to thank the contributors for their support and patience, and all those who attended the conference for making it such a memorable occasion. Finally we would like to thank John Davey of Edinburgh University Press for patiently steering the volume through to publication.

Christopher Smith
John Serrati
*University of St Andrews*

# LIST OF CONTRIBUTORS

**Dr Giovanna Ceserani** is a Postdoctoral Fellow in the Princeton Society of Fellows in the Liberal Arts, University of Princeton.

**Dr Thomas Harrison** is a Lecturer in Ancient History in the School of Greek, Latin and Ancient History, University of St Andrews.

**Dr Tamar Hodos** is a Lecturer in the Department of Archaeology, University of Bristol.

**Dr Robert Leighton** is a Research Fellow in the Department of Archaeology, University of Edinburgh.

**Dr Sian Lewis** is a Lecturer in Ancient History in the School of History and Archaeology, University of Cardiff.

**Dr Kathryn Lomas** is a Lecturer in Ancient History in the Department of Classics, University of Newcastle upon Tyne.

**Dr N. K. Rutter** is a Reader in the Department of Classics, University of Edinburgh.

**Mr John Serrati** is a Teaching Fellow in the School of Greek, Latin and Ancient History, University of St Andrews.

**Dr Gillian Shepherd** is a Lecturer in Classical Archaeology in the Department of Ancient History and Archaeology, University of Birmingham.

**Dr Christopher Smith** is a Senior Lecturer in Ancient History in the School of Greek, Latin and Ancient History, University of St Andrews.

**Professor R. J. A. Wilson** is Professor of Archaeology in the Department of Archaeology, University of Nottingham.

# LIST OF ABBREVIATIONS

## AUTHORS

| | |
|---|---|
| A. | Aeschylus |
| *Pers.* | *Persians* |
| Apollod. | Apollodorus |
| App. | Appian |
| *Sic.* | *Sicilica* |
| Apul. | Apuleius |
| *Met.* | *Metamorphoses* |
| Ar. | Aristophanes |
| A.R. | Apollonius of Rhodes |
| Archimel. | Archimelus |
| Arist. | Aristotle |
| *Ath. Pol.* | *Athenaion Politeia* |
| *Pol.* | *Politics* |
| Asc. | Asconius |
| Ath. | Athenaeus |
| Auct. | Auctor Ignotus (Anonymous) |
| *De Vir. Ill.* | *De Viris Illustribus* |
| Cic. | Cicero |
| *Arch.* | *Pro Archia* |
| *Balb.* | *Pro Balbo* |
| *Caec.* | *Pro Caecina* |
| *Div.* | *De Divinatio* |
| *Man.* | *Pro Lege Manilia* |
| *Pis.* | *In Pisonem* |
| *Planc.* | *Pro Plancio* |
| *Verr.* | *Verrines* |
| D.Chr. | Dio Chrysostomus |
| D.H. | Dionysius of Halicarnassus |
| D.S. | Diodorus Sicilus |
| Eutrop. | Eutropius |

| | |
|---|---|
| Fest. | Festus |
| Gel. | Aulus Gellius |
| Hdt. | Herodotus |
| Liv. | Livy |
| *Per.* | *Periocha* |
| Mosch. | Moschus |
| Naev. | Naevius |
| *Poen.* | *Bellum Poenicum* |
| Nep. | Cornelius Nepos |
| *Han.* | *Hannibal* |
| Oros. | Orosius |
| Paus. | Pausanius |
| Philist. | Philistus |
| Philostr. | Philostratus |
| *Vit. Apoll.* | *Vita Apollonii* |
| Pi. | Pindar |
| *Nem.* | *Nemean Odes* |
| *Ol.* | *Olympic Odes* |
| *Pyth.* | *Pythian Odes* |
| Pl. | Plautus |
| *Capt.* | *Captivi* |
| *Mil.* | *Miles Gloriosus* |
| *Trin.* | *Trinummus* |
| Plb. | Polybius |
| Plut. | Plutarch |
| *Alc.* | *Alcibiades* |
| *Dion.* | *Dionysius* |
| *Marc.* | *Marcellus* |
| *Mor.* | *Moralia* |
| *Nic.* | *Nicias* |
| *Tim.* | *Timoleon* |
| Polyaen. | Polyaenus |
| Schol. Aesch. | Scholia to Aeschines |
| Sil. Ital. | Silius Italicus |
| Sol. | Solinus |
| Strab. | Strabo |
| Suet. | Suetonius |
| *Aug.* | *Augustus* |
| *Cal.* | *Caligula* |
| *Claud.* | *Claudius* |
| Tac. | Tacitus |
| *Ann.* | *Annales* |
| Thuc. | Thucydides |

| | |
|---|---|
| Val. Max. | Valerius Maximus |
| Var. | Varro |
| L. | *De Lingua Latina* |
| Xen. | Xenophon |
| Ath. Pol. | *Athenaion Politaea* |
| Zonar. | Zonaras |

## COLLECTIONS AND PERIODICALS

| | |
|---|---|
| *ABAW* | *Abhandlungen der Bayerischen Akademie der Wissenschaften* |
| *Act. Tr.* | A. Degrassi, *Acta Triumphales*, in *Inscriptiones Italiae*, XIII. 1 |
| *AE* | *L'Année Épigraphique* |
| *AHB* | *Ancient History Bulletin* |
| *AION ArchStAnt* | *Annali Istituto Orientale di Napoli: Archeologia e Storia Antica* |
| *AJA* | *American Journal of Archaeology* |
| *AJPh* | *American Journal of Philology* |
| *ANSMusN* | *American Numismatic Society. Museum Notes* |
| *ASNP* | *Annali della Scuola Normale Superiore di Pisa* |
| *BICS* | *Bulletin of the Institute of Classical Studies* |
| *BPI* | *Bulletino di Paletnologia Italiana* |
| *BTCGI* | *Bibliographia Topographia della Colonizzazione Greca in Italia e nelle Isole Terreniche* |
| *CAH*² | *Cambridge Ancient History*, second edition |
| *CAJ* | *Cambridge Archaeological Journal* |
| *CÉFAR* | *Collections de l'École Français de Rome* |
| *CIL* | *Corpus Inscripionum Latinarum* |
| *CPh* | *Classical Philology* |
| *CQ* | *Classical Quarterly* |
| *Dd'A* | *Dialoghi di Archeologia* |
| *DHA* | *Diologues d'Histoire Ancienne* |
| *ESAR* | T. Frank (ed.), *An Economic Survey of Ancient Rome* |
| *FGH* | F. Jacoby, *Fragmente der Griechischen Historiker* |
| *IG* | *Inscriptiones Graecae* |
| *IGCH* | M. Thompson, O. Mørkholm and C. M. Kraay (eds), *An Inventory of Greek Coin Hoards* |
| *JHS* | *Journal of Hellenic Studies* |
| *JRS* | *Journal of Roman Studies* |
| *LC* | *Lindian Chronicle* |
| *LIMC* | *Lexicon Iconographicum Mythologiae Classicae* |

| | |
|---|---|
| *MDAI(R)* | *Mitteilungen des deutschen archäologischen Instituts. Romische Abeilung* |
| *MEFRA* | *Mélanges de l'École Français de Rome* |
| *MRR* | T. R. S. Broughton, *The Magistrates of the Roman Republic* |
| *NSc* | *Notizie degli Scavi di Antichità* |
| *OCD*[3] | S. Hornblower and A. Spawforth (eds), *The Oxford Classical Dictionary*, third edition |
| *OGIS* | *Orientis Graeci Inscriptiones Selectae* |
| *OJA* | *Oxford Journal of Archaeology* |
| *PBSR* | *Papers of the British School at Rome* |
| *PCPS* | *Proceedings of the Cambridge Philological Society* |
| *QuadMess* | *Quaderni dell'Istituto di Archeologia dell'Università di Messina* |
| *RBN* | *Revue Belge de Numismatique et de Sigillographie* |
| *RC* | C. B. Welles, *Royal Correspondence in the Hellenistic World* |
| *RE* | A. Pauly, G. Wissowa and W. Kroll (eds), *Real-Encyclopädie der klassischen Altertumswissenschaft* |
| *REA* | *Revue des Études Anciennes* |
| *REG* | *Revue des Études Grec* |
| *RevArch* | *Revue Archeologique* |
| *RIA* | *Rivista dell'Istituto Nazionale di Archeologia e Storia dell'Arte* |
| *RSA* | *Revista Storica dell'Antichità* |
| *SEG* | *Supplementum Epigraphicum Graecum* |
| *SHA* | *Scriptores Historiae Augustae* |
| *SIG* | *Sylloge Inscriptionum Graecarum* |
| *SicArch* | *Sicilia Archeologia* |
| *SNG* ANS | *Sylloge Nummorum Graecorum*, American Numismatic Society |
| *TAPhA* | *Transactions of the American Philological Association* |
| *ZPE* | *Zeitschrift für Papyrologie und Epigraphik* |

# LIST OF FIGURES

# 1

# INTRODUCTION

## *Christopher Smith*

THE GREAT NINETEENTH-CENTURY scholar and historian Edward A. Freeman summed up the peculiar nature of Sicily as well as anyone in the introduction to his monumental history of the island:

> In the view of universal history, the island of Sicily, the greatest of Medi-terranean islands, had a special calling laid upon it by its geographical position. Placed in the midst of the great inland sea, it is indeed in some sort an appendage to the central peninsula of Southern Europe; but it is some-thing more. It is something more in its geography; it is something more in its history. It is a breakwater between the eastern and western divisions of the Mediterranean; it parts the waters that wash the coasts of Spain and Gaul from the waters that wash the coast of Greece and Asia .... It parts, and at the same time it brings together, Europe and Africa, Eastern and Western Europe.

It was a place which was 'called to be ... the meeting place of the nations' (Freeman 1891: 1, 3).

It is interesting to remember that Freeman's intention in writing the history of Sicily was in fact to write a sort of history of Europe, for he is anxious to tell us throughout the first chapter that he always had the Norman conquest of the island in mind ('we cannot give their full historical significance to Pyrrhos and Timoleôn without looking forward to Roger and William the Good', Freeman 1891: 44), and that the island was the crucial scene for the struggle between east and west ('From Theoklês to Frederick there is an unbroken story', Freeman 1891: 48). This volume does not attempt so large an undertaking, but in its way reflects the same concern with the central issues of the experience of Sicily at the crossroads of the Mediterranean.

Throughout the first half, the Odyssean half, of Virgil's *Aeneid*, Sicily is present. Aeneas lands there first in Book 3, and his father Anchises dies at Drepana, before, in chronological terms, he is blown off course to Carthage, where he meets the Phoenician queen Dido, and the seeds are sown for the hatred between Rome and its Punic neighbour. He returns to

1

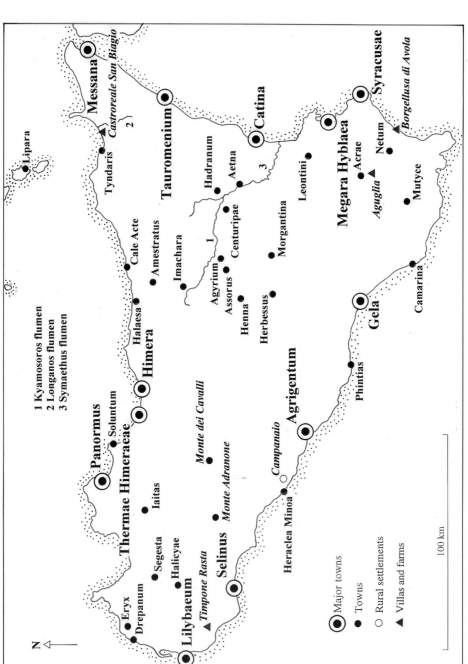

*Fig. 1.1* Map of Sicily (R. J. A. Wilson)

Sicily in Book 5 after leaving Dido to celebrate games at Segesta on the anniversary of his father's death, games which are full of strange foreshadowings of future Roman history, as when the unsuccessful Sergius, ancestor of the revolutionary L. Sergius Catalina of 63 BC, wrecks his boat. At the end the death of Palinurus, modelled on the death of Elpenor in the *Odyssey*, looks forward to Aeneas' descent to the underworld in Book 6. Nothing is concluded in Book 5, though much is hinted at; it is as though the games represent the ludic preliminaries to the more serious business that will come when Aeneas lands in Italy (Feldherr 1995).

This seems an appropriate way of approaching our subject, because the 'incompletion' of Sicily is part of its interest and importance. Sicily is always in the making, looking to its past and its future at the same time, and much recent scholarship of other places and periods has highlighted the relevance of the construction of identity in an age that is struggling with nationalism (see Colley 1992, for instance). Throughout this volume, local self-definition is a key issue; all of the chapters touch in one way or another on the ways in which Sicilians presented themselves at a given point in time, and there is a sense of experimentation and inventiveness that is inspiring as we face the challenge of inventing positive identities in a new age, and also instructive for other case studies in antiquity.

As we have already seen, Sicily occupies a central and crucial position in the Mediterranean world; it is an island at the heart of the many cross-currents of trade, people and ideology that flowed unceasingly through the ancient period. This makes any evidence from Sicily interesting as a test case for our views of the models of change, adaptation, acculturation and identity that currently dominate many areas of research into antiquity. Sicily was home to many peoples, most of them not originally from the island; Phoenicians, Greeks and then Romans made a home there, and sought ways of expressing their hybrid identities. Many people observed Sicily in antiquity; no less than mainland Greeks, or the Romans, the Sicilians were concerned with their image and their distinctive contribution to the achievements of the age. Between image and reality, there is room for a scholarly debate of the interpenetration of the two, the ways in which Sicily became its image, shaped its realities, and was situated in art and literature 'in between' – a place in which different worlds met and were recreated.

In this volume, ideas of identity, image and acculturation are central themes, and the contributions combine both the detailed investigation of the archaeological finds in which the island abounds, and also the profoundly interesting and understudied tradition of history and literature on and about the island. The aim of the volume is to provide both a diachronic account of the island's history, as far as possible, through Serrati's summaries (Chapters 2 and 9), and also a series of discussions on the nature of Sicilian identity; to show Sicily at the centre of affairs from the Iron Age through to the beginning of the Roman empire, a centrality achieved in part by being on the edge, on the outside of what were canonically the most important, the most privileged arenas of antiquity.

Chapters 2, 3 and 4 form a section on the archaic period, focusing in different ways on the evolution of society among the native Sicilians, and the incoming Greeks. Leighton (Chapter 3) and Hodos (Chapter 4) deal directly with the difficulties of assessing local traditions from the archaeological record, and of isolating the subtle distinction between the conscious choice to adopt and adapt, and the consciously imposed necessity to adapt and disappear. This deeply controversial question for Sicily is also key for the interpretation of many other areas and relationships in the ancient world, and therefore has a much wider methodological significance. Shepherd (Chapter 5), by focusing on religion as part of the relationship between colonies and mother-cities, and reinterpreting the evidence as indicative of an arrangement which was used by the colonies and part of the range of choices they had about their loyalties, reminds us that the Greeks who went to Sicily were to some extent moving away from mainland Greek concerns, and that there can be no straight interchange between 'native' and 'Greek' when the Greekness of the colonies, the ways they express it, and the goals for which they use it were from an early period aspects of an evolving identity. Shepherd's conclusion also warns us not to overlook the possibilities for defiance and resistance within what have been seen as one-sided power relationships; in a sense it is the colonies who are in control of the relationship with their mother-city, and who have transformed their earlier dependence.

The creation of an identity, and the way that identity related to the actualities of ancient Sicily, are also issues in the next section on classical Sicily. In his detailed analysis of Sicilian numismatics, Rutter demonstrates the ways in which, through an extremely subtle and sophisticated employment of iconography and symbolism on coinage, the Sicilians developed a medium of exchange in a literal sense into a medium of metaphorical and ideological exchange, to pass on complex information about themselves. The match between the coinage and the poetry of Pindar is extremely important; Leslie Kurke (1991) has written of the 'traffic in praise' and Sitta von Reden (1995) has recently explored further issues of parallelism between the reciprocities of economic and literary activity. We are reminded of the significance of Sicily within the wider Greek context – of its place within larger currents of history, and not simply as a periphery.

Harrison (Chapter 7) and Lewis (Chapter 8) consider the construction of Sicily as somehow different from a mainland Greek norm. Lewis looks at the persistence of tyranny in Sicily after it had become a largely discredited political form elsewhere. Here again, Sicilian Greeks make virtues of their difference in the way that figures like Hieron and Dionysius I adapt the more favourable aspects of the tradition on tyrants for their own purposes, whilst for outsiders, the Sicilian tyrants become exemplars of the worst aspects of despotic rule, and in some way shape accounts of earlier tyrants, thus influencing the historical tradition about figures whom they had to a degree emulated. Harrison explores another aspect of this historiographical reciprocity through the parallelism between Herodotus' account of the Persian Wars, and Thucydides' version of the Sicilian expedition. This was more than a simple exercise in literary borrowing; it reflects deep issues about the ways in which both authors viewed events of the past and present. Taken together with Lewis's demonstration of the fertility of the Sicilian imagination, Harrison's parallels may also indicate the development of analogous thinking in Sicily about their position in the larger scheme of world history, encouraged by the conflict with Carthage.

In the last section, the impact of the Romans is discussed. Serrati (Chapters 9 and 10) examines the contribution of Sicily to Roman efforts to defeat Carthage, particularly in terms of the Roman exploitation of Sicilian agriculture. There can be no doubt that as Rome's first province, Sicily was also a tremendous learning experience for the Romans, and thus helped create some of the abiding patterns of Roman imperialism. Again, the relationship is complex. Wilson (Chapter 11) re-examines the evidence from the first century BC. If one were to believe Cicero's denunciation of Verres for ruining the province, one would not expect to see the wealth and prosperity which the archaeological record reveals. Image and reality are at odds; the image, developed for a Roman audience, is an almost purely rhetorical one, but works to the advantage of the provincials as well as the prosecutor. Lomas (Chapter 12) looks ahead; under the Roman empire, the Sicilians reshape their identity again, and repeatedly, to relocate themselves within the cultural politics of the time. Epigraphic and archaeological evidence reveal the curiously hybrid outcomes.

The last chapter, which serves as a coda to the volume, is an account of the way that the identity of Sicily has been perceived and described in scholarship from the sixteenth century onwards. Ceserani (Chapter 13) reveals that modern scholarship constructed Sicily as a centre of debate from the beginning, its identity related in problematic ways to its history of invasion and displacement. It was precisely the boundedness of Sicily as an island that encouraged attempts to fix an identity, which in fact was permanently changing because of the permeability of those boundaries. Sicily the island and Sicily the crossroads are one and the same, and modern scholarship developed from the outset this dichotomy of attention. Within this volume the focus is constantly shifting from local initiative to external pressure, preserving and extending the dialectic.

Much previous debate on the ancient world has developed the model of core and periphery. This volume as a whole pushes to the fore the idea that the ancient world was fundamentally regional. There were too many centres and peripheries, and relationships were far too multiple and disparate, to allow simple dualisms. Sicily itself cannot readily be constructed as either central or peripheral; rather it was and must still be viewed through its relationships with other parts of the classical world, and through the choices made by individuals and states as to how they wished to be seen. Taken as a whole, the arguments presented here suggest that one cannot privilege the *longue durée* over microhistory, or economic structure over individual choice, but that one must develop a more complex engagement with the island's history, continuing the tradition of the historians with whom Ceserani ends. Sicily – and its many different inhabitants – then offer us the challenge of identifying and valuing individual choice within the grander forces of history, a challenge that brings us back to the recognition of the vital relevance of the history of Sicily as a case study for ancient history, and much more besides.

# Part I

# SICILY AND COLONISATION

# 2

# SICILY FROM PRE-GREEK TIMES TO THE FOURTH CENTURY

## *John Serrati*

The Trojans … came in boats to Sicily, and settling on the borders of the Sikans, they were called, as a people, Elymians. The Sikels, again, fleeing from the Opicans, crossed over from Italy, which was their home, to Sicily. Even now there are still Sikels in Italy; and the land was named Italy after Italus, a Sikel king. These crossed over to Sicily in great numbers, and, upon conquering the Sikans in battle, they pushed them into the southern and western parts of the island, thus it came to be called Sikilia instead of Sikania. The Sikels settled there after they had crossed from Italy, and occupied the most fertile lands for nearly three hundred years before the Hellenes came to Sicily.

(Thuc. 6. 2. 3–5, quoting Antiochos of Syracuse)

THE BELIEF OF THUCYDIDES that pre-Greek Sicily was divided among three peoples – the Sikels in the east; the Sikans in central Sicily; and the Elymians in west – was shared by most ancient writers. The fifth-century logographer Hellanicus of Lesbos also considered the Elymians to be of Trojan descent, coming to Italy as part of the Sikel migration that had begun around 'the third generation before the Trojan War' (*ap*. D.H. 1. 22. 1–3). However, in terms of archaeology there appears to be very little cultural difference between the indigenes of the island, thus blurring any rigorous ethnic divides. Finds of native writing, using Greek characters, on potsherds would appear to demonstrate that the early inhabitants of Sicily spoke an Indo-European dialect, but the evidence is in no way conclusive. Italians are materially present in Sicily from the eleventh century, mostly in the northeast. These people, along with those of the Ausonian culture of the Aeolic Islands, are known to have traded heavily with Italy, and links have been revealed with Italian culture as far north as the Apennines.

Settlement evidence has been found on Sicily dating back to the Palaeolithic period, and the island shared in the agricultural revolution in the Neolithic Age from the sixth millennium BC. The Copper Age is well represented on the island with pottery, metal ware, and burials in rock-cut chamber-tombs. The Bronze Age began in Sicily about 1800. By all accounts, the island had always possessed a highly rich soil base, giving the early inhabitants a healthy source of food and abundant material with which to establish early overseas trade links. From 1600 Greek goods begin to become visible in the Aeolic Islands and within two centuries they had penetrated into Sicily in growing numbers. Mycenaean ware is found in Sicily over the next few centuries, and there also seems to have been a prosperous trade with both Cyprus and Rhodes. The native cultures of Sicily in the latter half of the second millennium were, at least economically, firmly part of the Mycenaean Greek world. This contributed largely to what archaeologists have termed the first 'proto-urban' settlements that sprang up at this time. By the eleventh century, the upheavals in Greece that brought about the end of Mycenaean culture had shifted the emphasis in Sicily back to the western sphere. The island was now economically and culturally closer to Italy. This continued until the coming of the Phoenicians and Greeks in the eighth century. And the latter contact would, in the coming centuries, transform and eventually absorb the native cultures of Sicily (Leighton 1999).

In 734 a group of colonists from Chalkhidia founded the first Greek settlement on Sicily at Naxos, on the east coast. From this point onwards, the landscape of Sicily would be changed forever. The island, or at least the eastern and southern coasts, was now clearly a part of the Greek world; and materially, culturally and linguistically Sicily began more and more to look towards the eastern Mediterranean. Over the next century and a half, the Greeks would come in significant numbers, and establish a series of colonies, including Syracuse (733), Zankle (Messana) (730), Catania (729), Gela (688), Selinus (628) and Akragas (Agrigentum) (580).

This had a drastic effect on the native inhabitants of the island. Many were driven from their lands, while those who remained were often forced to become subservient to the new Greek overlords. However, on at least one occasion, at Leontini, founded in 729, there appears to have been a peaceful co-operation between colonists and natives. Once the Greeks had firmly established themselves, however, the processes of cultural amalgamation of the indigenous population took place with alacrity. Only in the interior did native culture, and presumably language, remain; material remains demonstrate that many local native traditions did in fact survive well into the sixth century.

The Greeks had settled on Sicily in such large numbers for one main reason – the richness of the island's soil. They immediately began to exploit the agricultural productivity of Sicily, especially with the growing of grain. This crop was traded with the Greek east in abundance, as the substantial presence of Corinthian, Laconian and Attic ware illustrates. Large markets were also to be found in Africa, southern Italy, Campania and, from the late sixth century, Rome. Just as Europeans of the sixteenth to eighteenth centuries saw the Americas, Sicily to the Greeks was a vast, largely untapped resource filled with abundant land. The aforementioned trade brought wealth to the colonies at an early stage; coinage was introduced, and rapid urbanisation and great construction projects occurred from the early seventh century onwards.

In the west of the island, the Phoenicians had first established themselves at Motya in the late eighth century. Other early settlements included Panormus and Soluntum (Soloeis). However, these were primarily trading *emporia*, and at first posed little threat to the Greeks on the other half of the island. But by the sixth century the Phoenicians had been assimilated into the Persian empire; their western possessions, most notably Carthage, had gradually become independent; and many of the old trading centres had developed into cities in their own right. Gradually, Carthage asserted its control over the Phoenician settlements in Sicily, and used them to guard its trade hegemony on the western Mediterranean. Carthage concluded treaties with various states that either forbid or restricted trade with the Punic cities of western Sicily (our best example of such a treaty comes from the pact between Carthage and Rome concluded in 508 and recorded in Plb. 3. 22–3). Carthaginian strength in Sicily centred on the island of Motya off the west coast, whose settlement had been founded in the eighth century and was now home to a significant Punic population.

The sixth century brought with it the first of several violent clashes between the Greeks and the Carthaginians over Sicily. These clashes were a contributory factor in the rise of tyranny in the Sicilian Greek states. The fighting with Carthage brought with it internal stasis and often led to the rise of a *strategos autokrator*, a general with exceptional powers. The road to tyranny for these generalissimos was a short one. Hippocrates (498–491) of Gela was the first of several great Sicilian tyrants; in just seven years he carved out an empire for himself that incorporated most of southeast Sicily and stretched as far north as Naxos. He was succeeded by Gelon (491–477), who expanded the empire and managed to take Syracuse in 485, making it his new capital. These early tyrants were also engaged in the forcible migration of Sicilian citizens within their realm. One of the largest movements came when Gelon transferred half the population of Gela to Syracuse. This action marked out Syracuse as the new centre of Greek power in Sicily, while at the same time it greatly diminished the prestige of Gela, which ceased to play a major role in the island's affairs.

Gelon was arguably the strongest ruler in the Greek world at this time. He vigorously challenged the Carthaginians for control of Sicily. Realising the military potential that might come from Sicily, King Xerxes of Persia, who was about to invade mainland Greece, asked the Carthaginians to attack Greeks of the island. The Punic government needed little persuading to continue the struggle, and a major Punic force landed in 481. This was met the following year by Gelon at Himera, where the tyrant decisively defeated the Carthaginians, supposedly on the same day as the Greek stand at Thermopylae (D.S. 11. 24. 1). Gelon now established himself as warlord of all Sicily, though in the end he was unable to drive the Carthaginians completely from the island.

The victory precipitated a time of relative peace on Sicily, and in this period classical Greek culture reached its zenith on the island. This epoch saw the greatest penetration of hellenism within the Punic west and the native communities. The peace was interrupted in 466 by the largest and longest rebellion by native forces opposed to Greek rule. The fight centred on the person of Ducetius, a hellenised Sikel leader who pursued a policy of capturing Greek cities and expelling colonists. In 453 he founded the Sikel League and in 451 inflicted a major defeat on the combined forces of Akragas and Syracuse. However, in the following year he was beaten on the battlefield, and his support quickly fell away. Sikel power was now broken and Ducetius was sent into exile at Corinth.

The Second Peloponnesian War began in earnest in 431 and Sicily, being a major supplier of grain to the Greek world, was bound to get pulled into the fighting at some stage. The Athenians made an alliance with Leontini and sent a force to the island in 427, but were unable to achieve much before withdrawing three years later. Another attempt was made in 415, this time at the behest of Segesta. The Athenians sent a large force in hopes of breaking the power of Syracuse, the most powerful city in Sicily and a major trading partner of Corinth, Athens' enemy. The expeditionary force was initially successful, defeating the Syracusans before the city's walls, but the strength of the latter prevented the Athenians from taking the place, and the Athenians settled in for a siege. The Spartans now came to the aid of the Syracusans and sent their general Gylippos to Sicily to co-ordinate the defence efforts. He was immediately successful in preventing the Athenians from completing their planned contravallation of the city. More help then arrived in the form of a Corinthian fleet, which combined with the Syracusan navy to defeat the Athenians in 413.

Reinforcements arrived from Athens, but the situation had already reached a critical point for the invaders. While the Athenians debated their next move, the Corinthian–Syracusan navy utterly destroyed the Athenian fleet in the harbour at Syracuse; the two naval defeats constituting a stunning series of reverses, considering the power, reputation and experience of the Athenian navy. The invaders now abandoned their sick and wounded and attempted to escape overland. They were hunted down by the Syracusans. Those who were not killed were condemned to the stone quarries of Syracuse, while the remaining Athenian generals were executed. The collapse of the Sicilian expedition was a major blow for Athens; an entire fleet and as many as 50,000 men were lost. One of the greatest military disasters in history was a turning point in the Peloponnesian War, since Athens would never fully recover from this defeat and would be slowly ground down by Sparta before surrendering in 404.

Carthage now took advantage of the weariness of Syracuse and lauched a campaign in 409, seeking revenge for Himera. The Carthaginians immediately succeeded in levelling the latter, and by 405 Akragas and Gela were in their hands. During this period of anarchy, a soldier named Dionysius (405–367) seized power at Syracuse and installed himself as tyrant. He was initially unsuccessful against Carthage, and was forced to accept the Peace of Himilco in 405, in which Syracuse had to give up all of its possessions. After emerging successfully out of several internal disputes, Dionysius returned to the battlefield and between 402 and 399 won back much of the lost territory.

The Carthaginians now renewed the war, and laid siege to Syracuse in 398. But Dionysius managed to repulse them, inflicting heavy losses. The following year he invaded the Punic west and proceeded to destroy Motya. He retreated under the threat of a new Punic force and was besieged in Syracuse until 395, when a combination of Corinthian and Spartan aid coupled with a plague managed to defeat the Punic army. Resuming the offensive, Dionysius invaded Italy, before a serious mutiny in his army forced him to conclude a peace with Carthage. He took Rhegium in 387 after a three-year siege and assumed control of south-western Italy; in the next few years he founded several colonies in Italy and extended his empire to the Adriatic. From 383 to 375 he fought a major war against the combined forces of Carthage and the southern Italians, which ended inconclusively. He renewed the war in 368 and unsuccessfully besieged Lilybaeum, the new Punic stronghold in western Sicily that had replaced Motya, before concluding another peace.

Dionysius was the greatest of all the Sicilian tyrants, and was perhaps the best non-Macedonian general to emerge from the Greek world. As an innovator he was heavily influential upon Philip and Alexander; he introduced Phoenician siege techniques, including artillery and engines, into Greek warfare, and was the first to use the quinquereme. He was a great patron of the arts, and his court was home to many famous names from his time, including the historian Philistus. Before Dionysius' death in 367 he was voted Athenian citizenship, and one of his plays won first prize at the Athenian Lenaia festival.

Political anarchy in Sicily followed his death, as various cities within his empire broke away under petty tyrants. These vied for control of eastern Sicily while intermittently fighting with Carthage. In desperation, Syracuse asked its mother-city, Corinth, to provide a tyrant to restore

order. Timoleon (344–336) was sent to Sicily, and he quickly took Syracuse and deposed Dionysius II (367–357, 346–344) as tyrant. Almost
immediately, Timoleon was forced to fight the Carthaginians, who had
once again invaded Sicily, hoping to take advantage of Greek political
disunity. They laid siege to Syracuse and managed to take most of the city
before plague once again decimated their forces. Their remnants were
crushed by Timoleon at the Crimissus river in western Sicily in 341. He
now turned his attention to ridding the island of most of its petty Greek
tyrants, and was largely successful. The Syracusan constitution was
then reformed, and many cities were repopulated. Having experienced a
material decline in the first half of the fourth century, the Sicilian economy
appears to have undergone something of a renaissance under Timoleon,
which would continue well after the tyrant's peaceful retirement in 336.

The archaic and classical periods saw Sicily develop from a far-off land
on the fringes of the Greek world to being a fully developed and powerful
westward extension of Hellas. Materially, the island's grain production
made it one of the richest places in the Mediterranean; land was plentiful,
and on the whole life in Sicily appears to have been relatively prosperous.
This fertility and Sicily's position as a gateway between the eastern
and western Mediterranean were what brought both the Greeks and the
Phoenicians there in the first place, but these facts have also, and permanently, had the effect of making it one of the most fought-over lands in
both ancient and modern times. As a result, prosperity was frequently
interrupted by warfare with a large and well-organised foreign power at
Carthage. This precipitated the rise of a class of generals who usually
seemed to be the only ones who could rid Sicily of what was, to the
Greeks, the Punic menace. Times of peace saw unrivalled wealth on the
island, but these were always short-lived. The Hellenistic Age brought
with it more tyrants and more wars with Carthage, and it would be left to
a new power in the north, Rome, finally to imprint a lasting settlement
upon Sicily.

# 3

# INDIGENOUS SOCIETY BETWEEN THE NINTH AND SIXTH CENTURIES BC:

## territorial, urban and social evolution

### *Robert Leighton*

## INTRODUCTION

ETHNICITY, ACCULTURATION AND RELATIONSHIPS between Greek settlers and indigenous people feature prominently in studies of the late prehistoric and early historical periods in Sicily. The discussion usually begins with the early Iron Age, or *prima età del ferro*, also known as the Pantalica III ('South') or pre-colonial period and dated from about 900 BC until the foundation of Naxos, the first Greek colony, in 734 BC (according to Thuc. 6.4). This is followed at indigenous sites by a *seconda età del ferro* (late Iron Age, from about 734 to 650 or even 600 BC), called the Finocchito period in eastern Sicily after a large indigenous site in the Hyblaean hills, typified by the persistence of local traditions, albeit influenced by contacts with nearby Greek colonies that were still at an early stage of development.

The Finocchito complex is superseded by or gradually merges into the archaic period, which is associated with more abundant evidence of Greek cultural traits at indigenous sites further inland between about 600 and 500 BC (whence the concept of acculturation or 'hellenisation').[1] Paolo Orsi regarded the site of Licodia Eubea as emblematic of the transformation, and the term 'Licodia Eubea facies' is still sometimes used to describe the material assemblage of indigenous groups in central–eastern areas at this time. The Iron Age is also designated *protostoria* in Italy, although the English equivalent (protohistory) is a rather neglected term, avoided by some, perhaps because of its overly evolutional implications and because it might seem to exaggerate the importance of the really rather scanty historical sources for the period. In sum, this variable and inevitably awkward nomenclature for the ninth–sixth centuries BC reflects different academic traditions and an attempt to account for contrasting territories and cultural provinces; notably that of the Greek colonial sphere (mainly coastal initially) and the rest of the island. The relationship between the Phoenicians of western Sicily and neighbouring native populations, thought to have been relatively circumscribed initially, although still poorly documented or understood, lies beyond the scope of this chapter.

Whether or not perceived to be protohistoric, this period should be a *luogo d'incontro* for prehistorians and classical archaeologists. In theory, the circumstances are improving for fruitful dialogue as, in practice, those mutual suspicions and academic divides which have been amusingly caricatured by Whitehouse and Wilkins (1985: 89) are beginning to be crossed more frequently in pursuit of interdisciplinary enlightenment and in recognition of the fact that an understanding of the later period will be influenced by an assessment of the preceding, if not vice versa. More persistent obstacles include the narrow range and uneven quality of evidence, and our limited knowledge of the early Iron Age and of different sites and territories, which clearly did not all develop in the same way or at the same pace. Moreover, Orsi's excavations were a model for the nineteenth but not for the twenty-first century, while several key sites of inland Sicily excavated in recent decades are largely unpublished.

This chapter begins with a brief review of chronology and recent attempts to define early Iron Age society, followed by a sketch of the shifting balance between territories variously within the orbit of Greek colonies or indigenous sites, while the concluding discussion concerns the development of settlement and urban structures. Viewed from the standpoint of indigenous culture, this is a somewhat neglected subject, since most recent studies, in the wake of old traditions of excavation, have concentrated on the more conspicuous evidence of burials. Rather than a comprehensive survey, the discussion draws on a few examples which serve to exemplify different approaches to cultural change in colonial or indigenous settings. While the history of occupation and development of individual sites during this period may have followed different trajectories, which were partly determined by proximity to and relations with Greek coastal towns, the identifiable patterns reinforce the conclusion, likewise emerging from complementary lines of inquiry (notably that of funerary practice), that indigenous communities, especially those further inland, maintained their traditions for longer than has sometimes been recognised.

## CHRONOLOGY

The existing scheme of late Bronze and early Iron Age chronology is less secure than often assumed and possibly erroneous in certain respects. Many supposedly pre-colonial tombs of the Pantalica III period (conventionally 850–734 BC) would be better dated between the late eighth and early seventh centuries BC.[2] While the style of the local pottery in some of the Pantalica South tombs argues for this later date, it is also becoming increasingly clear from several contexts (at Mendolito, Pantalica, Finocchito, Butera) that the serpentine fibula, which has always been regarded as a diagnostic artefact or 'type-fossil' of the early Iron Age, was still current in the late eighth and seventh centuries BC and, therefore, can no longer be taken as a sure indication of a pre-colonial date.

The dates of several tomb-groups and settlements could be lowered: for example, indigenous contexts beneath the first colonial dwellings in Ortygia, dated between the tenth and mid-ninth centuries BC (Frasca 1983), could well belong in the late ninth/mid-eighth century BC; the Iron Age tombs of Pozzo di Gotto and Longane, where there are local versions of *oinochoai* with geometric and metopal decoration, are dated in the early eighth century BC (Bernabò Brea 1967), but could more logically be placed in the late eighth or seventh centuries BC. The Morgantina Iron Age tombs with iron serpentine fibulae, which convention would place in the ninth/early eighth centuries BC, could also be dated in the late eighth or even early seventh centuries BC (Leighton 1993a: 106).

A lowering of the chronology would also be consistent with the historical situation: it would be quite remarkable if indigenous people in the interior of Sicily, well beyond the *chorai* of fledgling Greek colonies, had suddenly abandoned their traditional crafts or styles of dress. Since the chronology depends on the computation of Thucydides' foundation dates and associations with Greek pottery, Iron Age contexts without Greek imports can be problematic. They tend to be assigned, almost by default, to a pre-colonial period, even though the absence of Greek imports could be due to lack of interaction. This is a general problem with Italian Iron Age chronologies, which are too influenced by an expectation of contact or rapid cultural change among indigenous people (Leighton 2000). In Sicily, the main problem is in regions furthest from colonial centres, where there is little evidence for any profound transformation of indigenous culture until the sixth century BC. It is also noteworthy that the indigenous pottery of the Licodia Eubea facies, which has been neglected until recently (Albanese Procelli, 1996b), is not yet datable with much precision.

## ANCIENT ETHNONYMS AND MODERN DEFINITIONS

The early Iron Age communities of east–central Sicily, represented for example at Mulino della Badia, Morgantina and Leontini, have several similarities with their counterparts in Lipari and southern Italy, even though they may be said to have a more specifically 'Sicilian' identity as a result of local evolution. At the simplest level, the existing patterns can be accounted for in terms of greater cultural divergence from the peninsula in relation to greater distance from it: the Aeolian and northeastern complexes have closer counterparts in Calabria, whereas those of central and southeastern Sicily have more evidence for local traits.[3] All have been loosely referred to as 'Ausonian', following and extending the terminology of Bernabò Brea (1957: 137–47), although this should not be taken literally to mean that they belong to a single or distinct ethnic group. The term 'Sikel', with its analogous connotations of peninsular origins (Strab. 6.1.6), is often used equally loosely to describe any or every group in eastern Sicily, while Sikans or Elymians are generally placed in western Sicily, following the literary sources. It may seem over-fastidious to reject these labels when discussing archaeological material, but it is important not to be misled by them: we do not know to what extent or in what way such terms were used by indigenous people themselves, nor can we identify or accurately associate the supposed geographical locus of these putative ethnic groups with archaeological assemblages.

As regards more recent attempts to define local groups in terms of socio-political structures, the idea has been evolving over many years that late Bronze Age communities in Sicily, or at least those represented by larger sites, such as Pantalica, might be described as 'chiefdoms'. This term may also apply to socially stratified middle Bronze Age societies with settlements of varying size and complexity, characterised at one end of the scale by large harbour sites with fairly elaborate residential and funerary structures (Thapsos), suggesting an unequal distribution of wealth, an intensification of local specialist craft production and an elitist or aristocratic ideology stimulated by long-distance trade in prestige goods (Leighton 1996b). The transition to the early Iron Age may be defined in terms of social, economic and political realignments and the return of Sicily to a western sphere of interaction, encouraged if not caused solely by the demise of the international trading network in which Mycenaeans and other eastern Mediterranean societies had played a leading role.

The early Iron Age societies of eastern Sicily might be described as 'tribal' or segmentary entities, typified by more uniform or less ostentatious burials and grave goods. A move away from the elitist ideology of the previous period, perhaps towards a more collectivist or egalitarian ethos, may also be reflected in the wider diffusion and distribution of practical and utilitarian products, as opposed to exotic luxuries. Settlement patterns suggest a more decentralised world or one in which at least the coastal sites of the previous period, although not abandoned, had lost their former pre-eminence as the main centres of economic and political power. While it is hard to find any real evidence that indigenous society was evolving autonomously towards a form of centralised or hierarchical state organisation (at least not of the kind that finally did emerge), neither does it seem to have been reverting to a 'Dark Age'. In fact, the Iron Age in Sicily (and much of southern Italy) saw the re-elaboration or re-definition of social and gender roles, including those which appear to be symbolised in burials by the goods and rites associated with adult males, females and children, such as weaponry, spinning or weaving equipment and items of personal adornment. A limited division of labour may also be inferred from the wider spectrum of economic (trading and craft) activities, which included advances in the quality, range and intensity of metal-working, the continued production of wheel-made pottery, and possibly more diversified and productive forms of subsistence agriculture.

Of course, terms such as 'chiefdom' and 'tribe' have been used in different ways in European prehistory and can be misleading if applied arbitrarily. The 'tribal' epithet for Iron Age societies may invite criticism on the grounds that it is often also applied to the very different societies of the Neolithic, while such relativisms as 'complex' or 'simple' hardly illuminate the structure and character of the societies in question. Problems of terminology aside, more explicit assessments require a better use of archaeological evidence rather than a priori concepts. At present, there is no label which convincingly characterises the societies in question.

A glance at contemporary Iron Age communities in Greece shows that the technological disparity between the first settlers in the eighth century BC and those whom they encountered in Sicily cannot have been very great, albeit occasionally noticeable in some aspects of artefact production.[4] Bulk survival as well as chronological and aesthetic considerations have kept fine painted pottery at the forefront of discussion, to the extent that the spread of Greek imports has almost become a leitmotif for an apparently inexorable process of hellenisation, even though the diffusion or adoption of different kinds of pottery does not necessarily imply any profound change in cultural tradition, let alone in ethnic identity. In any case, Sicilian and Italic communities, one suspects, generally regarded metal rather than pottery as worthy of elaborate treatment. Of course, all the social, economic, political or generically aesthetic and cultural experiences of the parties may have a bearing on forms of interaction in a colonial context. It is important to recognise the complexity of this subject (its potential variability over space and time, selectivity, reciprocal but often asym-metrical nature), the risks in hasty conclusions based on limited categories of evidence, and the tendency to underestimate the many possible facets of interaction or to view relations between groups simply in terms of cultural colonisation, dominance or cores versus peripheries.

## WRITTEN SOURCES

The primary concern in this chapter is with archaeological evidence. It must suffice to say that limited information can also be gleaned from the written sources, which inevitably reflect a Greek point of view, but nevertheless contain intriguing references to indigenous sites variously taken by force (Syracuse), attacked (Omphake, identified with Butera or Dessueri), conceded by local rulers (the story of Hyblon and the Megarians) or shared by some form of compromise (Greek and native coexistence at Leontini).[5] Scrambles for land, shifting alliances, rivalries (from which emerged tyrants with ambitious and ruthless schemes of expansion), squabbles or more serious conflicts between colonists or with local people, and competing claims by small, opportunistic and independently minded groups lacking the organs of state administration with a predetermined 'colonial policy', characterise a complex and rapidly evolving scenario, which makes it hard for us to predict the nature or propose any single model of interaction.

Written sources may also selectively mention activities of indigenous people in the sixth–fourth centuries BC and indigenous toponyms, although not always easily identifiable with archaeological sites; information which can be as hard to ignore as it is to use. For example, one might note references to the role of Sikels from the Ragusano as allies of Camarina against Syracuse in the late sixth century BC, to Phaeax, the Greek ambassador, who crossed 'Sikel territory' on his journey from Gela to Catania, to Ducetius' exploits as self-proclaimed leader of disgruntled natives in the central–eastern region in the mid-fifth century BC, to the persistence of indigenous culture in certain regions, and so on (e.g. Holloway 1990). Of course an acritical reading of archaeological evidence through the lens of selective and biased literary evidence is to be avoided, as often remarked. However, it is noteworthy that the written sources do not proclaim or imply any rapid hellenisation of Sicily and even point to a tangible political dimension to the term 'Sikel' in the fifth century BC, which is reinforced by the evidence of inscriptions in the native language.

We habitually paraphrase literary sources in speaking of the founding of 'colonies' (a loaded English word), whereas in several cases, such as Syracuse and Leontini, a transformation of a pre-existing native settlement occurred. One challenge for archaeological research would be to assess whether this came about as a result of violent and sudden actions or evictions, as stated by Thucydides (6.3) in the case of Syracuse, or through other possibly more gradual forms of accommodation. A relevant and recently popular subject of discussion concerns the presence of indigenous people in these places, once denied by some scholars, but of whom there are at least hints from burials, for example at Syracuse, Naxos, Gela, Megara Hyblaea and Mylai.[6] There is also a growing awareness on the part of a post-Dunbabin generation of classical archaeologists that the Sicilian Greek colonies were not as faithful to or constrained by the traditions of the motherland as once believed (Shepherd 1995; this volume; De Angelis 1998). Relations between homeland and colony may therefore also have a bearing on Greek and native interaction, since they represent a filter through which exogenous traditions were introduced and possibly modified.

## INDIGENOUS VERSUS COLONIAL TERRITORIES

The modalities of interaction between indigenous people and Greek colonists and the 'spheres of influence' which have traditionally been ascribed to them varied in different times and places. Pre-existing communities on or near the eastern coast were obviously affected sooner and more directly by the foundation of the first colonies (Naxos in 734, Syracuse in 733, Catania and Leontini in 729, Megara in 728 BC, following Thucydides 6.1–4), than their neighbours inland, while the later foundations on the southern and northern coasts of Sicily (Gela in 688, Himera in 649, Selinus in 645 or 628, and Agrigentum not until 580 BC) imply a lesser degree of contact in these regions prior to the later seventh century BC (figures 3.1, 3.2). Assessments of territorial relationships have tended to follow in the steps of Dunbabin (1948), using a mixture of historical and archaeological information. Modern field-survey techniques have been used only recently in Sicily, their results are yet to be evaluated, and there is no direct archaeological evidence for land divisions and boundaries for early Sicilian colonies of the kind from Metaponto in Apulia, which suggests that the *chora* of this Greek town extended for not more than about 15 km inland (Whitehouse and Wilkins 1989 with references).

The relationship between Syracuse, the most powerful of the Sicilian colonies, and its Hyblaean hinterland is usually treated as a special case. Finocchito and Pantalica, the main indigenous sites in the region, show significant developments during the late eighth and early seventh centuries BC. Finocchito emerged as a major centre, reflected in the large numbers of chamber-tombs (Steures 1980), which implies a process of centralisation, possibly caused in part by a move away from the coastal belt as a result of colonisation. Expansion by synoecism or the absorption of smaller nearby communities, such as Cozzo delle Giummare, Grotta del Murmuro and Monte Alveria, has also been suggested (Frasca 1981: 93). From a political standpoint, one explanation for this may be that it was advantageous to conduct relations with the more unified entity represented by the developing *polis*, and evidently a rather aggressive one in this case, from the comparative security of an indigenous stronghold. Concerns with security are also suggested by defensive structures (below). Likewise, from an economic standpoint, the formation of an indigenous

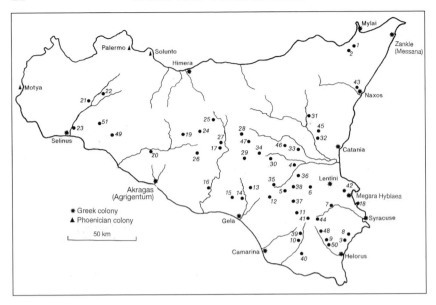

*Fig. 3.1* Greek and Phoenician colonies and indigenous sites (R. Leighton)
*Key:* 1 Pozzo di Gotto; 2 Longane; 3 Avola; 4 Ramacca; 5 Mulino della Badia;
6 Ossini; 7 Pantalica; 8 Cassibile; 9 Finocchito; 10 Ragusa; 11 Monte Casasia;
12 Monte San Mauro; 13 Monte Bubbonia; 14 Dessueri; 15 Butera; 16 Monte
Saraceno; 17 Sabucina; 18 Thapsos; 19 Polizzello; 20 Sant'Angelo Muxaro;
21 Monte Castellazzo; 22 Monte Maranfusa; 23 Montagnoli; 24 Marianopoli;
25 Terravecchia; 26 Vassallaggi; 27 Capodarso; 28 Calascibetta cemeteries;
29 Montagna di Marzo; 30 Morgantina; 31 Mendolito; 32 Paternò; 33 Monte
Turcisi; 34 Rossomanno; 35 Monte Balchino; 36 Palike; 37 Licodia Eubea;
38 Mineo; 39 Castiglione; 40 Modica; 41 Monte Casale (Casmene);
42 Villasmundo; 43 Cocolonazzo; 44 Palazzolo Acreide (Akrai); 45 Civita;
46 Monte Iudica; 47 Cozzo Matrice; 48 Tremenzano; 49 Caltabellotta;
50 Giummarito, Murmuro; 51 Monte Adranone

metropolis, permitting greater efficiency in the administration and production of storage and surplus, would also have facilitated trade with the
new and correspondingly more centralised markets represented by Greek
colonies. The tomb goods at Finocchito show that Greek pottery and
luxury items were valued locally and probably obtained from Syracuse
and Helorus, a sub-colony, founded before the end of the eighth century
BC and well placed to trade with the indigenous site.

A similar pattern may be observed at Pantalica, which was already a
prominent centre during the late Bronze Age, although it has relatively
few early Iron Age burials. If some of the South tombs belong in the late
eighth–seventh centuries BC, as suggested above, then a re-emergence
of Pantalica as a major centre in the early colonial period can also be

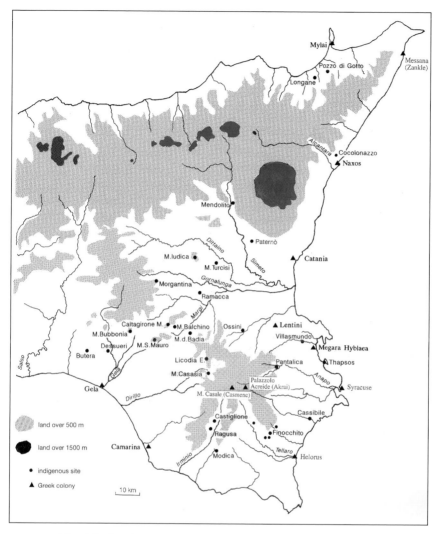

*Fig. 3.2* Greek colonies and indigenous sites in eastern Sicily

postulated. That both Pantalica and Finocchito lost their independence by the later seventh century BC, if they were not abandoned altogether, was doubtless due to the intervention of Syracuse, culminating in the foundation of outposts at Palazzolo Acreide (Akrai) and Monte Casale (Casmene) around the middle of the seventh century BC, which truncated relations between Greeks and natives in this particular region after less than a century. One must therefore look to other areas in order to study the subsequent development of indigenous centres.

Until recently, it was generally believed that the neighbouring Chalkidian colonies, Leontini and Catania, pursued a less aggressively expansionist policy at the expense of local groups in their hinterlands and that their relations developed along largely pacific and economic lines between the late eighth and early sixth centuries BC (Vallet 1962). For example, native sites obtained drinking cups and jugs of Greek type, presumably in exchange for local products, although there is no reason to believe that a pronounced alteration or abandonment of their traditions occurred as a result. Subsequent developments are more controversial. In view of the more consistent evidence for Greek materials and cultural practices (burials and religious structures) from the mid-sixth century BC, it has often been suggested that native communities in the hills extending from Leontini westward to the Enna region absorbed settlers from the Chalkidian sites, and that this led to more profound cultural changes. However, the manner and extent of adoption by indigenous groups of Greek cultural traditions at this time has only recently begun to be evaluated afresh. Whether the arrival of settlers is really a necessary or logical inference in order to explain changes at inland sites, such as Morgantina, is questionable (e.g. Antonaccio 1997), as noted below.

It has also been suggested that relations between Leontini or Catania and native sites in their vicinity were not always respectfully confined to the economic sphere (Procelli 1989). Some sites in the region of Leontini, such as Ossini and Monte Casale, seem to have been abandoned in the course of the seventh century BC. This is also true of small native sites near Megara and Naxos, such as Villasmundo and Cocolonazzo, where there seems to have been an initial but relatively short-lived period of trade, represented by imported vases in native burials, followed by abandonment or decline in the late eighth/early seventh centuries BC; possibly a reflection of the growing intolerance of neighbours by increasingly assertive colonies, although whether the locals were absorbed by the latter or moved away is open to question. The adoption of a more expansionist policy by Leontini and Catania, at least from the late seventh century BC, has also been inferred from the following: the appearance of fortification walls at several native sites (Mineo, Palike, Monte Balchino, Monte San Mauro, Civita and Mendolito), albeit often difficult to date accurately; the destruction levels at Ramacca in the early sixth century BC; and the creation of a *phrourion* or Greek outpost at Monte Turcisi (Procelli 1989). By the end of the sixth century BC, it is suggested that Leontini and Catania had gained control or a strong influence over a large territory extending westward as far as the Enna region, bordered to the south by their rival, Syracuse.

While the Catania plain, the largest alluvial basin in Sicily, probably facilitated contacts with inland groups, the relationship between Naxos and its hinterland must have been more circumscribed by rugged terrain. Nevertheless, the Alcantara river presents a thoroughfare between the northern edge of Etna and the southern side of the Peloritani, and it is probably no coincidence that the earliest significant Greek influence, implying more than just trade contacts, dates to the second half of the sixth century BC and comes from sites in this area, such as Sant'Anastasia (Greek burial practices) and Francavilla (Greek votive terracottas). However, the central–western Etna region, with historically important and well-defended indigenous centres at Mendolito and Paternò, seems to have remained a stronghold of indigenous culture well into the fifth century BC. Unfortunately, we know little about these sites from an archaeological point of view, although the vitality of indigenous metal-working in the seventh century BC is seen in the huge hoard from Mendolito (Albanese Procelli 1993), where P. Pelagatti has alluded to the survival of traditional Ausonian pottery forms into the late eighth century BC and where the persistence of the indigenous language is proclaimed by a public inscription on the city wall, projecting an assertive if not hostile attitude towards neighbouring communities (Albanese Procelli 1989, with references).

Similar considerations should apply in the mountainous hinterland of northeastern Sicily, which may have seemed relatively uninviting to the inhabitants of Zankle (Messana), unless they were also interested in the metallurgical resources of the Peloritani, recently brought to attention by Giardino (1996). Control of the northern coastal plain may conceivably have been a source of contention in this region. Chronological revisions mentioned above would allow us to infer coexistence between the first generations of settlers at Zankle or Mylai (Milazzo), where there is evidence of mixed traditions in the cemetery (Domínguez 1989: 116, with references), and indigenous communities in the nearby foothills of the Peloritani, represented by chamber-tomb burials at Longane (Rodì) and Pozzo di Gotto, which could represent indigenous groups that maintained their funerary traditions, while adopting some Greek pottery forms. The maritime vocation of Zankle and Mylai and the lack of historical references to relations with indigenous people may lead one to infer an essentially peaceful coexistence in this region, where it would appear that more profound cultural changes occurred in the sixth century BC, with the spread of Greek burial practices.

Another bastion of indigenous culture, beyond easy reach of Syracuse, is associated with the limestone tablelands and hilltops of the Ragusano, as also suggested by the literary sources. Some early imports of Greek pottery are known from Modica, while important indigenous centres such as Ragusa (Hybla Galeatis), Castiglione and Monte Casasia probably benefited from regular trading relations with the coastal emporium at Maestro and the prosperous Greek foundation at Camarina. Once again, the evidence consists mainly of burials: growing Greek influence in the sixth century BC is suggested by the appearance of trench graves, possibly of Greek residents, although the graves contain much local pottery, while multiple burial in some tombs also points to the survival of local traditions.

Prior to Greek colonisation, there were several large centres in the hinterland of Gela. Dessueri is usually thought to have been abandoned well before Greek colonisation, although recent discoveries (Panvini 1997; and below) may not be much earlier than the foundation of Gela. Here again, accurate dating of the new finds in the light of chronological revisions could be significant. By contrast, Butera provides an interesting example of a site with indigenous roots and an increasingly mixed population within the orbit of a Greek colony (Gela), which expanded in the late eighth and seventh centuries BC. Adamesteanu (1994–5) has argued recently that the seventh-century BC necropolis (layer II) is essentially Greek and reflects the arrivals of Cretans who practised the rite of head-removal (*akephalia*). However, there are persistent elements of native tradition (plumed pottery, metal grave goods) in the cemetery, while domestic assemblages and residential quarters may have maintained local traditions more faithfully.

In what was still a vast swathe of indigenous territory across central Sicily during the first two centuries of Greek colonisation, late Bronze and early Iron Age settlement patterns had given rise to a system of hilltop settlement, frequently commanding lines of communication along river valleys. There may also have been valley-bottom sites (not enough survey work has been done), but it is clear that the hilltop locations were the ones to emerge as major native centres during the early colonial period, and some of them subsequently became important towns. Traces of early Iron Age occupation are known at several sites, such as Sabucina, Capodarso, Monte San Mauro, Polizzello, Morgantina and the cemeteries around Calascibetta, although there are also hilltop sites of the seventh–sixth century BC, especially in western Sicily, with no evidence of prior occupation, such as Monte Castellazzo, Monte Saraceno and Monte Maranfusa. The seventh century BC therefore saw continuity in settlement location and an intensification of an earlier pattern with pre-existing sites growing in size and some new centres also appearing. The explanation may again be sought in a combination of those factors (insecurity, economic and political motives) already noted in connection with Finocchito.

However, cultural change in these regions has traditionally been charted in terms of the penetration of the hinterland by a virile Greek culture emanating from coastal centres using the main river valleys, led either by Greek traders, settlers or military expeditions (e.g. Adamesteanu 1962b). Once Gela had quickly gained control of the coastal plain, the Gela and Salso river valleys and their tributaries served as thoroughfares

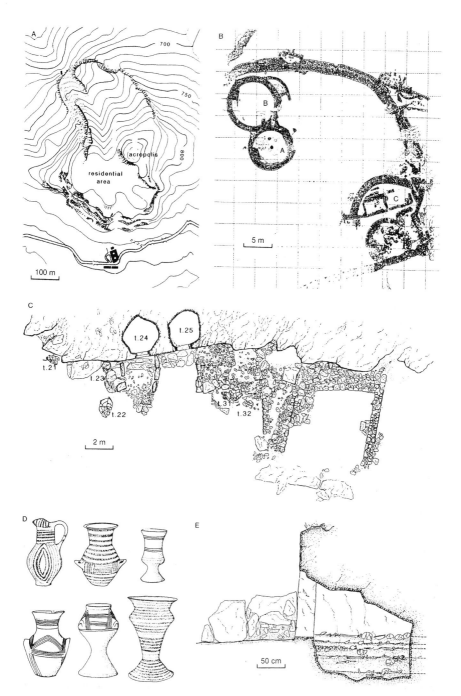

*Fig. 3.3* (A) Polizzello contour plan, (B) acropolis sanctuary, (C–E) indigenous chamber tombs and pottery (after de Miro 1988)

inland to sites such as Monte San Mauro, Monte Bubbonia, Monte Saraceno, Sabucina, Polizzello and Sant'Angelo Muxaro (Orlandini 1962). One possible criticism of this approach is that the colonies are assumed to be the sole agents of change, always dictating the pace, while inland centres are little more than passive recipients of 'influences civilisatrices' (Vallet 1962: 47). In fact, the inland centres of indigenous origin, which adopted some customs of the colonies in the course of the seventh and sixth centuries BC, could equally have been the initiators of contact, and certainly active participants when commerce or trade was a primary concern. As local centres and markets for rural populations in territories where native traditions and language were predominant, they must have been influential crucibles of cultural interaction.

It is also increasingly clear that more consideration should be given to forms of interaction in which religion and cults, both Greek and indigenous, played an important part. Much of interest has been written about the role of religion in Greek colonisation (Malkin 1987) and, for example, of Greek non-urban sanctuaries not just in defining and proclaiming the *chora* of an expanding *polis*, but also in more subtle processes of mediation and acculturation between Greeks and non-Greeks (e.g. De Polignac 1991: 95–127). The recent finds from the prominent hilltop sanctuary at Polizzello are now shedding new light on the unexpected scale and complexity of indigenous cult areas and activities during the seventh-sixth centuries BC at this site (fig. 3.3), where votive offerings include articles of fine indigenous craftsmanship as well as imported Greek items, luxuries and high-value materials obtained by trade (de Miro 1988, 1988–9). It may be suggested that indigenous cults, and those individuals of undoubtedly high or special status who administered them, could also have regulated economic transactions and exerted considerable influence over indigenous attitudes and behaviour towards Greek colonies: for example, by providing an ideological focus for the accumulation and distribution of wealth and by playing an active part in establishing relations between local elites and their potential rivals or partners.

In general, hilltop sites seem to have expanded in the seventh century BC, while receiving trade goods, which stimulated local craft production, with more profound changes visible from about the mid-sixth century BC in burial practices, cults and other aspects of domestic life. The challenge remains to analyse changes at these sites from a wider range of evidence, including the rather neglected areas of subsistence economics. Continuity of settlement location is also a likely premise for continuity in the more mundane aspects of everyday life.

## URBAN STRUCTURES AND SPACE

To what extent and in what way was early Iron Age society urban? Many of the practical and theoretical problems encountered in attempting to answer this question recur in discussions of urbanisation throughout western Europe in the Iron Age. At present, hierarchical patterns are hard to detect in Sicily, although late Bronze Age centres, such as Pantalica, with smaller sites in their territories have been postulated (above). Early Iron Age settlement systems or heterarchies must have existed, linking hilltop sites with those nearer the coastal plain and possibly harbours. Examples could be the distribution of settlements along the southern edge of the Catania plain (Leighton 1993a: 132), or sites on the Hyblaean canyons (*cave*), which lead to the coast. River valleys must have been used as natural lines of communication inland before the foundation of colonies and new trading relations led to an increase in traffic.

Apart from the fact that the main cemeteries were usually located on perimeter slopes or near the valley bottom, only limited information is available about the internal layout of late Bronze and early Iron Age sites, particularly with regard to zoning or activity areas, public versus private space, working and living quarters, or street systems. The limited extent of excavation and difficulties in proving that different buildings were contemporary hinders an assessment of size, even though some sites might have been quite large, as suggested by the numbers of tombs (at Pantalica, Dessueri and Cassibile, for example) or by the scatter of material or structures over a potentially large settlement area (Thapsos, Morgantina). Rather than assume criteria identical to or evolving towards those governing the layout of classical towns in historical times, the Iron Age tradition should be evaluated with reference to middle–late Bronze Age sites. Some well-preserved examples are on Sicily's satellite islands (fig. 3.4A): agglomerations of single or subdivided dwellings at Mursia on Pantelleria (Tozzi 1968) and in Aeolian Milazzese sites (Bernabò Brea and Cavalier 1968), and with more substantial courtyards, trackways and impressive fortification walls at I Faraglioni on Ustica (Holloway and Lukesh 1997).

Late Bronze–early Iron Age settlements on the acropolis of Lipari (Bernabò Brea and Cavalier 1980), the Metapiccola of Leontini (Rizza 1962) and Cittadella of Morgantina (Leighton 1993a) are represented by house clusters or individual houses, but without the urban geometry of regular plots. In such cases, local terrain and traditions, long-term occupation or reuse probably influenced developments. On Lipari, where the restricted area of the acropolis created a dense agglomeration, some buildings had curved and straight walls with erratic alignments, probably designed to fit available spaces between pre-existing structures, although at least one large building of symmetrical form is known (a2), and some

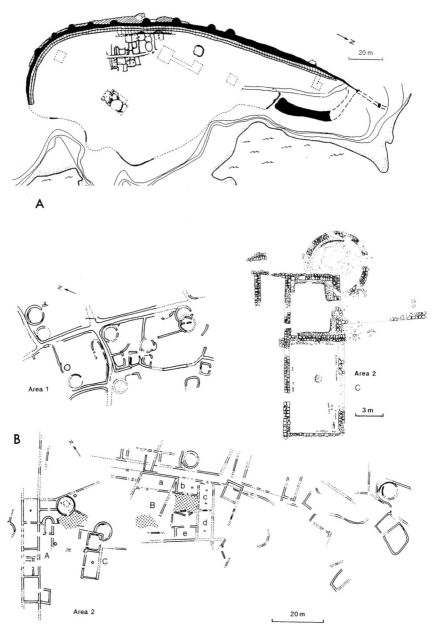

*Fig. 3.4*  (A) I Faraglioni, Ustica (after Holloway and Lukesh 1997);
(B) Thapsos (after Voza 1973; 1984–5)

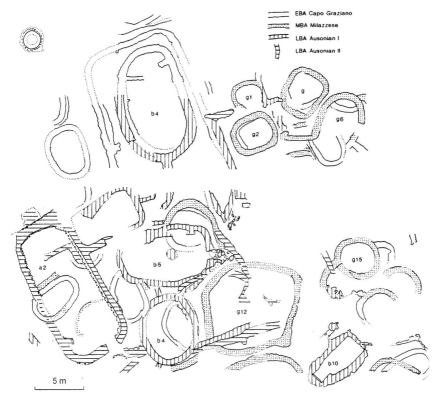

EBA Capo Graziano
MBA Milazzese
LBA Ausonian I
LBA Ausonian II

*Fig. 3.5* Lipari acropolis (after Bernabò Brea and Cavalier 1980)

structures shared walls (fig. 3.5). At Leontini, Morgantina and perhaps other inland hilltops without pressures of space or pre-existing structures, there were probably clusters of dwellings in different locations, which would allow a large area or a series of interlinked hillocks to be occupied, perhaps with an eye to security. Arrangements of multiple nuclei are also widespread in peninsular Italy.

The situation probably differed at coastal sites on flatter land. Thapsos has middle–late Bronze Age round-houses arranged in quadrangular courts or plots, flanked by rectilinear pathways, as well as substantial multi-roomed rectangular structures with courtyards (phases 1–2; Voza 1973), which echo sporadic developments in urban planning at certain coastal sites in the central and eastern Mediterranean in the thirteenth–twelfth centuries BC (fig. 3.4B).[7] The last (third) phase, of the final Bronze or possibly early Iron Age, includes a sizeable rectangular structure with two doorways and rooms perfectly aligned, giving onto what may be a corridor or a street (fig. 3.4B, area 2C), perhaps part of a more symmetrical layout (Voza 1980–1: 677–9). New evidence from Dessueri also shows the existence of substantial subdivided rectangular structures with

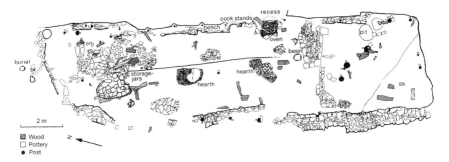

*Fig. 3.6* Morgantina trench 31 (after Leighton 1993a)

stone foundations, aligned and flanked by cobbled pathways, located on the slopes of the hill, which look like part of a more regular plan (Panvini 1997).

The size and design of single units also varies markedly. Several sites have large individual buildings (18.75 × 4.25 m at Morgantina, tr. 31; 13.8 × 5.5 m, Lipari a2), most of which appear to be dwellings, sometimes subdivided internally (figs 3.4–3.6). The floors may be covered with a tough lime plaster and set below the exterior ground surface, the walls built up to a certain height with stone, timber-lacing and interior plaster, perhaps with a superstructure of wattle, daub and thatching, flanked by low benches, areas for cooking (with terracotta cooking stands, ovens, millstones) and storage, sometimes with flagstone pavements. A wide range and large quantity of pottery (fine wheel-made painted and coarse handmade wares) are found, with domestic implements and utensils, including spinning and weaving equipment. Such buildings are typical of the late Bronze and early Iron Age and are not so different in their principles of design or level of sophistication from some of the post-Mycenaean domestic architecture of Greece, where 'long-houses' with apsidal ends and internal benches are also encountered (e.g. Mazarakis Ainian 1997); perhaps reflecting similar environmental adaptations, use of analogous raw materials and a comparable level of socio-economic organisation and development. In Sicily, similar designs probably persisted into the seventh century BC at some inland sites, as suggested, for example, at Morgantina (trench 2A/F) and at Monte San Mauro, where elliptical buildings with internal benches are dated tentatively to the late eighth and seventh centuries BC (Wilson 1996: 75).

The next phase at Monte San Mauro (roughly mid seventh–early sixth centuries BC) is represented by a large two-roomed building (the so-called *magazzino* found near the *naiskos* or '*anaktoron*') built in traditional style with a sunken floor and internal bench, and by another long subdivided building (11.8 × 4.6 m) with an apsidal end and stone wall foundations (fig. 3.7A), probably built up with daub or mud brick and thatched (Spigo

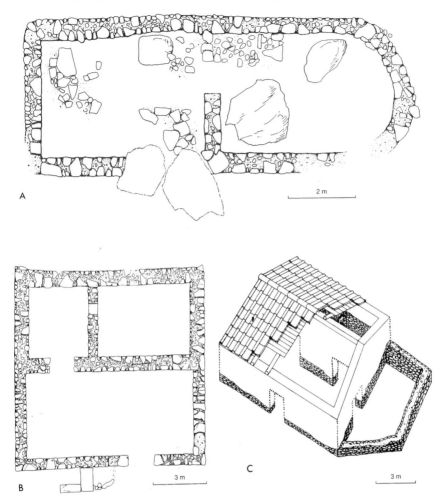

*Fig. 3.7* (A) Monte San Mauro apsidal building; (B) house 1 plan;
(C) house 2 reconstruction (after Spigo 1980–1; 1986)

1986).[8] At this and other indigenous sites, more significant changes
in domestic architecture, discussed below, did not occur until between
approximately 580 and 550 BC (fig. 3.7B, C). The diversity of local architectural traditions at the time of colonisation and the apparently flexible
attitude of indigenous people to building design are further illustrated by
circular structures at Montagnoli in western Sicily, including one (10 m
diameter) with an internal bench (Castellana 1992) – a form with countless predecessors in Bronze Age sites – while massive retaining walls, and
round and rectangular cult buildings, characterise the surprisingly elaborate plan of the indigenous sanctuary on the acropolis of Polizzello
(noted above; fig. 3.3) during the seventh–sixth centuries BC.

While our knowledge of indigenous structures is growing, one apparently exceptional building that has most famously been associated with the Sicilian late Bronze Age, the so-called *anaktoron* (or 'princely palace') of Pantalica, may have to be omitted from further discussions, despite the careful work of Bernabò Brea (1990). Brief but pointed observations by Messina (1993; cf. Leighton 1999: 155–7) suggest that it might well have been a fortified farmstead of Byzantine date. Likewise, it was argued many years ago (Adamesteanu 1955) that other buildings on inland hilltops at Monte San Mauro and Monte Bubbonia, which Orsi mistook for indigenous chiefly residences, were probably Archaic shrines (*naiskoi*). Not long before these serious doubts emerged about Orsi's original *anaktoron* at Pantalica, La Rosa (1991) used the term to describe no more than a few tracts of middle–late Bronze Age walls at Serra del Palco, while new discoveries at Dessueri are being hailed as evidence of a 'palace' (Panvini 1997). In view of the limited documentation and range of comparative evidence, aside from past confusion and errors of judgement in relation to the *anaktora* of Sicilian prehistory, it would be prudent to drop the term altogether.

Were new urban developments encouraged at Finocchito and Pantalica by contact with colonists? Unfortunately, the residential quarters of these sites are unknown. Since the form of burial did not alter one should probably not expect major changes in the domestic sphere either. Frasca (1981: 93) suggested that the residential zone at Finocchito consisted of separate clusters in correspondence with various groups of chamber-tombs spread around the hillside, which would be consistent with a local tradition.

Ortygia (Syracuse) would be a key site for the investigation of urbanisation and comparisons between the indigenous and colonial worlds if only the opportunities for excavation were not so restricted. A pre-colonial deposit (Orsi's 'Sikel layer') is encountered over a wide area between Archaic layers and bedrock, although indigenous buildings are only glimpsed in a few soundings (Orsi 1918; Frasca 1983). Tracts of broad stone foundation walls with internal benches attest fairly large structures, either round, elongated or elliptical with rounded ends, not unlike those at Morgantina or Leontini. These are overlain in places by small quadrangular dwellings (usually about 4×4 m) of early colonial date (late eighth century BC), flanked by a narrow lane, and regarded as part of an embryonic town plan of the first Greek settlement (fig. 3.8) (Pelagatti 1982).[9] The design of the latter was perhaps imported from the Greek homeland, where similar structures were beginning to appear at about this time, and they undoubtedly reflect the modest socio-economic status of early settlers (Fusaro 1982; Vallet 1984–5). Subsequent developments, traced at Megara for example, including the elaboration of plot divisions, the separation of public from private areas and the gradual evolution of

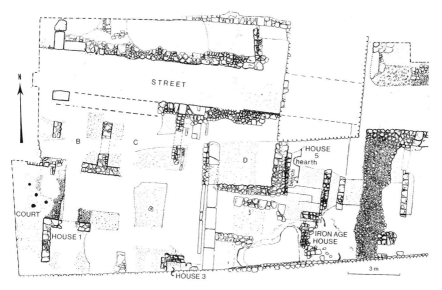

*Fig. 3.8* Ortygia (Syracuse) early colonial buildings, Prefettura excavations
(after Pelagatti 1982)

monumental architecture, obviously reflect the evolving needs and character of the *polis*.

Given the apparent lack of continuity, changes in layout and design, as
well as the limitations of the evidence, one cannot claim that the early
colonial dwellings on Syracuse were modelled on indigenous buildings.
However, there are similarities as regards fixtures, materials and techniques of construction: wall foundations of rough stones, flatter surfaces
facing outward; floors levelled or cut down, sometimes into the bedrock
and laid with lime mortar; a low bench on the inside wall and sometimes
a hearth, oven or cooking installation against the bench; and thatched
roofs. These are all standard features of indigenous early Iron Age
dwellings. If exterior floor surfaces, courtyards, wells or linear trackways
could be found at indigenous sites, which is by no means unthinkable,
then the similarities would increase further.

However, surveys of urban development in the early Greek colonial
world have rarely and only recently countenanced the possibility of
indigenous influence or connections.[10] Emblematic of the traditional
premise of discussion is that early colonial dwellings, however modest or
simple in size and design, are '*case*' (houses), whereas the (often larger)
native residences are '*capanne*' (huts). Likewise, any structures with
corner walls at 90° associated with Greek settlers tend to be admired as the
earliest examples of 'rational' urbanism. It is tempting to invert or subvert
this hellenocentric convention and surmise, subjectively of course, that
the little box-rooms characteristic of the first phase at Naxos, Megara and

Helorus, as well as Syracuse, would not have seemed particularly worthy of imitation to indigenous people (whereas the fine painted pottery used in them might well have been admired and even seemed incongruous). In fact, there is no evidence that such a design was adopted.

On the other hand, there are occasional examples in the Sicilian colonies of another type of residence, with a more elaborate design of two or three rooms linked by a longer lateral room or vestibule, known as a *pastas* house in Greece, and encountered in Sicily at Megara and Naxos just before the mid-seventh century BC, where it is regarded as a form of prestigious architecture, perhaps used by higher-ranking individuals and not just as a dwelling (e.g. Cordsen 1995). Of approximately similar design, but with modifications and additions, are four structures at the indigenous site of Monte San Mauro (fig. 3.7B, C), dated between about 580 BC and the beginning of the fifth century BC, associated with several developments at the site, including the appearance of Greek pottery and artefacts in significant quantities, modifications in burial customs, religious practices and a Greek inscription of a political or legal nature (Spigo 1986). First regarded by Orsi (1911) as a centre of mixed character ('sicula-greca'), the archaic site, located in the Heraean hills near the outer limits of Geloan, Chalkidian or Syracusan territory, has now been re-labelled a *centro greco* and a probable Geloan foundation (Spigo 1980–1: 775). The idea of local continuity has been reduced to a minimum, if not entirely negated.

At first glance, the houses look new. Domestic structures prior to this date were of different shape, as noted above, and yet despite the appearance of roof tiles and the presence of Greek artefacts, there are many elements of continuity with early Iron Age practices, for example in the layout and domestic concerns reflected by the contents and fixtures. In fact, the arrangement of the individual units is not orthogonal, but dictated by the sloping terrain; hearths or cooking installations with layers of clay on stones are traditional; the floor surface is not paved; lava millstones were used and large *pithoi* set into the floor for grain storage; loomweights are very common, and the presence of a loom can be inferred in at least one house; the botanical remains from the *pithoi* suggest the persistence of traditional agriculture (barley, spelt, vetches and beans), rather than olive or grape cultivation. One should also consider, in order to avoid familiar preconceptions, that the appearance of roof tiles, bath tubs, amphorae, Greek pottery and *arulae* (to which most attention is given in the preliminary reports) are simply concessions to modernisation in a world which was becoming more cosmopolitan and in which one did not need to be Greek in order to appreciate wine, fine pottery and the other artefactual trappings commonly associated with hellenisation (Leighton 1999: 253). The adoption of a new and larger house type in the sixth century BC (whose surface area is not much greater than that of many early Iron Age long-houses) could be regarded as part of a general change in the style of urban living, which was occurring over a wide area of the western Mediterranean at this time (cf. Whitehouse and Wilkins 1989), even if Greek coastal centres were active in its promulgation.

Various chains of inference can be formulated in order to account for the changing character of Monte San Mauro and its inhabitants in the course of the sixth century BC. In theory, an influx of settlers importing the customs of coastal colonies could have accelerated a process which had already begun in the seventh century BC. With or without new arrivals and regardless of their ethnic origin, the main point is that the local residents probably adopted this new style of residence; otherwise we would have to find them elsewhere carrying on in traditional manner, or assume that they were evicted or eliminated. A question that follows is whether these new home-owners were of elevated rank. If so, then the dwellings of the less well-to-do have yet to be found. This line of inference could reinforce the proposition that an indigenous upper class played an important role in a process of acculturation, which may account for the spread of wine drinking and 'cultivated' pursuits, such as literary skills and a taste for prestigious exotica at sites of local origin (Albanese Procelli 1996b). If these houses are not unusual for the period, it may also be suggested that the tenor and quality of domestic life at inland sites were as high as or even higher than in the coastal *metropoleis*.

Similar questions arise at other, if not all, inland sites of this period, although progress will be limited to those where the evidence is reasonably well, although nowhere yet fully, published. For example, the two-roomed house at Ramacca of the late seventh/early sixth centuries BC (fig. 3.9) might be regarded as a rather ordinary dwelling with a bench, a hearth and a lime-plaster floor (Procelli and Albanese 1992). The proximity of Leontini would lead one to anticipate stronger Greek influence here than further inland. However, the excavators do not automatically assume the presence of Greeks, but note the changing range of rather mixed elements and traditions over time: the pottery includes both indigenous ware and Greek imports (such as Ionic drinking cups and amphorae); long-distance trade items (Etruscan bucchero); mixed burial rites (chamber-tombs, trench and amphorae burials); a suggestion of Greek cult buildings (from architectural terracottas) after the mid-sixth century BC; fine wares (mainly late sixth–fifth-century BC Attic cups) with scratched Greek letters, but probably representing Sikel names or words. Even everyday artefacts, which should provide clues to changes in local culinary traditions, give a rather mixed message: there are both Greek (late sixth–early fifth century BC) and indigenous cooking-pots.

Likewise, Morgantina and many other inland sites (such as Monte

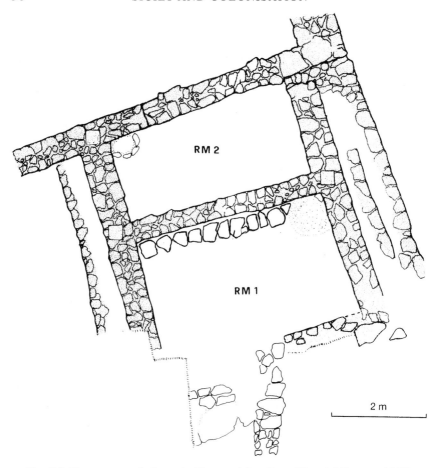

*Fig. 3.9* Ramacca, archaic period house (after Procelli and Albanese 1992)

Bubbonia, Monte Saraceno, Vassallaggi, Sabucina) show significant changes in layout only from about the mid-sixth century BC, with the appearance of public or religious buildings of Greek design.[11] There is an on-going discussion in connection with Morgantina, perhaps incapable of resolution, as to whether this represents the arrival of ethnic Greeks or a stage in the hellenisation of resident Sikels, or both. Attention has centred on burials (Lyons 1996a, 1996b) and has recently extended to other categories of evidence from domestic contexts and inscriptions, which also indicate that indigenous traditions survived for longer and that the adoption of cultural traits was more selective than has usually been assumed (Antonaccio 1997). There are large quantities of unpublished painted or plain wares of local tradition at the site, and some sixth-century BC houses include fixtures, cooking wares and installations reminiscent of early Iron Age forms.

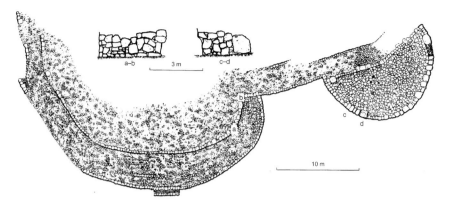

*Fig. 3.10* Finocchito fortifications (after Orsi 1897; Bonacasa Carra 1974)

Finally, one may note that similar questions are raised at indigenous sites with regard to defensive works, usually bedevilled by chronological uncertainties and conflicting opinions as to whether the various banks, ditches or more elaborate stone constructions reflect Greek influence. Most authors have assumed this to be the case. However, the construction of the fortification wall at Finocchito (fig. 3.10), although not dated directly, could logically be associated with the need to delimit and defend an indigenous stronghold in the context of growing insecurity and a souring of relations between Syracuse and its hinterland. As such, the impressive stone bastions (up to 7 m wide) should belong to the late eighth or seventh centuries BC and represent indigenous workmanship, as Orsi (1897) first suggested. By contrast, Dunbabin (1948: 98) was unwilling to countenance the possibility of indigenous fortifications and vaguely postulated 'the influence of Greek military architecture of later date' or even a Byzantine construction.

In recent decades it has become clear that substantial turreted fortification walls were not uncommon at various times during the Sicilian Bronze Age (for example at Thapsos, Petraro, I Faraglioni) and therefore the presence of indigenous fortifications at a site like Finocchito should not be discounted. However, even those more willing to regard the Finocchito fortification as indigenous seem to assume that the local people must have been helped by 'accorgimenti appresi dai Greci della costa' (Adamesteanu 1956: 359; Orsi 1911: 743). At many other inland sites of indigenous origin, which subsequently adopted Greek customs and were involved in various later conflicts of Sicilian history, accurate dating is vital. In view of the range of sites and defensive structures, the whole subject needs to be tackled on a case-by-case basis (Bonacasa Carra 1974, for a survey), although interpretation need not always be reduced to a choice between the role of Greeks or locals educated by Greeks; another instance of the teacher–pupil model which has dominated the study of Greek and native relations.

## CONCLUSIONS

Plainly, much remains to be discussed in the Sicilian arena of cultural interaction, where domestic contexts, dwellings and the subsistence economy merit further attention. Rather than more hasty reconstructions of the invisible and usually most uncertain parts of structures (upper walls and roofs), which is characteristic of some recent work at prehistoric sites in Sicily, or the emphasis on a few Greek artefacts of aesthetic merit to the exclusion of much of the rest, which has typified publications of archaic sites, one hopes for fuller and broader consideration of socio-economic factors in future, with detailed recording and full publication as the proper springboard for interpretation or further elaboration. From such a stand-point, the house or the household is a potentially very illuminating context for study.

In some ways, the archaeological evidence for the eighth–seventh centuries BC differs little from that of earlier periods, given the lack of contemporary historical documents and the persistence of small-scale pre-state societies, and does not easily lend itself to the reconstruction of what a Braudelian approach would call a '*histoire événementielle*'. Of course, the accelerating pace of economic, political and demographic change between the eighth and sixth centuries BC is very striking throughout the western Mediterranean, and local developments also reflect a supra-regional evolution. New centres of power capable of strategic calculations and alliances of international scope were beginning to influence events or deploy military forces on a scale without parallel at a prior date. However, questions of interaction require a contextual study using a wide range of archaeological evidence; much evidence exists already, while more would not be hard to obtain. The nature or degree of acculturation also needs to be defined with care, since it may range from full and rapid assimilation or adoption of cultural traits (which, as I have attempted to show, is not typical of the situation in Sicily, contrary to popular belief) to more selective forms of cultural borrowing or entrainment. Likewise, the locus of interaction may be either restricted or extended across various social, economic, political and ideological spheres, and involve contacts that vary from indirect to direct, active to passive, voluntary to enforced. A further impetus for reassessment may therefore derive from the growing dissatisfaction with old and often simplistic approaches and paradigms and a greater willingness to challenge them, as expressed by both pre-historic and classical archaeologists in recent years.

# 4

# WINE WARES IN PROTOHISTORIC EASTERN SICILY

## *Tamar Hodos*

## INTRODUCTION

THE FACT OF THE acculturation of the native peoples in Sicily within 300 years after the first Greeks settled is hardly a new observation. The preliminary periodisation of native ceramics of the Bronze and Iron Ages was established over 100 years ago by Paolo Orsi, who noted that by the end of the fifth century there were no ceramics which could be identified as native. While subsequent refinements to the chronology have been made, the basic outline remains unchanged.

Literature, on the other hand, tells us of native cultural identity continuing and thriving during the fifth century, including the ethnic self-identification of the Sikels, the native people who lived in southeastern Sicily. Diodorus tells the story of the Sikel leader Ducetius, who allied the Sikels against the Sicilian Greeks and punished those whom he felt were in danger of losing their Sikel identity; one such example is the settlement of Morgantina.[1] Ducetius' army was defeated by Syracuse in 446 BC, but he spent the remaining six years of his life establishing Sikel communities. Frequent reference is made to the Sikels in Thucydides' account of the second half of the fifth century, as they are often called upon to assist a particular Greek settlement against another. For instance, during the seventh year of the Peloponnesian War, in 425 BC, we are told that the Sikels came down from the surrounding mountains to assist Naxos against Messina (Thuc. 4.25.9). Diodorus recalls that at the end of the fifth century, Dionysius I destroyed Naxos and returned it to the Sikels (D.S. 14.15). As confirmation of recognised Sikel participation, an inscription found in the Athenian agora which dates from the time of the Peloponnesian War lists the Sikels as allies of the Athenians (*IG* I[3]: 291; Meritt 1957). While we have literary and epigraphic references to an ethnic group, archaeology provides us with little to supplement these, for by this time material remains which can be identified as culturally Sikel are simply no longer found: in traditional indigenous contexts, native ceramic

41

forms, for instance, seem to be replaced by types of Greek and colonial origin and manufacture. For this reason, it is generally accepted that Sikel Sicily was materially hellenised. Indeed, this circumstance is not unique to the Sikels but is shared by the other indigenous cultures in Sicily by this time, too, although they have been less well examined archaeologically than the Sikels.

Prior to hellenisation, we have a very complicated picture of Greek–native relations. The material remains in many settlements display a mixture of cultures. Architecture and burial customs reveal a blending of Greek and indigenous traditions (Albanese Procelli 1996a: 169–73), and too often, there is no consensus amongst scholars as to whether a particular site is a native settlement or a Greek outpost. One such example is Morgantina, where it remains uncertain whether the post-destruction rebuilding during the first half of the sixth century represents a hellenised Sikel settlement with commercial contact with the Greek coastal cities or a secondary Greek colony (Tsakirgis 1995: 126; Lyons 1996a; Antonaccio 1997). By this time even primary Greek colonies clearly had native residents. At Naxos, for instance, from a sixth-century house in the Greek settlement comes a traditional Sikel carinated bowl made in local clay with one horizontal handle and a bulge on the opposite side, a Sikel form which predates Greek colonisation (Naxos Museum number XI39996). The decoration on the shoulder is of wavy vertical metope lines, a motif common to traditional Sikel wares although unfamiliar in such a syntax on Greek wares. It is undoubtedly of Sikel manufacture and implies the continuing production of traditional Sikel wares. No factor of prestige acquisition is associated with this vessel because it is simply not a prestigious object. Thus its presence in an archaic house at Naxos is best explained by the suggestion that Sikels were somehow co-resident, although the status of non-Greek inhabitants within Greek settlements remains uncertain.[2]

Most of our evidence for indigenous culture during the sixth century actually comes from sites in the interior of the island, although few settlements can be considered purely native by their ceramics or buildings, and the preponderance of Greek wares in cemeteries may mask the identity of the interred. Although the tombs at Morgantina largely maintain traditional burial rites, the use of Greek religious votives suggests the presence of ethnic Greeks at the site (Lyons 1996b: 187). Similar developments are reflected in other archaic-period graves at traditional Sikel sites such as Licodia Eubea (Orsi 1898, 1902), Modica, Ragusa (Dunbabin 1948: 107–9) and Monte Casasia (Di Stefano 1987: 153–7).

## ACCULTURATION STUDIES

Acculturation has been defined as the interaction of two cultures leading to the exchange and adaptation of information and the adoption of traits by one or other culture (Millett 1990). The question at hand, therefore, is whether it is possible to identify evidence of acculturation in the centuries between initial colonisation and material assimilation by clarifying those elements representative of the persistence of cultural difference and ethnic self-consciousness (after Jones 1996: 77, n. 5). There are several difficult-ies which arise with such an exercise. One is that the process of accultur-ation is not a continuously paced development. Changes in material culture can represent any number of different aspects of development at different times. The essence of the problem is to gauge which changes might carry a secondary level of implication and might be related to new factors in the identification of local populations. It is not always clear, however, which cultural motifs deserve a specific ethnic label (Curti et al. 1996).

While it is often assumed that distinctive material cultures can be equated with ethnic groups, this can be problematic (Bradley 1997: 35). One reason is that, with specific regard to archaeology, remains are fre-quently interpreted in the light of literary attestations of ethnic groups and may only appear distinct because of this (for a further discussion, see Whitehouse and Wilkins 1985). Literary evidence, because written at a different time and possibly with a particular agenda, can also misinterpret earlier ethnic situations; written representations of ethnicities may not necessarily be a reflection of the basic structures of a society but instead one of transient political alignments (Dench 1995: 186–9; Hall 1997: 51, 60, 76; Alston 1997: 83). This may hold true for some ethnic groups in Sicily, such as the Elymians, who are less well supported by archaeo-logical means than literary. But enough material evidence exists to allow concordance with literary records and to identify the main culture living in southeastern Sicily during the period of Greek colonisation as Sikel.[3] Furthermore, literature seems to suppose some sort of social differen-tiation between the Greeks and others, and perhaps the traditional priority of Greek culture in today's interpretations of literary and archaeological evidence can be traced back to the ancient sources. Historians such as Thucydides refer to the Greeks through their *polis* affiliation, such as Naxians and Messenians, while the 'others' are distinguished by their ethnicity: the Sikels, the Elymians. It is unclear whether these distinctions were imposed by the Greeks themselves, encouraged by the Sikels and other ethnicities, or were the historians' subsequent colouring. Neverthe-less, these literary distinctions have affected modern interpretation and encouraged scholars of Iron Age Sicily to search for material differences to correspond with literary ethnic differentiation where little has been otherwise apparent, or to have sought a literary ethnic identity for a distinct material culture (Leighton 1999: 217).

Acculturation studies have largely focused upon Greece itself, or upon the romanisation of Italy, but it is only very recently that such attention has been directed towards Sicily.[4] These studies have been preliminary and have concentrated upon using settlements, cemeteries, inscriptions, manufactured goods and exchange, and food production as a means of seeking signs in the archaeological record of acculturation and understanding their meaning.[5] The circumstances of the acculturation process in Sicily are markedly different from Greece, where ethnic groups strove for self-identification and self-assertion in response to the rise of the *polis*, or romanised Italy, where Rome took vast regions by violent force and imposed a Roman framework upon the local cultures.[6] No such occurrences took place in protohistoric Sicily. Sicily was colonised, not conquered (by the Greeks), and thus material changes observable in the local, indigenous communities are reactions to different circumstances from those either by emerging *poleis* in Greece, or by local Italian peoples in response to the might of Rome.

This appropriation of aspects of another culture does not necessarily entail the assumption of an identity that is not traditional, however (Gallini 1973; Curti et al. 1996: 182). When elements are labelled 'Greek', for instance, reference is made to nothing more and nothing less than an abstraction, an ideal (Curti et al. 1996: 181). Furthermore, as Lyons has noted, the term 'hellenisation' is usually applied to the transformation of the life-ways of non-Greek residents in the Greek colonial sphere of influence but fails to account adequately for the reciprocities of inter-cultural contact (Lyons 1996a: 132). Thus, 'hellenised Sicily' reflects an interpretation based only upon acculturated native material remains, but it does not address any notions of development in Greek culture through contact with native Sicilians. Furthermore, while observable changes in native culture may be viewed as signs of native acculturation, it remains unclear whether they reflect a subconscious reaction to a changing economy or a conscious reaction of self-preservation in response to a perceived threat of Greek culture.

The best documentation of the development of a non-Greek culture in Sicily comes from Sikel contexts. A greater number of non-Greek sites which have been excavated have been identified as Sikel, and the typological development of Sikel ceramics and other objects is well published. Furthermore, the area of initial Greek contact and penetration was primarily within Sikel territory, along the eastern coast of Sicily and into the Hyblon mountains of the southeast. It seems most sensible, therefore, to focus a study of early interaction between the colonists and indigenous peoples upon the Sikels.

## GREEK–SIKEL CERAMIC EXCHANGE

During the Finocchito period (traditionally 735–650 BC), when the Greeks first established themselves along eastern Sicily, the ceramic repertoire of the resident Sikels altered under influence from their new neighbours. Greek geometric motifs were adopted and adapted into the local repertoire in both incision and dipinto techniques. Often these decorative influences can be traced back to the mother-city of the local colony.[7] Greek objects themselves, particularly ceramics, have been found in native *necropoleis* and generally are of the same types as vessels from the earliest levels of the Greek colonies. On the other hand, hardly any Sikel vessels have been found in contemporary colonial contexts. The impression is of the Greeks overrunning indigenous creativity.

On closer inspection, however, a somewhat different picture emerges. First, it must be pointed out that during this early colonial phase, most of our evidence for the native cultures is limited to funerary contexts, so our understanding cannot be as thorough as for contemporary colonial sites. No doubt if contemporary indigenous settlement evidence were available, our understanding of the distribution of Greek and native pottery would be quite different. Second, there are surprisingly few Greek vessels, or types of Greek vessels, at this time in the native cemeteries. Thapsos and Thapsos-type[8] *skyphoi* are the most common; they are found at Thapsos, Modica, Villasmundo, Avola-Cassibile, Ossini and Finocchito. Another early Greek vessel shape is the Aetos 666 *kotyle* appearing at sites such as Modica, Villasmundo, Ossini and Cocolonazzo di Mola.[9] In addition, there are chevron *skyphoi* and the pendent semi-circle *skyphos* from Villasmundo.[10] Other examples of Protocorinthian *kotylai* and *skyphoi* have been found at sites such as Finocchito, Ossini, Morgantina, Sant'Aloe, Centuripe (Centuripae) and Modica.[11] The neck fragment of a Protocorinthian *oinochoe* has been identified at Avola (*BTCGI*, 3: 348), and an early Attic SOS amphora was found at Modica (Di Stefano 1987: 152). Additional Euboean imports include *skyphoi* from Castelluccio and an example from the La Rocca collection, originally from the Modica area.[12]

It is interesting to observe that no Corinthian *aryballoi* have been found in any of these Sikel contexts, with the exception of one poor example from Ossini (T30: Lagona 1971; Orsi 1909: 83), although Proto-Corinthian belly and transitional ovoid–piriform examples are well represented amongst the earliest tombs in the Fusco necropolis of Syracuse and at Megara Hyblaea, as well as in the respective settlements. In fact, it is from the distribution of the *aryballos* shape in the colonial graves in Sicily that its seriation and typological development has been determined (Neeft 1987). Furthermore, no imitations of this shape in either native or colonial sites have been found except for one of the transitional shape in local fabric from the settlement at Megara Hyblaea.[13] There is no similar small unguent shape in the Sikel repertoire. What this implies is a selective exchange between the colonists and their Sikel neighbours during the eighth and first half of the seventh centuries, and it suggests no interest on the part of the Sikels in small flasks or their contents. Furthermore, this contrasts significantly with evidence from Etruria (Ridgway 1992a: 88) and southern Italy (de la Genière 1995: 36), where Corinthian perfume flasks have been found in indigenous graves, although, as in Sicily, there is no small unguent shape in the traditional repertoire of either region.

In the microcosm of a single site, such a pattern of selective import can be seen more clearly. Finocchito is the site best representative in publication of the Sikel culture during the early colonial period. Using the fabric assessment of the ceramics conducted by Steures (1980) and following the typological classification of Frasca (1981), a total of 205 vessels of ninety-four different types date to the colonial period. Of these, only thirteen examples can be accepted as imports and eighteen identified as of colonial manufacture.[14] In other words, Greek and colonial-manufactured vessels account for only 15 per cent of the total number of vessels of the colonial period. The shapes are limited to the drinking and pouring shapes of *oinochoai*, *skyphoi*, *kotylai* and a *hydria*. From the funerary remains of other Finocchito-period sites, there is no evidence that the Sikels were interested in Greek commodities which required transport in large containers or miniature vessels, such as oils or perfumes; this contrasts with the use of such vessels by the colonists, who frequently included vessels ranging from large amphorae to miniature unguent containers amongst their burial *corredi*.

Over time, however, the nature of the evidence changes. The Sikel ceramics of the later seventh and sixth centuries become more limited in shape and decoration when compared with the variety of Greek wares. The repertoire of forms consists mostly of large shapes, such as amphorae, *oinochoai*, large bowls and *askoi* (see Fouilland et al. 1995: 334, for instance). The decorative patterns are almost always geometric. This contrasts greatly with the rich variety of shapes and motifs found on contemporary Greek wares, many of which are frequently found in graves in hellenised Sikel settlements. Sikel wares draw no inspiration from the Orientalising influences prevalent in Greek imports of this time, continuing to utilise geometric designs. No filling ornaments and, perhaps more importantly, no animals other than stylised birds are found decorating Sikel vases of this period (files of birds are a remnant of the Greek Geometric era, however). The complexity of the process of acculturation means that this long-term development, or change in ceramic production, may be interpreted as a sign of acculturation through decreasing traditional output, or else as a reaction against acculturation, with ceramic shapes and decorative styles adhering to more traditional forms as a method of resistance to current Greek influences.

## WINE WARES

The fact that primarily *skyphoi* and *oinochoai* of Greek and colonial manufacture were imported into Finocchito and other contemporary Sikel sites suggests an early interest in the drinking of wine. The import and local imitation of such vessels are common in the hinterland of the colonies at this early period, but not elsewhere in Sicily (Albanese Procelli 1996a: 168–9), most probably due to the nascent nature of contact, which had not yet developed into longer-distance trade or territorial expansion. Thus, the inclusion of wine-drinking vessels in graves at sites in the interior is seen only later, during the sixth century, where a greater variety of wine-related vessels of Greek and colonial manufacture has been found (at sites such as Morgantina: Lyons 1996b: table 1). The fact that the earliest Greek vessels in which the Sikels are interested are related to the Greek cultural practice of the symposium is extremely suggestive.

The introduction of Greek customs of wine drinking must have influenced Sikel customs. Following the pattern suggested by Whitehouse and Wilkins for southern Italy, in which they have proposed that the native elite organised the exchange of prestige objects for motivations of status rather than profit (Whitehouse and Wilkins 1989: 114), it is possible that within Sikel Sicily wine drinking was viewed as a status activity.[15] The non-Sikel vessels, in addition to their practical function as drinking cups, may have been used also as expressions of wealth and power, and they may have possessed a symbolic role, independent of or in addition to their function. In turn, this may have provided the incentive to produce local, Sikel-made, imitations (as Herring has suggested for Southern Italy: Herring 1991: 129). A similar sense of 'value' may explain the adoption of Greek decorative motifs on Sikel wares of traditional shape. As Albanese Procelli has written, 'With regard to forms of acculturation … in addition to the diffusion of drinking vessels, [imitation] points to the spread of wine-drinking as an important element in the process' (1996a: 169).

Albanese Procelli's statement gives the impression that the Sikels did not drink wine prior to the arrival of the Greeks. There is no archaeo-botanical or residual analyses which would allow one to substantiate a claim for or against the consumption of wine before the Greeks arrived, but it seems unlikely that the Sikels did not know about wine prior to the end of the eighth century BC. Although there is no evidence of actual viticulture, the presence of wild grapes during the prehistoric period has been identified (see Leighton 1993a: 23–4, n. 9, and Costantini et al. 1987: 400). It is possible that the Mycenaeans introduced wine to Sicily; Mycenaean vessels are well documented in Sicily, including those suitable for wine consumption (Jones and Vagnetti 1991; Vagnetti 1993; Leighton 1996b). The native peoples may have adopted some of these shapes into their own repertoire, particularly those suitable for drinking, pouring and mixing liquids.

Albanese Procelli has recently observed that during the colonial period the earliest imported amphorae were for oil and that wine vessels do not appear in Sicily until the end of the seventh century (Albanese Procelli 1997a: 8–9), but it is not impossible that Corinthian Type A and Attic SOS amphorae were used to transport wine as well as oil. The image of Dionysus carrying an SOS amphora on the sixth-century François Vase reinforces a relationship between the vessel type and wine consumption which may reflect a traditional connection (see Foxhall 1998: 302). It is also possible that local wine was readily available for colonial consumption, although such containers, which may have been organic, have not been archaeologically preserved. It seems very unlikely that the colonial Greeks did not consume wine for a century.

## WINE WARES AS EVIDENCE OF ACCULTURATION

Wine drinking has been used as a means of observing acculturation because the customs of wine drinking in Greek culture are well known: the occasions for such ritualisation, where such events were held, who the participants were, the customs and format which they followed, and the specific vessels that were used for mixing, pouring and drinking (Murray 1983, 1990).

Thus, when these vessels appear in a different cultural context, scholarship concludes that there is Greek influence upon that other culture through the introduction of the culturally Greek symposium. In Etruria, for example, banqueting has assumed a central role in our understanding of the process of acculturation. The appearance of Greek sympotic elements in Etruscan culture has led to the general acceptance that the symposium was adopted by the Etruscans (d'Agostino 1989; Cristofani 1987; Murray 1990: 10; Pontrandolfo 1995; Rathje 1995; Small 1994), although it was not adopted outright. There are important elements of the Etruscan banqueting rituals which differ from the Greek, such as the conjugal symposium (d'Agostino 1987, 1989), a concept unheard of in contemporary Greece and later discussed with disgust by writers such as Theopompus (*FGH* 115 fr. 204 *ap*. Ath.12.517d–e). Elsewhere in Italy, women play an important role in the Italian symposium – amphorae and

sympotic services have been found in tombs in Latium identified otherwise as belonging to women, suggesting they had a more involved role
than their Greek counterparts (Gras 1983: 1069).

In other words, the Etruscans and Latins did not follow the Greek
models of banquets and the symposium in full but used selective elements
where they fitted into their own needs. In all likelihood, Etruscan and
Latin drinking did not have the identical ritual and/or social connotations
that the symposium had for the Greeks. In fact, Rathje has identified
important Near Eastern elements in sympotic representations and assemblages in Italy which suggest a direct Phoenician ideology of the entire
banqueting concept, of which the symposium is only one aspect.[16]

Additional differences between the Greek and Italian ideologies regarding the symposium can be seen in the archaeological remains at various
sites. None of the Greek tombs from Posidonia, for instance, contained
a sympotic service, not even a *krater* (Pontrandolfo 1992: 225–44), yet a
range of vessel shapes appropriate for use in the symposium has been
recovered from urban contexts throughout the settlement (although the
vessels may not necessarily have been used exclusively for the symposium; Greco and Theodorescu 1983, 1987). In contrast, banqueting
sets, including sympotic services, are uncommon outside of funerary contexts in non-Greek Italy (Rathje 1983; Tagliente 1985).

Evidence for the symposium in Sicilian contexts is equally complex. In
central Italy we have artistic representations as well as sympotic services,
and possible parallels with Homeric rituals have been drawn with regard
to princely tombs, but a similar hypothesis cannot be made for Sicily.
There are no Sikel artistic representations of banqueting or drinking,
weapons were not commonly buried, and no princely tombs have been
identified thus far (or even any notable wealthy burials such as have been
identified not only in Italy but also in Hallstatt Europe: Dietler 1989).
Furthermore, in contrast to Greece, where the evidence for banqueting
structures is plentiful (see, for instance, Bergquist 1990; Cooper and
Morris 1990), the absence of significant settlement evidence for the
Finocchito period so far means that structures which may have been used
for banqueting in Sikel Sicily cannot be identified.[17] Finally, burials of
members of other Italian native groups of high rank exhibit *krateres* and
*oinochoai*, as well as Etruscan wine amphorae (Greco and Pontrandolfo
1990; Pontrandolfo 1995), the inclusion of the forms lending status to
their users (Stoddart 1989). In Sikel Sicily during the Finocchito period,
however, it seems to be primarily *skyphoi* and *oinochoai* which were
buried, sometimes in association with locally made amphorae (Finocchito
N52, for example, contained a local amphora and a Thapsos-type
*skyphos*).

The social circumstances in Greek culture in which wine was used and consumed are well known. In contrast, little is known of such Sikel traditions, but given that the Sikels have their own set of pouring, mixing and drinking vessels – including various jug shapes, large stemmed basins and primarily one-handled bowls – from long before the Greeks arrived, it is probable that wine drinking played a role in Sikel life. Much has been made of wine drinking as a process of acculturation during the archaic period (Antonaccio and Neils 1995; Albanese Procelli 1996a; Antonaccio 1997), but little attention has been paid to the presence of such vessels in native contexts during the eighth and seventh centuries and to the implications for the roots of the subsequent acculturation.

We have three circumstances as evidenced by the ceramic remains in Sikel contexts with regard to wine drinking during the Finocchito period: (1) the Sikels import from the Greek colonists vessels of which they have their own traditional forms – trefoil *oinochoai*, the form of which is generally thought to appear during the preceding Pantalica South period;[18] (2) the Sikels also import vessels of which they do not have traditional forms – the *skyphos*; this might suggest an interest in exotica, except that (3) the Sikels choose not to import other vessels of which they do not have traditional forms – the *aryballos* – even though it perhaps better represents an 'exotic good' than the *skyphoi* and *oinochoai* they did import. The selectivity of the Sikels in choosing some, but not all, new forms available, and some, but not all, that replaced or replicated native forms, requires explanation.

On the one hand, the importing of these vessels could be evidence of nothing more than early exchanges between new settlers searching to establish themselves with their far more numerous, long-existing neighbours, by offering items which the Sikels would have viewed as exotica. Yet those vessels which the Sikels obtained were not the only things the Greeks had to offer: the corpus of *aryballoi* in the colonial settlements and cemeteries and virtual absence of the vessel in Sikel contexts thus far suggests that the Sikels were interested in selected items, those which are used for wine drinking and are associated with the Greek symposium. If the Sikels were interested in exotica, why were they not more attracted to the *aryballoi* and their perfumed contents, items unfamiliar in the Sikel culture?

Another explanation could be that the Sikels simply utilised some of these new drinking vessels as emblems of status. This is difficult to substantiate, as presently there is no evidence for Sikel class structure during the Finocchito period based upon the funerary remains, and the elite cannot be identified at any particular site. Nevertheless, it is possible that an elite was beginning to emerge at this time, encouraged by the status-enhancement of foreign goods, used irrespective of the function and implications of these vessel types in Greek culture. These vessels may also represent nothing more than the Sikels using Greek vessels in their own Sikel way, irrespective of class or status. This suggestion may be supported by the fact that the *krater* was not a popular form amongst the Sikels. If they did not mix their wine, they would have had no use for such a mixing vessel. Thus they selected those vessels which accorded with their own customs of drinking. The hypothesis fails to explain why the Sikels did adopt Greek drinking cups, however, another form which they did not have prior to the arrival of the Greeks.

The fact that the Sikels took only selected wine vessels and none of the other Greek ceramic forms available, particularly when they already had their own selection of suitable vessels, implies that the Greeks were offering something more than mere objects. It is possible that they offered the concept of a social custom which required special wares which only the Greeks could at first supply, until the Sikels began to make their own imitations, but for use in that same social custom of ritualised wine drinking: the symposium. The local imitation of the *krater* form at Villasmundo (Voza 1978: pl. 26.2), the site with the earliest Greek vessels in Sicily, lends further support to this hypothesis, suggesting that the full format of the symposium may have been attempted initially by the Sikels.[19] The shape was not widely adopted, but its early imitation is significant. The fact that the Sikels appear to have been interested only in some of those vessels associated with the Greek symposium must be more than mere coincidence.

## CONCLUSIONS

Above all, these circumstances raise the question of whether or not it is even fair to identify the various sympotic elements found not only in Sicilian but also in other Italian cultures as representative of the adoption of the symposium. Only selected elements of the Greek symposium seem to have been utilised throughout Italy, and those aspects differed between regions. Thus, while in Sicily, the *krater* remains a less common vessel in sympotic services throughout the archaic period in favour of drinking and pouring shapes (cf. Lyons 1996b: table 1 and Fouilland et al. 1995: 511–12), in Etruscan funerary art, representations of the symposium eventually become reduced to the 'simple exaltation' of the *krater* (d'Agostino 1989: 7–8), indicative of the symbolic importance of that single vessel as emblematic of not only the symposium but also the high status which participation in it in Italian society offered. In contrast to both examples, in Latium, a banqueting service found at Ficana had several mixing vessels but virtually no pouring shapes or ladles, and the majority of objects were drinking cups (Rathje 1983, although the collection itself may be somewhat anomalous).

It is clear that there are some basic difficulties in the translation of the Greek symposium into another culture, and hence its identification. For example, as Small has observed with regard to Etruria, the conjugal symposium is an oxymoron in Greek terms because it contradicts one of the basic requirements for a symposium in Greek usage – that the participants, if not restricted to men, include only *hetairai*, not wives (Small 1994: 85). Is it still fair to call this event a symposium, then? Certainly, if it is identified as an Etruscan symposium, utilising elements of the Greek symposium in a manner in concordance with local tradition. Therefore in Sicily, where the early evidence for sympotic ritual is limited to the presence of certain sympotic vessels in Sikel contexts, the use of ritual vessels for drinking wine may also be viewed as a sign of the adoption of the symposium, even if not in its full – Greek – format.

It could equally be argued that perhaps it is no longer appropriate to use a Greek term such as 'symposium' to describe the outcome of the adoption of selected elements of the banqueting custom into another culture's ritual (see, for instance, Antonaccio 1997: 182–3). It is unknown if there were pre-existing drinking rituals in the Sikel culture, for which there is evidence in Etruria, but to discard the use of a Greek term to describe what may be an indigenous tradition with new Greek elements would remove the significance of the contribution of the Greek symposium to indigenous drinking customs. Reference to such events as a Sikel or Etruscan symposium recalls that these are customs with regional variations and adopted aspects of Greek culture and tradition, although ideally these should be called hellenised Sikel (or Etruscan, etc.) drinking rituals, to demonstrate the chronological priority of the indigenous tradition.

A parallel example of the blending of Sikel and foreign traditions can be seen with the development of written Sikel, which utilises the Greek alphabet to express the Sikel language,[20] as a result of increasing Greek infiltration during the sixth century. It has been noted that at interior sites such as Morgantina, Montagna di Marzo and Ramacca, graffiti appear on imported and Sikeliote cups more frequently than on other forms or wares, evidence of an exchange network throughout eastern Sicily which emphasises the significance of wine and wine drinking and may imply the status of the owners/users (Antonaccio and Neils 1995: 275–6). Some view the use of the Greek alphabet to record native languages as a sign of hellenisation as a result of first having learned the Greek language and then the Greek script before adapting the script to the Sikel language (Domínguez 1989: 539; see also Albanese Procelli 1996a: 173). To others, this is viewed as a means of expressing ethnic identity (Antonaccio and Neils 1995: 274; 276) and therefore perhaps resisting hellenisation. In this respect, through the use of the Greek alphabet to maintain their own language and separate identity, the Sikels would have been able to show their resistance to hellenisation, which the adoption and outright use of the Greek language would not have allowed.[21] Some scholars have gone further away from a Greek relationship to the Sikel alphabet altogether and focus upon elements of Oscan in the script, which to them imply an Italian route of dissemination (see Parlangèli 1964–5; Prosdocimi and Agostiniani 1976–77; Leighton 1999: 221). Thus, the motivations behind written Sikel, whether subconscious action or conscious decision, remain subject to interpretation (Cusumano 1994: 57–61), and none of this reflects spoken language use.

Both the early importation of sympotic vessels and the implications behind the adoption of the Greek alphabet for the Sikel language recall Herskovits's expression of acculturation as a concept which 'comprehends those phenomena which result when groups of individuals having different cultures come into continuous first-hand contact, with subsequent changes in the original cultural patterns of either or both groups' (Herskovits 1948: 523). Bitterli has observed that many archaic peoples responded to such contact selectively, and that individual components are frequently met with very different degrees of receptivity (Bitterli 1989: 49). Thus it can be argued that the Sikels adopted selective elements of the Greek symposium to use in a framework consistent with their own traditions. Elsewhere, however, different elements of the symposium were adopted for disparate reasons. Nevertheless, in the case of the Sikels, the introduction of elements of foreign practice paved the way for additional aspects to enter Sikel culture, until ultimately it becomes impossible to distinguish Sikel material from the corpus of Sicilian goods. By this time we are left only with tales of Ducetius, endeavouring to preserve Sikel continuity in reaction to the 'frustrations of cultural contact' with Greek society in Sicily.[22]

In keeping with the notions of the selective adoption of cultural elements, there is another way to consider Ducetius, which reconciles the discrepancy implied between the material acculturation and literary ethnic distinction of the fifth century. Although Ducetius phrased his campaign in terms of Sikel ethnic identity and acculturation resistance – his self-perception as a Sikel – his asylum in Corinth and subsequent return to Sicily upon advice from a Greek oracle suggest that not only was he treated and thus perceived by the Greeks as a Greek in terms of culture, but also he used this perception to serve his own purposes. In all likelihood, his dispute with the Sicilian Greeks was one of territorial rights and political and economic power, but he played off the perceptions of himself from Greek and Sikel perspectives to achieve his own aims. Material acculturation, therefore, clearly does not preclude ethnic identity, and this reminds us of the complexity of the nature of our evidence for both acculturation and ethnicity. Nevertheless, it seems likely that the seeds of Sikel acculturation began to take root immediately upon the arrival of the Greeks, when the first colonists introduced a significant element of Greek culture into the lives of the Sikels, the ritual of wine consumption.

# 5

# GREEKS BEARING GIFTS:
## religious relationships between Sicily and Greece in the archaic period

### *Gillian Shepherd*

AN IMPORTANT THEME IN the study of Greek colonisation has been the nature of the relationship that existed between a Greek colony and its mother-city. A common view is that in antiquity there existed on-going, active relationships between colonies and mother-cities which were based upon common origin and reinforced by sentiment. This chapter seeks to examine the evidence for such relationships, particularly as it applies to the colonies founded in Sicily in the archaic period, which together with their mother-cities provide some of the best case studies relevant to this issue.

That ancient colonies could interact with their mother-cities and maintain a relationship of some sort after foundation is clear. Quite apart from the fact that the identity of the founding city could survive to be recorded centuries later by ancient authors, there is the amount of evidence giving details of the involvement of two cities with each other apparently on the basis of a familial relationship. Determining the exact character of this relationship, however, is more problematic.

The evidence is largely documentary and falls into two main categories: that describing political/military interaction and that describing religious. It is the latter which will be discussed here, since it is in the field of ritual and religion that most modern scholars have detected the real bond between colonies and mother-cities, upon which other encounters were based. Religion, it is argued, was the underlying structure through which close colony and mother-city relationships were maintained and articulated.[1] Unlike the odd political incident, religion would have constituted a perpetual and continually reaffirmed link.

Before looking at the religious evidence, however, it may be worth saying a few words about the nature of the political or military involvement of colonies and mother-cities. For the Greek colonies in the west, examples of co-operation are very few and almost entirely limited to Corinthian circles, especially between Corinth and its Sicilian colony

Syracuse in the fifth century. These include, for example, the dispatch of the troublesome Sikel Ducetius to Corinth – where so little attention was paid to him that he soon made his way back to Sicily (D.S. 12.8) – or the request from Syracuse to Corinth for aid against the Athenians in the Peloponnesian War, a request made on the basis of their family relationship but most likely granted as a result of Corinthian hatred of Athens (Thuc. 6.88.7–10; Salmon 1984: 389; Graham 1971: 144). These examples are fairly typical: other instances of encounters between a colony and a mother-city illustrate similar features of either an absence of real commitment or outlay on the part of the benefactor state or assistance granted purely on the basis of its advantage to the conferring party.[2] They may be sporadic episodes which just happened to be recorded, the tips of an iceberg of a genuine and continuous relationship; on the other hand, the consistent pragmatism and self-interest of the parties involved may indicate that they are isolated instances where an otherwise dormant relationship was deployed as a justification when required by convenience and ostensibly acknowledged if the situation was likely to provide express benefit to the party called upon.

The nature, quality and consistency of any underlying religious relationships may provide the answer here. One type of interaction between colonies and mother-cities, which in some ways bridges the categories of politics and religion, is the practice recorded by Thucydides of colonies requesting an oikist from the mother-city when founding a sub-colony (Thuc. 1.24.2). On the secular side, this is a diplomatic episode which like others involves little effort on the part of the mother-city, but which from the colony's point of view was a worthwhile piece of flattery which might be put to some use at a later date.[3] The oikist, however, apparently also had a religious role in that he obtained an oracle, laid out the sanctuaries of the new foundation and, it seems, acquired his own cult after he died.[4] The evidence for oikist cults is rather scanty, but in fact one of the most compelling pieces comes from Sicily: this is an early fifth-century Attic *kylix* found on the Acropolis at Gela, bearing the inscription, '*Manistheles anetheke Antiphemoi*' – 'Manistheles dedicated me to Antiphemos' (Orsi 1900: 272–7; Malkin 1987: 194–5). Antiphemos is, of course, the Rhodian oikist recorded for Gela (Thuc. 6.4.3).

There are two opposing interpretations of the oikist cult. One is that the oikist represented the mother-country and hence his cult was effectively derived from the mother-city: as such the oikist cult constitutes a bond with the homeland, indicative of the close and continuing relationship between colony and mother-city (Dunbabin 1948: 11). The other, put forward by Irad Malkin, is that since the oikist cult was not transplanted but created after foundation, it was a cult specific to the colony and one route by which a colony could gain religious independence and self-identity

(Malkin 1987: 189; 201–3; see also Humphreys 1966: 915). If this is the correct interpretation, which seems likely given the Greek use of individualised pantheons for state self-definition, then it gives a rather different slant to the practice of oikist requesting, which is often regarded as a prime piece of evidence for the close relationship between mother-city and colony. The question here, then, is whether or not other evidence for interaction in the field of religion between colonies and mother-cities is open to reinterpretation also.

The texts most frequently cited as attesting to an on-going relationship between mother-cities and colonies, which was manifested through religion and which gave the colony a subordinate postion, are the passages in Thucydides where the historian explains the reasons behind the Corinthian hatred of Corcyra. Although they were Corinthian colonists, says Thucydides:

> the Corcyraeans ... neglected the mother-city. For neither at their common festival gatherings would they concede the customary privileges to Corinthians, nor would they begin with a representative of Corinth the initial rites at sacrifices, as the rest of the colonies did, but they treated them with contempt.
>
> (Thuc. 1.25.4)

The passage is a little unclear in that we are not told where the 'common festival gatherings' were held, but the Greek implies public festivals in Corcyra,[5] and in any case it does not much matter here, since the important point is that the Corinthians wanted – but were not getting – the upper hand in religious matters. A little later on, Thucydides makes the Corinthians expand upon their cause for grievance:

> But neither did we colonise them to be insulted by them, but to be their leaders and receive from them all due reverence. The rest of our colonies, at any rate, honour us and by our colonists we are more beloved than is any other mother-city.
>
> (Thuc. 1.38.2)

These passages, along with some other sources discussed below, are often taken to reflect a universal relationship existing between colonies and mother-cities, involving certain religious observances and in particular regular dedications made by the colony to the mother-city (e.g. Graham 1971: 160–1, 216; Jeffery 1978: 56). As is usual for the archaic western colonies, the sources are later than the events, but there is an additional problem here in that Thucydides is not even claiming to be describing events of the past: these are fifth-century issues and attitudes. The question is whether we are entitled to retroject this sort of situation into the eighth, seventh and sixth centuries.

In the first place, it is necessary to take into account the nature of

Corinthian colonies in the fifth century BC. The two earliest Corinthian colonies were Corcyra and Syracuse, both founded in the eighth century. The other Corinthian colonies were somewhat different: they were founded later, under the tyrants, and were less far flung, including establishments like Leukas, Ambracia and Anaktorion. These colonies seem to have been set up under somewhat different conditions: the employment of tyrants' sons as oikists and a degree of political connection between the colonies and Corinth implies imperial aims and more formal relationships with the mother-city than those which existed for Syracuse and Corcyra (Graham 1971: 30–1, 148, appendix I). Such a relationship may well have had expression through the medium of religion. The two settlements in the west, on the other hand, were founded under different auspices and lacked such formal ties and hence any associated obligations. Whether filial piety was ever voluntarily rendered by them is another matter: certainly by the fifth century it seems unlikely. From the Corinthian point of view, Corcyra had obviously been behaving badly for some time, and had maintained a consistently hostile attitude towards Corinth, especially since the period of Corinthian control of Corycra under Periander (Hdt. 3.49; Salmon 1984: 394). The Corinthians' complaints indicate that Corcyra actively refused to engage in a relationship with its mother-city where the colony was subordinated; for Syracuse, at the beginning of the Peloponnesian War, such a relationship is simply not very plausible. By then, Syracuse had a democracy, but had previously been under various tyrants of the Deinomenid family from Gela since the 480s, who would have had no desire to accept subordination to Corinth, even if only symbolically. This is indicated by Gelon's reaction to the request from Greece for help against the Persians in 480 (Hdt. 7. 158), and we are also told that Gelon introduced a mixed population at Syracuse with his resettlement of several thousand of his own mercenaries, Geloans, Megara Hyblaeans and the inhabitants of Camarina (Hdt. 7. 156; Finley 1968: 51–2, 60). Corinth would have held little interest for these groups. The assertions of Thucydides' Corinthians therefore surely only have real relevance for the later foundations of Corinth and would not have applied in practice to a powerful state like Syracuse, however much wishful thinking there may have been on the part of the Corinthians. Such religious relationships may then be mechanisms constructed for the later tyrant colonies, including Corcyra under Periander, for the maintenance of political control, rather than institutions dating back to the later eighth century.

Other pieces of evidence for religious relationships analogous to that described by Thucydides are few, although admittedly common practice may not have warranted mention by ancient authors. As with the Corinthian example, there are difficulties in applying them to the archaic western colonies simply because they are late or refer to rather different colonies, or both. The best cases for regular colonial dedication are to be found in a foundation decree from Brea and in inscriptions relating to Milesian colonies. Brea was a fifth-century Athenian colony, and the Brea decree sets out the regular offerings to be made by the colony at major Athenian festivals (*IG* I³: 46; Graham 1971: 62, 228–9). Brea, however, was part of an empire and was not politically independent: its subservient position would have been most effectively underlined by regular contributions to Athenian religious celebrations – a situation which seems very similar to that likely for later Corinthian colonies.

The evidence for the Milesian colonies concerns regular dedications to be made to Apollo of Didyma. It has been suggested that arrangements for mutual citizenship existed between Miletus and its colonies (Graham 1971: 98–110), in which case again there would be formal legal connections which might be demonstrated in ritual. The evidence is also mainly confined to the hellenistic period, and therefore chronologically as well as geographically remote from Sicily and the west. While it may reiterate a long-standing tradition, there is also the possibility that we are seeing late innovations designed to meet some particular situation. This has been suggested as the explanation for two other decrees providing for dedications from colonies to their mother-cities. One is a fragmentary fifth-century decree referring to Argos and two Cretan cities, Tylissos and Knossos. By the classical period, it seems, these two cities had adopted the view that Argos was their mother-city and found it expedient to turn to Argos for mediation in a Cretan quarrel: hence the provision in the decree for sacrifices to Argive gods in addition to Cretan ones (Graham 1971: 154–60). The second inscription detailing possibly late innovative measures is a fourth-century one concerning Epidauros and its colony Astypalaea (*IG* IV²: 1.47). Here, along with the arrangement that the Astypalaeans will sacrifice to Epidaurean gods and send offerings to Epidauros, we have the granting of the privileges of *ateleia* (tax immunity) and *asylia* (inviolability) to the Astypalaeans, on the basis of their status as colonists and benefactors of Epidauros. As Graham suggests (1971: 164), all this looks like a new stage in the relationship between the two, which up until the time of decree was not necessarily particularly close.

All these inscriptions attest to religious arrangements between colonies and mother-cities in the classical period and later, and describe the sorts of ritual connection which may have existed between colonies which were already bound legally and politically, or those which were made to answer a particular diplomatic situation. It is not clear that similar practices can be ascribed to the politically independent colonies founded in the west in the archaic period.

There is, however, some evidence which relates more directly to the archaic period. An archaic inscription records an expensive dedication made by two men from Perinthos, a Samian colony on the Propontis, to Hera of Samos. We are still a long way from the western colonies here, but at least the period is right. Unfortunately, it appears to note a private dedication rather than a state one, and, as it stands, the inscription is not therefore necessarily related to any form of regular, on-going relationship between Perinthos and Samos. Despite suggestions to the contrary, there are no compelling reasons to regard it as anything more than a one-off donation.[6]

The other piece of evidence which relates – or at least purports to relate – to the archaic period is one which is frequently cited in discussions of colonial religious practices and which takes us, at last, to Sicily. This is the inscribed stele found at Lindos on Rhodes in 1904 and known as the *Lindian Chronicle* (Blinkenberg 1941). It is one of the very few pieces of textual evidence which relates directly to the western colonies and which claims to record events of the archaic period – in this case, dedications sent from Gela and Akragas to the sanctuary of Athena Lindia on Rhodes. As such, it has been enthusiastically cited by various scholars as proof of the sort of on-going religious relationship implied by Thucydides for Corinthian colonies.[7]

The *Chronicle* is best described as an imaginative document. The mention of the priest Teisolos dates the inscription to the very early first century BC and it was composed by a Rhodian called Timachidas, although his reasons for doing so are not clear. The stele gives a list of dedications in chronological order made to Athena Lindia, starting with those donated by legendary figures and going as far as the third century BC. Chronological distance between descriptions of objects and the objects themselves is very familiar to classical archaeologists and historians, but here the usual reservations one might have about a document such as this are far from allayed by its announcement that most of the votives listed were in fact destroyed along with the temple by a fire which is thought to have occurred in the mid-fourth century BC (*LC* D38–42; Richards 1980: vii). The catalogue of mythical figures who visited the sanctuary is to be expected, but even given this standard piece of sanctuary self-aggrandisement there are a surprising number listed – and not just the usual sprinkling of heroes and Trojan War figures. Even such eminent pre-Trojan War personalities as Kadmos and Minos put in an appearance at Lindos.[8] Finally, the *Chronicle* as a whole is derived from a range of twenty-one authors, and while many of these are otherwise completely unknown, all the information relating to Sicily comes from the early hellenistic historian Xenagoras, whose accuracy has been doubted.[9]

All this does nothing to inspire confidence in the inscription. Let us for a moment, however, play along with Timachidas and assume that his record is accurate, in order to examine the nature of the dedications claimed to have been passed from Gela and its sub-colony Akragas in the west to Rhodes, the historical mother-city.

The first reference is also the most important: it refers to a *krater* dedicated in the seventh century to Athena by the Geloans on the occasion of their conquest of 'Ariaiton' – most probably a place of unknown location, but possibly a person (*LC* XXV; Dunbabin 1948: 113 with n. 2; cf. Richards 1980: xi). It is the earliest mention we have of an offering from a colony at a homeland sanctuary, and much significance is placed on the wording 'the Geloans to Athena of the fatherland', indicating that the *krater* was a state donation and mentioning the 'fatherland' (Graham 1971: 161–2). Next we hear of a *krater* from Akragas made – naturally – by Daidalos and dedicated by the sixth-century tyrant Phalaris (*LC* XXVII). A few lines later comes a wooden gorgon with a stone face, dedicated by Gelon's father Deinomenes in the second half of the sixth-century (*LC* XXVIII). Dedications of *kraters* in the seventh and sixth centuries and an acrolithic *gorgoneion* in the late sixth do, admittedly, sound plausible for the periods claimed for them but equally they are not beyond the bounds of specious invention. Finally, the Akragantines sent a *palladion*, part of their spoils from their victory over Minoa (*LC* XXX).

It is immediately obvious that these dedications divide into two categories: state dedications made on the occasion of a military victory in Sicily and dedications made by private individuals, which in the case of the tyrant Phalaris at least may effectively be viewed as state dedication also (Graham 1971: 162). Indeed, Phalaris may give us a clue as to how these dedications should be interpreted.

Rather like the *Chronicle*, Phalaris has a high degree of associated mythology and scores low in the credibility stakes. In antiquity, he was most famed for commissioning a bronze bull in which he roasted his enemies alive, and he was renowned for his cruelty (D.S. 9. 18.19; 23. 14. 3). The historical Phalaris, however, seems for a time to have been highly successful: following his coup at Akragas, he seized control and became the city's first tyrant towards the middle of the sixth century. His expansionist policy resulted in many wars against the local Sikans and the acquisition of considerable territory for Akragas (D.S. 19. 108. 1–2; Finley 1968: 46). The anecdotes surrounding him may, if nothing else, at least reflect his ruthless approach. It is difficult, to say the least, to see such a character as being overly concerned with maintaining religious obligations which placed himself and his state in a position secondary to that of the mother-city or the grandmother-city. There may be a more plausible explanation. The assertion of his power and the display of his wealth are likely to have been high priorities for Phalaris, in which case the Daedalic *krater* dedicated at Lindos becomes easier to understand: it was a clear demonstration of his riches and success. Phalaris could have chosen to ignore Rhodes entirely: that he did not indicates that he thought it expedient to maintain some sort of contact with the grandmother-city. This may have been due more to the international character of the sanctuary at Lindos, which must have given it a reasonably high profile in international relations,[10] than its supposed relationship with Akragas, although the latter may have been worth cultivating with a view to possible future occasions when it could prove useful. The memory of the relationship may have been more strenuously maintained at the Rhodian end, in which case Phalaris may have felt the need to assert his status. Under the guise of piety towards the Old Country, Phalaris' *krater* arrived in Lindos full to the brim with political messages for Rhodes.

A similar interpretation may be placed upon the other dedications. Deinomenes was, if not a tyrant, then a very prominent Geloan and father of one of the most successful of the Sicilian tyrants, Gelon. The other two dedications were both made by states on the occasion of a military conquest which augmented the respective territories and power of the victors: Gela defeated Ariaiton and Akragas gained control of Minoa, the subject of hot dispute with Selinus. These are dedications made to commemorate specific events, and as such cannot be assumed to be part of a tradition of regular dedication between colonies and mother-cities intended to maintain links between the two. Like Phalaris' *krater*, they are better viewed as part of a programme of punctuated dedication designed to inform Rhodes of the successes of the western states and to display their disposable wealth.

Is there any other evidence from Rhodes which might suggest at least a background of regular dedication from the west against which the *Lindian Chronicle* donations may have taken place? The answer is that there is virtually none which can be detected archaeologically and unequivocally attributed to the west. Blinkenberg, who excavated the sanctuary of Athena Lindia, was surprised to find so little evidence of Sicilian material given the establishments there with Rhodian connections (Blinkenberg 1931: 43). What little there is is confined to a sprinkling of fibulae, with the total of eleven 'Italian' examples forming a negligible proportion of the total of 1,592 fibulae of identifiable type, mainly of island origin (Blinkenberg 1931: nos 103–5). Seven of the fibulae are of the type decorated with bone and amber (fig. 5.1, nos 1–2) which is now known to have been manufactured at Pithekoussai (Ridgway 1992b: 93–5) and is the type most commonly found at Greek sites; three are of the common 'navicella' type (fig. 5.1, no. 3), and the last is a fragment of a serpentine fibulae (similar to fig. 5.1, no. 4). The significance of the western fibulae is further reduced by the fact that fibulae form the largest single category of votive for the archaic period at Lindos. Clearly, fibulae were a standard offering, and the few western models, inconspicuous amongst hundreds of

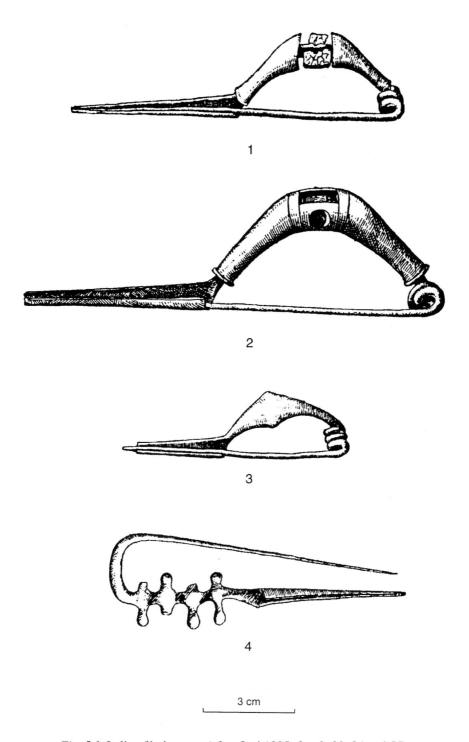

*Fig. 5.1* Italian fibula types (after Orsi 1895: figs 2, 32, 34 and 55)
*Key:* 1–2 bone and amber fibulae; 3 *navicella* fibula; 4 serpentine fibula

others, are more likely to be convenient dedicatory trinkets picked up by Rhodian traders wheeling and dealing around Italy and Sicily than a reflection of colonial piety towards the motherland and its gods. Even this was short-lived, since none of the fibulae is likely to date much after the end of the seventh century. On the present evidence, there is nothing to confirm long-term regular dedication from Gela and Akragas to Rhodes: the best that can be produced is the odd piece of jewellery, which can be paralleled at other Greek sites, and the isolated dedications of the *Lindian Chronicle*. The latter are better seen as specific communiqués between Sicily and Rhodes, and may indeed have as much in common with other international dedications to Athena Lindia as with any more particular connection with Rhodes: compare, for example, the linen corslet and two statues dedicated by Amasis of Egypt, which are, interestingly, recorded as being of stone by Herodotos (2.182) but gold in the *Chronicle* (*LC* XXIX).[11] Even this, of course, assumes that the *Chronicle* can be taken at face value, and it may be that it cannot: the *Chronicle* may well say more about what was going on in Rhodes in the first century BC and about hellenistic views of the past than it does about relations between colonies and mother-cities in the seventh and sixth centuries. But whichever way we look at it, neither the *Lindian Chronicle* nor the archaeological record gives us the required evidence of an on-going relationship between colony and mother-city maintained within the sphere of religion.

If we look for movement in the other direction, namely from Rhodes to Gela and Akragas, we do not fare much better, although again there have been strenuous attempts to demonstrate tight links between the mother-city and its descendants. The transfer of the cult of Athena from Rhodes to Sicily is not in itself of much significance, since the well-documented export of familiar cults to new settlements at the time of foundation is scarcely surprising and need not have any further implications for the relationship between two states. Other connections, however, have been suggested. Both Gela and Akragas have produced a collection of statuettes of seated female divinities wearing a polos and distinguished by a neck-lace of pendants strung across the breast and fastened with fibulae (fig. 5.2).[12] They appear to be locally made, and to date to the sixth and fifth centuries, and the type has become known as the 'Athena Lindia' type. In 1917 Blinkenberg attempted a reconstruction of the archaic cult statue of Athena at Lindos on Rhodes, on the basis of a very few references to it in the *Lindian Chronicle* and of this series of figurines from Gela and Akragas, which, he argued, represented Athena Lindia as the main god-dess of these Rhodian establishments, and for which he postulated an earlier prototype (Blinkenberg 1917: 25, 31; *LC* XXIII and XXXIV). The underlying assumption here was that either the cult statues at Gela and Akragas were replicas of that at Lindos – and hence the series of figurines

*Fig. 5.2* Early fifth-century 'Athena Lindia' figurine from Sicily, exact provenance unknown. London, British Museum inv. no. 1926.3–24.11.
© British Museum

at those sites – or the desire to maintain a link with the mother-country was so strong that the colonies produced images of the Lindos statue *in memoriam*, as it were, regardless of the appearance of their own cult statues. The first option is probably preferable to the second on purely logical grounds, especially if cult statues were manufactured at the time the cult was transferred. The statuettes then would simply be an independent Sicilian by-product of the customary export of cults, with no more specific connection with Rhodes. This is supported by the fact that such statues were apparently never dedicated at Lindos itself: the sanctuary there has produced mainly imported statuettes and has no locally produced assemblage of figurines which could claim to be imitations of a cult statue.

This, however, did not deter Orlandini from attempting to argue that the figurines at Gela and Akragas were specifically the product of Siciliot nostalgia for the Old Country and also the result of events on Rhodes.[13] In order to fill the awkward seventh-century gap, he endeavoured to create a continuous sequence of votive statuettes stretching back into the seventh century by inserting two earlier series ahead of the 'Athena Lindia' type, arguing that between the early seventh and mid-sixth centuries Gela and Lindos were linked by similar daedalic or sub-daedalic figurines, which were replaced for a very brief period with an Ionic type around the middle of the sixth century. The evidence for these two earlier series is not particularly convincing, since the examples given are too few and too fragmentary to constitute a series, and since the short-lived Ionic type at least could simply number one amongst the various types of east Greek figurine which made their way to the west in the sixth century. In addition, the appearance and large-scale production of the 'Athena Lindia' type at around 540 BC at Gela and Akragas still needed to be accounted for: the renovation of the Geloan sanctuary of Athena around the mid-sixth century would seem to provide sufficient reason (Orlandini 1968), but since, like Blinkenberg, Orlandini took the evidence of the *Lindian Chronicle* to reflect a long-standing, tight relationship between Lindos and the west, he looked beyond Sicily to Rhodes for an explanation. He found the answer in the reported reconstruction of the Lindian temple on Rhodes by the tyrant Kleoboulos: this, he argued, would not only have given new impetus to the cult at Lindos, but also have had repercussions for the cult at Gela and Akragas, given what he saw as their very high degree of adhesion to Lindos. Orlandini even went so far as to put forward the period *c*.540, the date of the introduction of the statuettes at Gela and Akragas, as a fixed point in the hitherto chronologically unanchored career of Kleoboulos (Orlandini 1968: 28).

These interpretations of the 'Athena Lindia' statuettes seem to be over-elaborate in their determination to shackle Gela and Akragas to Rhodes and Lindos, on the basis of the belief that colonies and mother-cities maintained tight links through religion and that the former were constantly looking to the latter for guidance and authority. The evidence of the *Lindian Chronicle* suggests that such links should be reinterpreted, and there are more simple explanations that can be put forward to account for the 'Athena Lindia' statuettes in the west. The absence of similar statuettes on Rhodes is surely significant and must at the very least reflect some difference in dedicatory practice between different sites, however trivial. The renovation of the sanctuary at Gela would provide a quite sufficient context for the introduction of the statuettes, if indeed a specific explanation is required other than the general sixth-century increase in the use of figurines at Greek sites. The fact that they occur in numbers at Gela and Akragas need not reveal anything more significant than a predictable similarity of cult, and indeed the figurines are not restricted to these sites. Although they are certainly most common at Gela and Akragas, they have in fact been found at a number of other sites around Sicily, including Grammichele (near Caltagirone, fig. 3.2), Selinus, Megara Hyblaea and Helorus – perhaps indicative of the generic nature of such cheap terracotta offerings.[14] They are most easily explained as an independent Sicilian development in cult practice, perhaps as a sideline for the healthy Geloan coroplastic industry. As archaeological evidence for close mother-city–colony relationships via religion, they are unconvincing.

Together, Rhodes, Gela and Akragas provide the best case study for investigating the religious relationships between archaic western Greek colonies and their mother-cities simply because – quite apart from the *Lindian Chronicle* – here we can match up major city sanctuaries for comparison. The circumstances of survival and excavation mean that this works less well, or not at all, for other Greek cities and their related foundations in the west. However, two other important sites in Greece have produced material from the west which may help throw light on the nature of the religious relationships existing between Greece and settlements in Sicily and Italy in the archaic period.

The first is the Corinthian sanctuary of Hera at Perachora, situated on the coast opposite the main harbour of Corinth. Its position led the excavator Humfry Payne to view it as a seafarers' sanctuary, attracting dedications from ships sailing in and out of Corinth (Payne 1940: 25). It has indeed produced a range of foreign dedications, of which Phoenician objects account for just under three-quarters (Kilian-Dirlmeier 1985: 225, fig. 8). However, despite the extensive trade in Corinthian products in Italy and Sicily, and the view that in theory western Greeks of Corinthian origins like the Syracusans should be making regular trips to Corinth, there is very little that can be identified as probable dedications from western Greeks. The evidence is confined to a mere twenty-seven fibulae of 'Italian' type, again mainly those decorated with bone and amber, which form a tiny proportion (only 2.5 per cent) of the total number of foreign dedications made in the archaic period (Dunbabin 1962: 439; Kilian-Dirlmeier 1985: 225, fig. 8, 245). There is unfortunately no evidence available from a sanctuary actually in Corinth, such as the temple of Apollo, which might be more revealing, but Perachora at least would seem to be sufficiently high-profile and cosmopolitan to attract Sicilian Greeks regularly making pilgrimages to the motherland and intent on displaying their piety towards its gods. Instead, what we have is a very few brooches, which can scarcely represent any regular pattern of dedication, and which are just as likely to be odd ornaments picked up by mainland Greeks on trading expeditions and deposited in return for a safe passage.

On this showing, Perachora does not look very different from Lindos with its eleven western fibulae. Further comparisons can be made with two other sanctuaries where the archaic foreign dedications have been quantified: one is the Heraion at Samos, where three 'Italian' fibulae and some other objects form 1.7 per cent of the total number of foreign dedications; the other is Pherai, which, like Lindos, was a sanctuary which attracted large numbers of fibulae as a standard offering, and, also like Lindos, comes up with a small number of Italian goods (2.6 per cent, including one fibula) amongst all the other foreign dedications (Kilian-Dirlmeier 1985: 217, fig. 1, 237, fig. 18, 244). We have here four different sanctuaries which, according to the model of special religious links between colonies and mother-cities, should also differ in their patterns of dedication: first, Lindos, a major city sanctuary with related cults in the west, and therefore supposed to show a high level of Sicilian Greek presence; second, Perachora, which as an important Corinthian sanctuary may be similar to Lindos, but which may equally be simply a traders' sanctuary; and finally, Pherai and the Samian Heraion, with no particular connections with the west. In fact they do not differ much at all as far as western Greece is concerned: we are hard put to make any distinction whatsoever in their levels of dedications from Sicily or Italy. The most likely explanation for the few 'Italian' fibulae at these sites is trade, and a putative relationship with a foundation in the west does not make any apparent difference to the dedicatory patterns.

This situation can be set against that of another type of sanctuary and the second important site in Greece: the pan-hellenic sanctuary of Olympia. Here, in the seventh and eighth centuries, objects from Italy or Sicily account for 8.9 per cent of the foreign dedications, a figure which is significantly higher than that for the other sanctuaries with quantified Italian dedications (Kilian-Dirlmeier 1985: 231, fig. 13). Furthermore, there is a far greater range of both fibulae and other objects than at the other sanctuaries, including rather more substantial offerings, such as a helmet, spearheads, shield fragments and an axe head. As has been pointed out before, the weapons look most like western Greek dedications advertising victory in one scuffle or another with the indigenous population[15] – typical material for Olympia, which was the standard arena in which Greek states reminded each other vociferously of their military and other successes. In the sixth century, Olympia was the recipient of even more substantial gifts from the west in the form not only of statues, but also of treasuries, most of which were donated by a colonial state – such as the earliest and ultimately the biggest treasury, that dedicated by Gela.[16]

This, then, is surely closer to the sort of pattern of regular dedication we should be seeing at the state sanctuaries of mother-cities if they had on-going religious relationships with their colonies involving attendance and participation at festivals. Instead, the focus of the colonial states seems to be on Olympia, and, to a lesser extent, Delphi.[17] Like other Greek states, the western Greek colonies seem to have used Olympia for showing off their various military victories, but there is evidence of more sustained interest in the sanctuary as well which is lacking in a sanctuary such as Lindos. If colonies were going to bother to dedicate at sanctuaries in Old Greece, it was done with a view to promoting their own interests and self-image: that was more efficiently and successfully achieved by maintaining a presence at an interstate sanctuary like Olympia than at a state sanctuary with its restricted audience. If we accept and generalise the evidence of the *Lindian Chronicle*, mother-city state sanctuaries could still be informed of specific successes and general prosperity from time to time and diplomatic channels could be kept open, but this was as far as the contact went: from the evidence which is available, there is nothing that suggests that religious activity on the part of archaic Sicilian colonies towards their mother-cites was ever more substantial than a calculated system of sporadic and informative dedication, where the familial relationship provided the excuse but not the reason.

In conclusion, the evidence for the religious relationship between a western colony and its mother-city indicates that the motive for that relationship and its nature may be open to reinterpretation. Religion, particularly in the form of dedication, was an essential aspect of the mother-city–colony relationship, but this did not necessarily take the form of constant or consistent interaction. Rather, it was an avenue used when appropriate to the aims of the colony and it was directed towards the most advantageous recipient, which was more likely to be an interstate sanctuary than a state one. Other, later colonies of different nature may well have maintained regular and regulated connections with their mother-cities through religion and ritual. As far as the archaic Greeks in Sicily are concerned, however, it may be more appropriate to generalise the Corinthians' peeved complaint of the Corcyraeans as recorded by Thucydides: 'they have constantly stood aloof from us' (Thuc. 1.38.1). Except, of course, when the Sicilian Greeks chose otherwise.

# Part II

# GREEK SETTLEMENT IN SICILY

# 6

# COIN TYPES AND IDENTITY:
## Greek cities in Sicily

### *N. K. Rutter*

## COIN TYPES AND IDENTITY

THE TYPES OF SICILIAN coins in the Greek period have always been of interest to students of ancient Sicily. They have contributed much to such areas of investigation as the religion and cults of the Greek cities, or the history and development of Greek art on the island: the types of Sicilian coins are well known for the very high level of the artistic quality they frequently achieved. They are also unique in the Greek world for the richness and variety of their depictions of elements of the natural world: 'fresh-water springs and rivers, products of the fertile soil such as an ear of barley or a grape cluster, creatures of the earth, the sky and the sea [are] portrayed in astonishingly accurate detail' (Rutter 1998a: 16). The word 'unique' introduces at the outset a contrast with the coins of the Aegean world, the world the colonists had left behind: the Siceliotes developed their own approaches to the business of creating coin types. Developed, notice, because in some cases their initial models were coinages of the Aegean area, as we shall see.

At the present time of course new interests and approaches to the study of ancient Sicily attract our attention. We are interested in the ways in which the many different peoples who lived together on the island interacted, in questions of ethnicity, of identity, and of how these concepts might have been expressed in the material record and how they might be recognised now. In this area too, as in the others mentioned earlier, coin types are a potentially rich resource that can be fruitfully exploited for information. Thomas R. Martin has recently observed that coin types 'could hardly escape expressing the identity of the *polis*' (Martin 1995: 281), and we can accept at the outset that what is shown on the coins ought to be able to tell us quite a lot about the values, interests and aspirations of the communities which issued them. But to put flesh on this basic idea it is obvious that we need to ask a number of questions. Why was a particular coin type selected, and, once adopted, to what extent did it continue in use? Why was it presented in a particular way, and to what extent did the manner of its presentation change over time? What other elements, for example of letter forms or language, accompanied it?

There are further questions to be explored, including that of the significance attached by the people of a particular *polis* to the messages conveyed by its coin types. Ancient literary and documentary evidence on this question is limited, but in the Sicilian context there is quite a lot of non-numismatic evidence that can be used to throw light on it. But 'self-identity' among the Greek cities, the *polis* identity as represented to itself, is only a part of the problem. Coins are artefacts that were created and used within one kind of society, in the case we are considering a Greek *polis* of coastal Sicily, and then in various ways moved, or were imitated, beyond the boundaries of the producer society, not only among fellow-Greek communities, but also among a variety of non-Greek communities in the Sicilian hinterland. The question arises of the message put out to those *using* the coin(s). To quote Martin again: 'These types would … necessarily reflect some component of the identity of the *polis*, as represented to itself *and to others*' (Martin 1995: 265, my italics). So when discussing questions of identity arising from coin types, there are at least two perspectives to consider: that of the issuing city, and that of the user(s) of its coins, whether its own citizens or not.

## COIN TYPES: AKRAGAS

By 500 BC at least six Greek cities in Sicily had issued coins, illustrated here by samples of three of them (fig. 6.1). From Himera (no. 1), the obverse type is a cock, joined after a little while on the reverse by a hen. From Naxos (no. 2), the obverse shows a head of Dionysus, the reverse a bunch of grapes. From Akragas (no. 3), the types are on the obverse an eagle, on the reverse a crab. Nos 1 and 2 illustrate something of the variation of style and of technique among early Sicilian coinages; no. 3 introduces points I wish to develop, particularly in relation to the reverse type. The crab is a constant feature of the typology of Akragas from the beginning of coinage there towards the end of the sixth century down to its end in 406. That fact already underlines its importance as an expression of the city's identity, and the crab is generally thought to symbolise the river of the same name above whose banks the city of Akragas was established (Jenkins 1990: 43). It certainly seems significant that in one of the very few cases where the crab does not appear as a type, its place is taken by the head of a young river god.[1]

The coin type is not the only evidence that draws attention to the importance of the river Akragas to its homonymous city. Among the standard themes of Pindar's epinician odes is praise of the victor's home city. Such praise is often quite brief, but may refer to a topographical

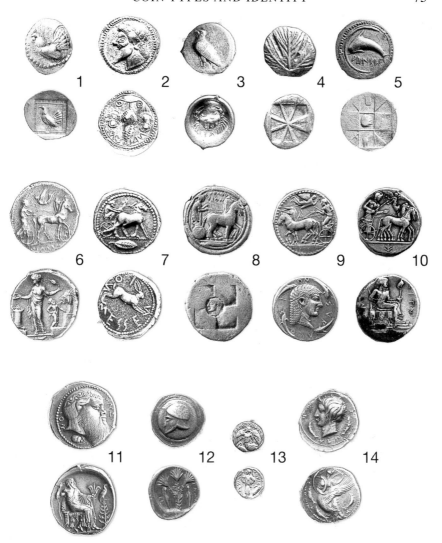

*Fig. 6.1* Sicilian coin types (British Museum, with the exception of nos 9 (Glasgow, Hunterian Coll. 3), 10 (Antikenmuseum, Basel, 250) and 11 (Brussels, de Hirsch Coll. 269))

feature of the city concerned. When Pindar came to write his odes celebrating the achievements and qualities of victors from Akragas at Delphi or Olympia, the feature of the city that he singled out for mention was precisely the river Akragas: at *Pythian* 6, line 6, he calls the city *potamios*, and at *Pythian* 12, lines 2–3, he again singles out 'the banks of the Akragas where the sheep feed' for special mention. Both *Pythian* 6 and *Pythian* 12 celebrate successes achieved in 490, by Xenocrates and Midas respectively, before Pindar's 'highly probable' visit to Sicily in 476 (Carey 1981: 104), and the detail of Akragantine topography he has chosen to mention was based not on autopsy but possibly on information communicated to him by others, perhaps, according to one suggestion, 'his patrons or their agents'.[2] The river is still singled out, though, in *Ol.* 2.9, composed in 476 for Theron of Akragas: the tyrant's forefathers acquired 'a hallowed home beside the river'.

There are three points here to bear in mind. The first is that we appear to have, both on a series of coins made in Sicily and in literature composed outside the island, the same reference to what was evidently for its inhabitants the most salient feature of one of its cities – a river. That raises in turn the question of the kind of information about Sicily and its cities that was available to those such as Pindar who did not live there. Finally, I note the importance of a river in the symbolism of a colonising people, an importance amply illustrated in the high incidence of river-god types in the coinages of Sicily.[3] Such a concentration of river-god types is unknown in mainland Greece, and once adopted, they tended to last a long time. Their significance for their respective cities has been compared with that of Athena for Athens (Weiss 1984: 21–3).

## SELINUS, ZANKLE, HIMERA

First, Selinus: the early coins of that city (fig. 6.1, no. 4) have as their obverse type a leaf of the *selinon*, the wild celery plant – an example of a 'canting' type in which the type expresses the name of the city. The fabric of these coins – broad, rather than chunky flans – and also elements of technique, particularly with regard to the reverses, on which the designs are commonly surrounded by a flattened area of metal, have been compared with those of the earliest coins of Corinth. Furthermore, the links between the early coins of Selinus and those of Corinth are not simply of technique. Overstrikes by Selinus on coins of Corinth have been recognised, and in a hoard of archaic silver – coins and ingots – from Selinus published quite recently, the bulk of the 165 coins came from the mints of Aegina (eighty-one) and Corinth (thirty-nine) (Arnold-Biucchi et al. 1988). So in the case of early Selinus we have evidence of the flow of silver westwards to a silverless island in the form of coins. That point of economic history is by now well recognised, but in terms of our present interest in questions of identity, it is worth noting the close relationship with mainland Greece evidenced by one of the earliest coinages, if not the earliest, of Sicily. The main connection is with Corinth, though with the coinage of Aegina substantially in the picture as well.

At Zankle, on the Sicilian side of the Straits of Messina (fig. 6.1, no. 5), the reverse design – a pattern of rectangles and triangles with shell in the centre – may have influenced a similar design at Syracuse. The obverse type is the first example of something that is often apparent in Sicilian coin types: the strong sense of identification with a place, a specific topography, and not only a river. In this case the place is the harbour of Zankle, with its distinctively circular shape. On the coin the harbour is represented by the sickle shape, reminding us of Thucydides' note (6.4.5) to the effect that the town of Zankle was so named by the native Sicels 'because the place is sickle shaped', the Sicel word for a sickle being *zanklon*. Again, there is a match between Sicilian numismatic evidence and literary evidence. The coin type, then, signifies a firm sense of place, but note that the name that accompanies it, so prominently displayed in the Chalkidian alphabet, is a native one. Even settlers with a strong sense of their own identity will regularly take over native names for places. Bill Bryson wrote (1991: 155): 'Despite the difficulties of rendering them into English, Indian names were borrowed for the names of more than half the American states and for countless thousands of rivers, lakes and towns.'

Another example of this Sicilian interest in place comes from Himera, in slightly later type, after the middle of the fifth century (fig. 6.1, no. 6). It is one of a series, again long-lasting, that was introduced in the 450s and carried on down to the capture of the city by the Carthaginians in 408:[4] the nymph Himera sacrifices, while at the right a satyr bathes under a fountain with a water-spout in the form of a lion's head. The reference is to the hot springs in the neighbourhood of the city, which according to a tradition preserved by Diodorus Siculus (4.23.1, 5.3.4–5) were brought into being by the nymphs of the place at the behest of Athena, to refresh Heracles on his journey west. For the hot springs of Himera there is another Pindaric comparison, just like the one at Akragas. Pindar composed the short *Olympian* 12 to celebrate a number of victories won by Ergoteles, a native of Crete but now a citizen of Himera. The ode was composed in 466.[5] What element in the environment of Himera did Pindar select for special mention? Precisely, the hot springs; in line 19 of the ode, he says to Ergoteles that having won his victories he is 'ennobling the Nymphs' hot bathing-places'.[6]

Returning to coinage in the cities on the Straits of Messina, I illustrate another, different aspect of the choice of coin types, and one that is unique among contemporary Sicilian coinages. Around 494 a tyrant, Anaxilas, appeared in Rhegium, on the Italian side of the Straits, and from about 488 he controlled Zankle too, changing its name to Messana. Soon after 480 he introduced both there and at Rhegium a coinage with the obverse type of a mule-car (fig. 6.1, no. 7). This type gives the only hint of the personal in the choice of a coin type in Sicily before the reign of Agathocles towards the end of the fourth century, and the reasons for that personal touch are not too far to seek. The type is significant for its reference to the

Olympic games, where Anaxilas had won a victory in the mule-car race, probably in 480.

Over and above the uniqueness of this coin type, a number of points about it deserve comment. One might say on the one hand that there is here an element of 'peer interaction', in that the mule-car of Anaxilas echoes the quadriga of horses that had been the obverse type of Syracusan coins for about twenty years. On the other hand, it is Anaxilas' own initiative and priority that should be stressed. Those Syracusan horses (see below) initially at any rate were not the issues of tyrants, but symbolised primarily an aristocratic lifestyle. In 480, Hieron and Theron had not yet won their victories in the pan-hellenic games, and when they did, in the 470s, they did not follow the example of Anaxilas in commemorating them on coins issued by their respective cities. Another interesting aspect of the mule-car type is that although it was introduced by a tyrant, and was abandoned at Rhegium in 461 when the tyrant family fell, it continued in use at Messana until the capture of the city by the Carthaginians in 396.

## SYRACUSE

At Syracuse the earliest coins, beginning about 500, were tetradrachms with a thick, chunky fabric (fig. 6.1, no. 8). The obverse type was a quadriga, with the name of the Syracusans above, either in full or abbreviated. Most of the reverses, as here, carry a small female head in a circular depression in the centre of an incuse square of mill-sail design: compare the design of reverses of Zankle referred to above. On one reverse, though, a simple square punch is divided into four smaller squares, like a window. The 'window' design appears on the reverse of coins of many north Aegean mints (for example, Abdera, Aegae and Acanthus) which began to strike coins in the late sixth century. Furthermore, the plodding 'cart horses' of early Syracusan obverses seem to have been inspired by similar animals on tetradrachms traditionally attributed to Olynthus (Cahn 1979). To these typological and stylistic links between early Syracusan coinage and several of those of the north Aegean region can be added the shared weight-standard, the Euboic–Attic.

What is the significance of these Syracusan numismatic connections with the northern Aegean? In the light of the earlier discussion of Selinus and its connections with Corinth, it is probable that at least some of the silver for early Syracusan coinage came from the northern Aegean. It is significant that in a number of early fifth-century hoards from Sicily and southern Italy, the only non-western coins are from Athens and Acanthus.[7] We do not yet have overstrike evidence from Syracuse, such as we have in abundance from Selinus, but the possibility of such evidence turning up should not be ruled out. From the point of view of our concern with identity, it is important to note that although the models chosen by Syracuse for its first types derived from the Greek world, they did not come from its mother-city Corinth, though the example of Selinus has shown that they could well have done so. What one might call economic factors seem to outweigh ties of sentiment. Thus the typological evidence from Syracuse raises again the question of the relations of the Sicilian colonies with their respective mother-cities. It can be analysed and set beside other studies such as that on the burial practices of the Sicilian colonies by Gillian Shepherd, who argued that in that aspect of culture the colonies diverged from their mother-cities; furthermore, the links that *can* be observed between them and old Greece, for example in the incidence of colonial dedications in mainland sanctuaries, represent not nostalgia but self-assertion (Shepherd 1995: 75; this volume). That is a point we too can pursue further, still in relation to the coinage of Syracuse.

The earliest phase of the coinage of Syracuse we have just been considering began around 500 and lasted for ten to fifteen years. The next phase began around 485, and can be associated with the early period of the rule of Gelon in Syracuse, before the battle of Himera in 480 (fig. 6.1, no. 9) (Rutter 1998b: 312). On the obverse the horses are now really race horses, and the charioteer is being crowned for his victory; on the reverse the female head is no longer confined in a small medallion in the centre of the die, but takes centre stage, surrounded by four dolphins and the name of the Syracusans. She is not named, but it has been persuasively argued that she is Arethusa, not Artemis.[8] The four dolphins are a constant element in the design, which never includes any attribute of Artemis: the naming of her as 'Arethosa' on the facing head by the engraver Cimon (in 405) signifies a change of *type*, a new representation of her, not a new divinity.

Arethusa, the famous fresh-water spring located beside the salt water and dolphins of the Great Harbour of Syracuse, is another example of something that has already been referred to: a highly developed sense of place reflected in a coin type. But as in the examples referred to above, we can push the discussion further than that. The phenomenon of a fresh-water spring on an island and near the sea was something special, and was explained by an aetiological myth. The myth of Arethusa survives in more than one version,[9] but in whatever form – whether it was the river Alpheus who flowed under the sea from the Peloponnese, or Arethusa herself, or both of them – it symbolises a close link with the Greek mainland, and in particular the Peloponnese. Furthermore, it is precisely this element of Syracusan topography which Pindar selects for mention, more than once, in his odes for Syracusan victors; see the opening of *Nemean* 1, composed for Chromios of Syracuse in 476: 'Holy place where Alpheus breathes again, green branch of glorious Syracuse, Ortygia'; or line 7 of *Pythian* 2, the first of Pindar's odes for Hieron, composed in late 477 or early 476 in honour of his victory in a chariot race at either Thebes or Syracuse. There are further references at line 69 of *Pythian* 3, composed in 474 for Hieron, and at line 92 of *Olympian* 6, composed in 476 or 472 for Hagesias of Syracuse.

## AITNA

Two issues of coins survive from Aitna (Aetna), the city founded (in 476 or not long after) by Hieron on the site of Catana. The first issue is represented by a single surviving tetradrachm, with obverse Athena driving a quadriga, reverse seated Zeus (fig. 6.1, no. 10; there is a drachm to go with this issue, again surviving in only one specimen, with obverse naked rider, reverse seated Zeus). The tetradrachm dates from the second half of the 470s (Rutter 1998b: 312–13), and both its types are iconographically fascinating, but note one small feature of the reverse: the eagle that sits with wings folded on Zeus' sceptre. Once again coin imagery is reflected in Pindar, in poems dating from the second half of the 470s. He twice refers to 'Zeus of Aitna' (*Nem.* 1.6, *Ol.* 6.96) and in the famous opening to *Pythian* 1, the eagle, king of birds, is lulled to sleep on the sceptre of Zeus, as he appears to be here on the coin. Both coin type and Pindar seem to refer to something important for the new colony, perhaps an element in a cult statue. Comparison with a second seated Zeus type from Aitna, to be dated a decade or more later (fig. 6.1, no. 11), does not suggest that either type copied any such cult statue precisely in all its details.

## CAMARINA

The fifth-century coinage of Camarina was issued in three distinct periods.[10] Fig. 6.1, no. 12, illustrates a limited issue of didrachms dated to the period between 492 and 485, with military types: on the obverse a Corinthian helmet superimposed on a round shield, on the reverse a palm-tree between two greaves. The second and third periods, dated respectively in the years after the refounding of the city in 461,[11] and between 425 and 405, both contain coins with types that are of comparable interest with those from other cities discussed above. The second period contains only *litrai* (fig. 6.1, no. 13). On the obverse a winged figure usually described as Nike hovers above a swan: on the reverse a helmeted Athena stands with shield to one side, holding a spear and wearing an aegis. The third period contains tetradrachms with obverse quadriga, reverse head of Heracles, and also a series of didrachms (fig. 6.1, no. 14). On the obverse these didrachms carry a beautifully conceived head of the horned river god Hipparis, while the reverse shows the nymph Camarina reclining on the back of a swan swimming or 'sailing' over waves (probably of her lake, as we shall see).

After what has been said above, it will not be surprising to learn that there is a splendid Pindaric parallel for several elements of these coin types. Two odes of Pindar survive, *Olympians* 4 and 5, that were written in honour of a victor from Camarina named Psaumis. It is possible that both poems celebrate a victory won in the mule-car race of either 460 or 456,[12] and the suggestion has been made that Pindar's first attempt, *Olympian* 4, may not have fully met the expectations of his patron: for example, it lacked any reference to praise of Camarina (Mader 1990: 14). That lack is amply made up for in *Olympian* 5, where the central portion, lines 10–14 of a twenty-five-line poem, is devoted to a detailed description of Camarina. In its fullness, if not in its details, this description has no parallel in Pindar:

> O Pallas, protectress of the city, he (Psaumis) sings of the holy grove that is yours, and the river Oanis, and the lake of the land, and the hallowed streams, with which Hipparis waters the people, and he swiftly welds together the soaring grove of firm-standing dwellings.

So far, so good. But at this point matters become more complicated. *Olympian* 5 happens to be the only one of Pindar's odes of which the genuineness has been questioned. Was it, or was it not, composed by him? Or was it perhaps the work of a skilled imitator? Discussion of the status of the poem started early, in the statement of a scholiast that it was not included in the original collection of texts of Pindar's poems made by Zenodotus, but that it *was* assigned to him from the time of Didymus. The question has not been conclusively resolved,[13] but in discussions of it the relevant numismatic evidence has barely been mentioned. To me what is really striking is the very close relationship between the evocation of Camarina in *Olympian* 5 on the one hand, and the coin types chosen for the city on the other.

Let us remind ourselves of the chronological relationship between city, poem and coin types. In the sixth and fifth centuries, Camarina had a chequered history of settlement, destruction and refoundation, but our concern is with the city refounded in 461. The victory celebrated in the poem dates from either 460 or 456, that is, early in the life of the new city. The *litrai* with obverse Nike and swan, reverse Athena, probably began to be issued about the same time. So already we have the Pallas of the poem, a figure whose pose on the coins suggests the representation in miniature of a cult statue (Westermark and Jenkins 1980: 26–7).[14] It is not possible in this instance to assign chronological priority either to poem or to coin type. They are approximately contemporary. On the other hand, the didrachms with obverse head of Hipparis, reverse Camarina and swan, were issued several decades later, in the last quarter of the century. Did the poem influence the choice of Hipparis as a type? The distance in time between the two seems to rule out that possibility, and in any case, speculation about influence(s) one way or the other seems to me to miss the point. In the light of what has been shown earlier about the relation between coin types and literature, it seems clear that what we are seeing at Camarina, in both poem and coin types, are references to religious and topographical elements that in turn symbolise what we might now legitimately call the city's official view of itself.

Before concluding, I should like to make one or two brief observations on the disputed question of Pindaric authorship of *Olympian* 5. Fuller appraisal of the numismatic evidence does not *prove* anything either way. On the other hand, it alerts us at the very least to the fifth-century context and content of the description of Camarina in the poem. Furthermore, the technique deployed and the interests displayed in lines 10–14 are, as we have seen from the material in other poems, entirely in the manner of Pindar himself; all the elements of the description of Camarina can be paralleled elsewhere in his poetry. Some of them – a guardian deity, rivers, and a lake whose waters support the people of the city – are very much of the kind we have met already; the description of the other element – the rapid development of a new city – is not exceptional: compare the description of Akragas at *Pythian* 12.2–3, '[you city], who on the banks of sheep-grazed Akragas dwell on your well-built hill'. It is true that these elements have been deployed here in a greater concentration than usual, and the length and detail of the description have sometimes been used as an argument against Pindar's authorship. The city was in a ruined state at the time of his visit to Sicily in 476, and he did not return; such an informed account could not have come from his pen, but was rather the work of 'a local Sicilian poet' (Bowra 1964: 419). But the imitator, if such he be, is here showing an awareness (more than 'external'?) of a special-ised and sophisticated element of Pindar's poetic technique, one that we have seen is consistently paralleled by coin types of the respective Sicilian cities.[15] Poems and coins both employ the same religious and/or topo-graphical motifs, a set of standard descriptors, to express a city's identity.

In exploring the theme of 'coin types and identity' in Sicily and linking it closely to expressions of pride in locality, identity with a specific local topography, I do not claim to have hit on an all-embracing theory that will serve to explain *all* coin types, either in Sicily or elsewhere. But it does seem to me that some of the evidence provided by coin types is at the very heart of current concerns of archaeological and historical inquiry, con-cerns, that is, with questions of identity, with how ancient peoples viewed themselves and wanted others to view them.[16] Official poems and official coin types from several Sicilian cities characterise each city by referring to the same feature of its local topography. Sicilian coin types do often share features with coins in other parts of the Greek world – for example, an interest in the pantheon of Greek divinities and a desire to be linked with them – but the interest, frequently a pictorial interest, in locality is stronger in Sicily than elsewhere. It is a distinctive feature of hellenism in Sicily.

# 7

# SICILY IN THE ATHENIAN IMAGINATION:

## Thucydides and the Persian Wars

### *Thomas Harrison*

THIS CHAPTER IS CONCERNED not with an episode in the history of events but with the imaginary history of those events, with the patterns into which events are moulded in the imagination of contemporaries. It is concerned, in particular, with perhaps the most charged, emotive episode in the imaginary history of Sicily, the Athenian expedition to Sicily as it is narrated by Thucydides, and with the ways in which Thucydides' account mirrors Greek representations of the Persian wars. These echoes have been traced before:[1] the purpose of this chapter is – by building on such earlier treatments – to make out a more convincing case for their existence. But I mean to do so not simply by amassing a greater number of such echoes – proof is, to an extent, cumulative – but by proposing a different, less purely literary, explanation of why they are there.

The Athenians' expedition to Sicily mirrors the Persian expedition to Greece not only in details but also in structure. Book 6 opens, like Herodotus' book 7, with a lengthy debate on the wisdom of the expedition (cf. Rood 1999): in both cases the decision to proceed with the campaign is flawed, in the Persians' case, because Artabanus' very reasonable doubts are overruled by a succession of apparitions in his own and Xerxes' dreams, and, in the case of Sicily, by the enthusiasm, the *erôs*, of the Athenians for the expedition; Nicias' strictures on the need for more men and more ships, intended to deter the Athenians, have the opposite effect of merely inflating the expedition and their confidence in its success. The contrast here – the absence of the divine in Thucydides' Sicilian debate – is as significant as the similarities: in both cases, however, there is the sense of human blindness, of the right turning having been missed.

Both Thucydides' Athens and Herodotus' Persia emerge also as powers driven to expand. Two impetuous young men theorise on this, translating imperial expansion into a matter of survival. Xerxes begins his proposal for the campaign to Greece with the words (Hdt. 7.8.α1):

Men of Persia, I will not be the first to introduce this custom among you, but shall adopt it, having received it from my forefathers. For, as I learn from older men, we have never remained inactive since we wrested the sovereign power from the Medes, and Cyrus overthrew Astyages; but the deity thus leads the way, and to us who follow his guidance many things result to our advantage. What deeds Cyrus, and Cambyses, and my father Darius have achieved, and what nations they have added to our empire, no one need mention to you who know them well.

Imperial expansion is seen almost as a form of propitiation of the deity.[2] Very similar arguments are used by Alcibiades in his response to Nicias (6.18): if Athens were to cease to expand it would become vulnerable, whereas every fresh struggle gives it experience. There is also the same appeal to the well-tried formula of their success, to the *nomoi* that have served them well in the past:[3] 'Those men live most safely who follow their own principles and customs most closely, even when they are worse' (6.18.7). The word 'most safely' (*asphalestata*) could not signal more clearly the Athenians' imminent reverse. Similarly in the case of the Persians, we, Xerxes' other audience, also remember how Cyrus', Cambyses' and Darius' imperial expansion ended.[4]

There is also a closer parallel between the motives of Persians and Athenians, a contrast in both cases between the ostensible and actual grounds for their campaigns. The Persians' campaign was allegedly in revenge for the Athenians' (and Eretrians') participation in the Ionian revolt (Hdt. 5.105, 7.8.α2–γ1, 7.138.1). Likewise the Sicilian expedition is directed against the Syracusans, although not in revenge. In reality, in both cases, the aggressors' real ambitions were much broader. As Thucydides and a number of speakers – Hermocrates, Alcibiades, Gylippus – emphasise, the Athenians' real ambition was to subdue all of Sicily, then the Peloponnese and the rest of Greece, and (in the judgement of Thucydides' Alcibiades and Plutarch, at least) Carthage and Italy as well (6.6.1, 15.2, 33.2, 76.2, 90.2, 7.66.2; cf. Plut. *Nic.* 12, *Alc.* 17.3), to have (in Gylippus' words) 'the greatest empire of any Greeks of our own or former times' (7.66.2). The Persians' aim, in Herodotus' and also in Aeschylus' view, was even more grandiose: to unite Asia and Europe, to create an empire 'bordering the *aither* of Zeus' (Hdt. 1.209.1, 7.8.γ, 19.1, 54.2, 8.53.2, 109.3; A. *Pers.* 189–99).

To be the ostensible object of such maniacal ambition can be turned to your own advantage, however. The queen of Aeschylus' *Persians* wonders aloud as to why her son should want to conquer Athens (A. *Pers.* 233): 'because all Greece would then become subject to the King', the Chorus reply (234). Athens holds the key to Greece (Hall 1996: 127; Paduano 1978: 26; Goldhill 1988: 190). A very similar claim is 'reported' by Thucydides (1.73.4–74.2) and made by the speaker of Lysias 2 (2.2).

Herodotus' self-consciousness in delivering the verdict that the Athenian contribution to the war was pivotal becomes, against this background, quite understandable (Hdt. 7.139). No great glory, one might think, to be merely the largest obstacle in the path of the Persian juggernaut. But, of course, it is only by virtue of Greek survival, as part of a debate – or more accurately perhaps a process of ideological posturing – as to which city was most responsible for the Persians' defeat, a process reflected most clearly in the Persian war epigrams (Simonides 20–1, 54, epig. 11 Campbell) and in Pindar (*Pyth.* 1.75ff), that such a claim becomes an object of pride.

And it is not only pride that results from being the object of such imperial aggression. 'These same Athenians', as Hermocrates tells the Syracusans, 'when the Mede was defeated in many ways contrary to reason, grew in power on the basis of the reputation earned by the Mede having attacked Athens. And this may very well happen to us also' (6.33.6). The Syracusans, as Hermocrates later remarks (7.56.2), 'would be regarded as the authors of this deliverance [of the Sicilians], and would be held in high admiration, not only with all men now living but also with posterity'. In the same way, Herodotus sees the Athenians' empire as rooted in the glory that they earned through their part in the Persian wars. What we see as a justification of empire was actually for Herodotus also a *cause* of empire (Hdt. 6.109.3, 9.102). Two very particular Athenian slogans are also projected onto the Syracusans. One has been introduced earlier: Syracuse is the key to Sicily as Athens was to Greece. According to Hermocrates, this is actually the reason for the Athenians' making Syracuse the first object of their hostility (6.33.2). Alcibiades in Sparta inflates the claim: if Syracuse is defeated, all of Sicily and then Italy will follow (6.91.3). The second such reflected slogan is, if anything, more potent: they were the first to go into battle against the Athenians at sea (7.66.2; cf. 7.21.4, 55.2) – as the Athenians had been the first Greeks to survive the sight of Median dress at Marathon (Hdt. 6.112.3).[5]

The gradual coming together of the cities of Sicily and the working out of Hermocrates' plan of uniting to conquer are, together with the relentless process of the isolation and destruction of the Athenian forces, the chief themes of books 6 and 7. The Syracusans must drum into the other Sicilians the real scale of the Athenians' ambitions (6.78.1). They must garner support by sending out ambassadors in all directions (6.34.1–3). They then succeed in creating a sense of Sicilian unity in the nick of time, just as the Greeks patched together their differences for just long enough to repel the Persians. Gradually all the cities of Sicily get drawn in to the conflict, so that – as in what we might call the original Peloponnesian War (the Sicilian expedition is repeatedly seen as another war, no less in size) – neutrality becomes impossible.

Whether or not this new-found sense of Sicilian identity was indeed a reality – as is commonly believed to be the case of Greek identity in the aftermath of the Persian wars – is another question. But Thucydides' Sicilian speakers repeatedly focus on the things they have in common, patriotic Sicilian themes: the need to 'save the whole of Sicily' (4.60.1, 4.61.2; cf. 6.37.2), always to combine against the foreign invader (*allophulous*, 4.64.4), to protect the 'common interests of Sicily' (6.79.2). They are all, Hermocrates tells them, neighbours together, living in one land, girt by the same sea, and called by one and the same name: Sicilians (4.64.3). The Athenian expedition constitutes an attack on the 'good things in Sicily which we possess in common' (4.61.3); the Sicilians are engaged in a 'beautiful contest … to pass on the freedom of all Sicily preserved' (7.68.3). This gradual coming together of Sicilians is observed by non-Sicilians also (7.15.1). Initially, just as Persians condemn the Greeks for their hopeless attachment to petty internal disputes (Hdt. 7.9.β1–2; cf. 5.49.8, 7.101.2, 103.3–4, 9.2.2), the Sicilians too are, in Alcibiades' view, a hopeless, shifting people unable to unite or resist the foreign invader (6.17.2–4).[6]

The Sicilians' unity is consistently undermined by Thucydides just as the Greeks' unity is undermined by Herodotus. It is implied throughout Herodotus' account of the Persian wars that the Greeks are fighting not only against the Persians but among themselves, jostling for the position they will hold come the peace.[7] Even as early as Marathon, Miltiades attracts the support of the polemarch Callimachus for fighting the battle by arguing that 'if the city were to win through, she would be the first of the Greek cities' (Hdt. 6.109.3). Similarly, Thucydides' reader knows in advance of the Syracusan agenda announced by Hermocrates that Sicilian unity is a veil for Syracusan ambition, that freedom from the Athenians will mean domination by the Syracusans.

The charge that the Athenians and their allies turned from being the liberators to the enslavers of their fellow Greeks is, of course, a hackneyed one, raised most famously against the Plataeans (3.61–7), but also by the Syracusan Hermocrates to – significantly – the people of Camarina rather than a home audience: the Athenians, he says, are trying to do to Sicily what they have done to Greece at the time of the Persian wars (6.76.3). Arguably, however, the better analogy for the Athenians' past aggrandisement is the Syracusans' rather than the Athenians' position. The shape of Syracusan ambition is clinically laid bare by the Athenian Euphemus (6.86–7): it is not us, he assures them, that you need to fear but the Syracusans themselves. Similar ironic light is cast on Sicilian unity just before the Athenians' attempt to break out of Syracuse harbour: in response to Gylippus' talk of the need to pass on the 'freedom of all Sicily preserved' (7.68.3), Nicias responds with like platitudes (7.69): the need to be worthy of their own past actions, not to obscure the virtues of their ancestors, the freedom of their city, that each man there (echoing Pericles' funeral oration) was free to live as he chose, and (to take up Thucydides' words):

> other arguments such as men would use at such a crisis, and which, with little alteration, are made to serve on all occasions alike – appeals to wives, children, national gods – without caring whether they are thought commonplace, but loudly invoking them in the belief that they will be of use in the consternation of the moment.[8]

One patriotic myth is born as another is buried.

Even the means by which the Syracusans gain their empire parallel the foundation of the Athenians' rule. The Athenians learnt to row almost by accident ([Xen.] *Ath. Pol.* 1.19–20); 'necessity drove every man to take up his oar'; each man, in the words of the messenger of Aeschylus' *Persians,* 'was lord of his own oar' (A. *Pers.* 378). Salamis is one of the founding myths of Athens' fifth-century democracy and empire.[9] By the time of Thucydides' writing, as we have seen, Athenian superiority at sea has become a settled fact of existence. But such superiority can be lost as well as gained – as the Corinthians note as early as book 1.[10] There is nothing innate, Hermocrates tells the Syracusans (7.21.3), about the Athenians' naval superiority – they had once been even greater landlubbers than the Syracusans – but they had been forced to become sailors by the Medes. Step by step the Syracusans believe this true;[11] and step by step they overhaul the Athenians: the Athenians' ships begin to rot in the water, whilst with experience the Syracusans gradually grow in confidence (7.12.3–5); they make alterations to their ships to make best use of the confined space, for example by strengthening their beaks (7.36); eventually they are confident that they now have the advantage at sea (7.41). This new fact of Sicilian superiority is acknowledged by both Demosthenes (7.47.3) and Nicias, in making the curious boast that the Sicilians would not have dared to fight with the Athenian navy when it was at its peak (7.63.4), but it is reflected most poignantly at the death of the expedition: asked to attempt a second break-out of the Syracuse harbour, the Athenian sailors refuse, as they no longer believe that they can win (7.72.4).

The death, when it comes, is all the greater for the size of the expedition (Connor 1984: 161). 'The whole barbarian force has perished' (A. *Pers.* 255): similar expressions pepper Aeschylus' *Persians.*[12] But the same conclusion is reached by both Aeschylus and Herodotus by rather subtler strategies: by magnificent lists of the peoples and commanders of the Persian army (A. *Pers.* 16–58, 302–30, 956–1002; Hdt. 7.60–100, 9.31–2), by Xerxes' perennial reviews of his forces, or by incidental anecdotes of the rivers drunk dry (Hdt. 7.21, 187.1–2) or of the seven days and seven nights that the Persian host took to cross the Hellespont (Hdt.

7.56.1). Similar strategies are employed by Thucydides to magnify the Athenians' fall. The Athenians knew nothing of the size of Sicily (unlike Plutarch's Athenians, busying themselves drawing pictures of Sicily in the sand, *Nic*. 12, *Alc*. 17.3) or of the number of those, Greek and barbarian, living there (6.1.1). This is, of course, the cue for Thucydides' description of the size and the peoples of Sicily (6.1–6). His conclusion to this description spells out the point unmistakably (6.6.1): 'Such is the list of the peoples, Hellenic and barbarian, inhabiting Sicily, and such the magnitude of the island which the Athenians were now bent upon invading; being ambitious in real truth of conquering the whole.' Thucydides' digression on the fall of the Athenian tyranny, with its tenuous overt link to the fear of tyranny engendered by Alcibiades and the mutilation of the Herms, takes one back to the point at which the period of democracy, and Athens' power, began, offering a pathetic contrast to their imminent destruction.[13] At a crucial point before the final denouement of the expedition, Thucydides reviews the forces on both sides; never, he introduces this final drawing-in of breath, had so many people settled in front of a single city (7.57.1).[14] Then, of course, there is his famous description of the preparations of the Sicilian expedition (6.30–2), the most costly and splendid force sent out by a Greek city (31.1), and its departure, viewed by the whole population (30.2). The Athenian forces, the pick of those available (like Xerxes' also: Hdt. 7.26), vied with one another for the beauty of their equipment (6.31.3–4), giving the appearance to the world that the expedition was more a display of Athenian power and resources than an actual expedition (6.31.4).

There are no precise parallels here, but the description recalls a number of episodes from the departure of Xerxes' expedition: most clearly perhaps the scene of Xerxes' reviewing his troops from a white marble throne at Abydus, calling himself blessed and then weeping at the sight of so many who would all be dead within a hundred years (Hdt. 7.46), in actual fact much sooner. There is the same sense of spectacle, of viewing[15] – only with the Persian King taking the place of the Athenian people – but also the same sense of pathos. At the close of the expedition, as the expeditionary force prepares to make its break-out by land, Thucydides makes the point (although not the analogy with Xerxes) explicit (7.75.6–7):

> This was by far the greatest reverse that ever befell an Hellenic army. They had come to enslave others, and were departing in fear of being enslaved themselves: they had sailed out with prayers and paeans, and now started to go back with omens directly contrary; travelling by land instead of by sea, and trusting not in their fleet but in their heavy infantry.

The greatest parallel with the situation of the Persians is that the size of both expeditions is quite useless. The Persians are obsessed with numbers;

Herodotus even observes their belief that numbers constitute strength in the course of his ethnographic 'digression' on the Persians in book 1 (Hdt. 1.136.1). How many ships, Aeschylus' queen asks the messenger (A. *Pers*. 333–6), do the Athenians have, that they think 'they could meet the Persians in a naval encounter'? 'You are not under the impression', the messenger replies, 'that we were numerically undone in the battle'; no, it was some god who was responsible; 'as far as the fleet was concerned you can be sure that the barbarians would have won' (337–47). Herodotus' Xerxes too is fixated with the number of his ships as if numbers were a guarantee of victory. This emerges most clearly in response to Artabanus at Abydus. Artabanus confesses to being afraid of two great enemies. Xerxes replies (Hdt. 7.48):

> Mysterious man, what are these two great enemies you say exist? Do you think that our army is at fault in its number, and that the Greek force will appear much greater than ours? Or that our navy will fall short of theirs? Or both of these things? If you think that our affairs are at all deficient in this respect, it would be quite possible for someone to collect another army.

He has, of course, missed the point, as Artabanus tells him in words closely paralleling those of the messenger in the *Persians* (Hdt. 7.49.1): 'King, no one of sense could find fault with this army, nor with the number of ships. Indeed, if you collected more, the two enemies of which I speak would be much greater. For these are the land and the sea.'

Thucydides' Athenians present only slightly variant symptoms of the same disease. The size of the Athenian force is increased as the result of Nicias' attempt to *dissuade* the Athenians from the campaign (6.20–6). Just as the Persians, with the exception of Artabanus, are too afraid to speak against the campaign for fear of the King (Hdt. 7.8.δ2, 10), so the Athenians are now afraid of the tyranny not of the king but of the democratic majority (Rood 1999): 'with this enthusiasm of the majority' – Thucydides earlier uses the word *erôs*, charged with overtones of tyranny (6.24.3)[16] – 'the few that liked it not, feared to appear unpatriotic by holding up their hands against it, and so kept quiet' (6.24.4). Even Nicias, however, is deluded in his faith in the power of numbers. If the people do vote him the absurd numbers of ships and men he demands, at least then, he reckons, he would be safe (6.24.1); the people too employ the same logic to conclude that the expedition is without risk (6.24.2).[17]

The Sicilians, though they too are prone to being awed by the number of their enemies – Demosthenes' reinforcements seem scarcely fewer in number than the force that they are come to join (7.42.2) – generally see the matter more clearly: the Athenians would not succeed, according to Athenagoras, even if their forces were twice as great (6.37.1). The size of the Athenians' forces indeed works against them. It is the size of the

Athenian effort that galvanises the Sicilians to join forces (6.33.4). Large armies, Thucydides adds later, are especially prone to panic (7.80.3). But the Athenians' numbers also have other consequences, more clearly reminiscent of the Persian wars. Artabanus at Abydus proceeds to detail the way in which the land and the sea will prove hostile (7.49.2–5): no harbours will be large enough to shelter the fleet in the event of a storm; the land will beget a famine. The Athenians suffer similar difficulties due to their distance from home: the fleet is split into three divisions so that they should not lack water, harbours or provisions (6.42.1). Just as with Darius' Scythian and Xerxes' Persian expeditions, the chief question that their failure poses is how they might escape, given the distance of Sicily from Greece: they are sailing, says Nicias, to altogether another land (6.21.2), in Thucydides' judgement the longest journey from home of any such campaign (6.31.6).[18] The many variant stories of the Persians' return – of the Persians eating the bark off trees from hunger, and then, when eventually they found food, dying from their immoderate eating (Hdt. 8.115–17), of the rivers drunk dry by the Persian army (Hdt. 7.21, 187.1–2), or of the crossing of the Strymon (A. *Pers*. 495–514) – are perhaps also reflected in Thucydides' description of the Athenians' arrival at the river Assinaros (7.84.3–5):

> Once there they rushed in, and all order was at an end, each man wanting to cross first, and the attacks of the enemy making it difficult to cross at all. Forced to huddle together, they fell against and trod down one another, some dying immediately upon the javelins, others getting entangled and stumbling over the articles of baggage, without being able to rise again. Meanwhile the opposite bank, which was steep, was lined by the Syracusans, who showered missiles down upon the Athenians, most of them drinking greedily and heaped together in disorder in the hollow bed of the river. The Peloponnesians also came down and butchered them, especially those in the water, which was thus immediately spoiled, but which they went on drinking just the same, mud and all, bloody as it was, most even fighting to have it.

The difference, of course, between the Persian and Athenian expeditions was that, in the first case, a substantial remnant survived to return to Susa.[19] However, despite the tradition of the return to Susa, despite Themistocles' allowing Xerxes to escape past the Hellespont, the Persian disaster is persistently portrayed as total.

In Herodotus and Aeschylus, the land and the sea conspire against the Persians in any number of ways, by the inadequacy of rivers and harbours, by cliffs resembling ships (Hdt. 8.107.2), by miraculous winds and storms (Hdt. 6.44.2, 7.34, 42.2, 8.12.1, 37–8), or by the island rocks echoing back the Greeks' paean at Salamis (A. *Pers*. 389–91). But the Persian numbers are particularly devastatingly counterproductive in the battles of the war:

at Artemisium, the Persian fleet 'by virtue of its size and number' destroyed itself as their ships rammed one another (Hdt. 8.16.2); the sites of Thermopylae and Salamis are chosen for the fact that there the Persians would not be able to make use of their numbers (Hdt. 7.177, 8.60α–β).[20] In the words of Aeschylus' messenger (A. *Pers*. 413–21):

> when the mass of their ships was crowded together in a narrow strait, [and] they could not bring any assistance to one another, they struck each other with their bronze-mouthed beaks, and shattered all the rowing equipment; the Greek ships judiciously encircled them and made their strike, and ships' hulls were turned upside down, and it was no longer possible to glimpse the sea, brimming with wrecked ships and dead men.

In Syracuse the circumstances of Salamis are inverted. Demosthenes wants to move into a broader place where the Athenians' skill serves them (7.49.2); it is a place, according to Gylippus, where they will gain nothing by their numbers (7.67.3; cf. 7.36.4–6). The Athenians in desperation try to force their way out of the blockade (7.67.4, 70), having adapted their mode of fighting to the enclosed space (7.62),[21] but still they collide with one another:

> In many quarters it also happened, by reason of the narrow room, that a vessel was charging an enemy on one side and being charged herself on another, and that two or sometimes more ships had perforce got entangled round one, obliging the helmsman to attend to defence here, offence there, not to one thing at once but to many on all sides; while the huge din caused by the number of ships crashing together not only spread terror but made the orders of the boatswains inaudible.

The blockade of Syracuse harbour itself provides a further ironic twist on the Athenians' predicament at Salamis (7.56.1–2, 7.59). The Persians' blockade, inspired by Themistocles' trick message to Xerxes, had been desirable in so far as it forced the other Greeks not to retreat to the Isthmus and the Persians to fight in a place where their superior numbers counted for nothing. Here the blockade for the same reasons worked against the Athenians. Themistocles' cunning trick finds its counterpart also in the message sent by Hermocrates to Nicias in order to block the Athenians' retreat by land: others in Syracuse shared his opinion that the Athenians should be prevented from retreat, but felt that such a plan was impracticable while the Syracusans were given over to celebrations of their naval victory. So, Hermocrates – already having shown a Themistoclean foresight in his preparations for the Athenian expedition – has a message relayed in a rather roundabout fashion to Nicias, advising him to wait until daytime to retreat as the passes were already blocked (7.73).[22]

As we have seen, Thucydides – like Aeschylus and Herodotus before him – builds up the impression of the scale of the expedition by a number of strategies. One particularly sharp echo of the Persian wars stands out. Themistocles famously replied to Adeimantus' taunt that he was a 'man without a city' (Hdt. 8.61.2) that the Athenians would have a city and a territory as great as the Corinthians' while they had 200 ships fully manned. The phrase is very probably alluded to in the *Persians* by the messenger's reply to the chorus that 'while men remain to a city, its ramparts are secure' (A. *Pers.* 349; Podlecki 1966: 16). Regardless of whether we see a precise debt to a historical remark of Themistocles, there is clearly a strong ideological affinity between such slogans. Both depend upon the famous Wooden Wall oracle given to the Athenians; both serve to turn the Athenians' evacuation of their territory into a source of pride. In the *Persians,* the slogan that a city consists in its men is the basis for a fundamental contrast between Athens and Persia: Susa and Persia are empty except for women and old men (A. *Pers.* 1–139; cf. Hdt. 7.11.1). Susa presents then a precise mirror image of Athens, as it possessed walls without men (Rosenbloom 1993: 191).

This myth of the Athenian evacuation outlives the immediate aftermath of the wars. The same pride is expressed by Thucydides' Athenian representatives in Sparta (1.74.2–4), alluding incidentally to Adeimantus' sneer (1.74.1; see Hornblower 1991–6 on 1.74.3): if, like others, they had given in to their fears for their territory, the war would have been lost. It is also satirised by Aristophanes in the *Frogs*, when he makes Aeschylus claim that the Athenians should consider 'their enemies' land their own and their own their enemies'' and treat ships as if they were the only true wealth (Ar. *Frogs* 1463–5). The Periclean defensive strategy of sitting tight behind Athens' walls and relying on the strength of its navy, the ideology of Athens as an island ([Xen.] *Ath. Pol.* 2.14–16; cf. Thuc. 1.93.7), are also founded upon this myth of evacuation: when Archidamus argues that the Athenians would never allow themselves to become the slaves of their land, the evidence for this is that they had famously turned their backs on it in the past (1.81.6).[23]

Thucydides then inverts this myth with deadly irony. He has Nicias tell the Athenians to understand that they must be prepared to found a city in a foreign land (6.23.2);[24] Thucydides himself describes the Athenians during their final attempted break-out by land as resembling 'nothing other than a beseiged city in flight, and this not a small one' (7.75.5). Even at this last stage Nicias – even after perhaps referring obliquely to the Persians, in talking of how other men have invaded others' land and suffered only tolerably (7.77.4; Connor 1984: 202) – still shows a dim belief in the power of numbers (7.77.4):

> And then look at yourselves, mark the numbers and efficiency of the heavy
> infantry marching in your ranks, and do not give way too much to despon-
> dency, but reflect that you are yourselves at once a city wherever you sit

down, and that there is no other in Sicily that could easily resist your attack, or expel you when once established.

'Men make a city and not walls or ships without men in them' (7.77.7).[25] 'Salamis holds all of Persia', Aeschylus' Persians intone (A. *Pers.* 595–7);[26] now, it seems, all of Athens has been left behind in Sicily. Aeschylus (and Herodotus) envisage the Persian defeat as leaving Asia open to, undefended against, all comers (A. *Pers.* 584–90, 751–2, 1018–24; Hdt. 7.11.2–3). Similar consequences are spelled out by Nicias before the attempt to break out of the Great Harbour (7.64): Athens' enemies will immediately sail against Athens, and it will be unable to repel them. They are 'the army and navy of the Athenians, and all that is left of the city and the great name of Athens' (7.64.2). Thucydides' final comments of book 7 are powerful enough for their simplicity, but against the background of the superlatives used in highlighting the totality of the Persian defeat,[27] they gain an extra force (7.87.6):

> This was the greatest Hellenic achievement of any in this war, or in my opinion in Hellenic history; at once most glorious to the victors, and most calamitous to the conquered. They were beaten at all points and altogether; all that they suffered was great; they were destroyed, as the saying is, with a total destruction;[28] their fleet, their army, everything was destroyed, and few out of many returned. Such were the events in Sicily.

Thucydides then comes back down to earth. The arrival of the news of defeat in Athens has much of the same pathos. Here there are echoes again of the versions of the news of Persian defeat reaching home that are found in Herodotus, Aeschylus, and Phrynichus' *Phoenicians*. However, as many readers have observed, the recovery of Athens in book 8 seems to sit uncomfortably with the disastrous climax of book 7.[29] When Thucydides reports the shock of the Euboean revolt, more terrifying even than the Sicilian disaster 'great though that had seemed to be' (8.96.1), the reader may even feel cheated. It is as if Aeschylus, after presenting the Persian disaster consistently as total, had calmly noted that the Persian empire was not, in actual fact, destroyed, but had survived to meet even worse terrors. Thucydides' events similarly, it seems, will not quite fit the pattern he imposes on them.

We too must come down to earth. Why does Thucydides evoke the Persian wars in this way? Is Thucydides' Sicilian Expedition no more than an isolated literary setpiece? I have no wish to deny that much of what Thucydides describes took place. Thucydides' account of the slaughter by the river Assinarus may be heavily coloured, even distorted, by association with the Persian wars, it may have been selected for extended treatment on the grounds of the potential it offered for such an implicit analogy, but that some such slaughter took place there is no reason to doubt.[30] The literary patterns that have been traced here also in no way preclude more sober historical judgements on Thucydides' – or indeed on our – part: the capture of Plemmyrium, he tells us, was the greatest cause of the Athenian expedition's ruin (7.24.3); in book 2, another such minimalist explanation is provided, the failure of the expedition's mother-city to offer proper support (2.65.11).[31]

At the same time, however, I have no difficulty with the proposition that some of Thucydides' original readers or audience may have been forced to recall passages of Herodotus, that Thucydides' echoes were deliberately planted for their effect. Aristophanes may – depending on one's view of the date (or dates) of Herodotus' publication – have taken for granted a degree of knowledge of his work on the part of a significant portion of his audience.[32] If such knowledge could have been taken for granted with a popular audience, why not in the elite reading clubs in which it is presumed that Thucydides' work was, at least initially, consumed?[33]

It would be wrong, however, to see such echoes as *purely* literary, as working against history (Macleod 1983: 145–6).[34] For one thing, many of Thucydides' echoes are of democratic Athenian slogans in common currency, ideological motifs that bridge Aeschylus, Herodotus, Aristophanes and yet other sources, and that must have had a life outside of these literary homes. Doubtless, there is something particularly idiosyncratic about what Thucydides does with these motifs – most markedly, in his implicit indictment of democracy – but he is none the less an important witness to this tradition – a tradition, an ideological current, it should be added, which is of historical value in its own right. The prominence given by Thucydides to the Sicilian expedition likewise cannot be presumed to be merely a matter of literary artistry.[35] As Colin Macleod (now famously) observed (1983: 146), 'History is something lived through; and part of the experience of the Sicilian expedition must have been the sense of a national downfall and the shock at the undoing of such might and splendour.' Thucydides' tragic scheme – incorporating his echoes of the Persian wars – was not, in other words, simply a way of writing about history but a way of thinking about it,[36] a 'mould of conception … inwrought into the very structure of an author's mind' (Cornford 1907: viii).

So, as Macleod continued to observe, was his 'technique of echo or reminiscence'.[37] Moreover, lest it be thought that the echoes traced here are merely fanciful, Thucydides is not alone in this instinct. Much of the best recent work on Herodotus has focused on similar submerged patterns in his text. Best-known perhaps – in that it has penetrated to non-classicists – is François Hartog's *Mirror of Herodotus*, on Herodotus' treatment of the Scythians, on the Scythians as inverting the norms of Greek society,[38] on affinities between the Scythian campaign and the expedition of Xerxes to Greece, between Darius' military approach towards the Scythians and the Archidamian war strategy of Pericles (Hartog 1988: 51, 203). A similar tendency to equate historical events can be seen in the murals of the Stoa Poikile, featuring Theseus and the Amazons and the capture of Troy with Marathon and the shadowy battle of Oinoe (Paus. 1.15), or in Pindar's praise of Syracuse for saving Greece from heavy slavery, setting the Syracusans' achievement at Himera alongside the Athenians' at Salamis and the Spartans' at Plataea (*Pyth*. 1.75ff). Pindar can hardly be accused of being anything other than rarefied. But a popular parallel to his equation of Himera with Plataea and Salamis is the synchronism of Himera with Salamis or Thermopylae that survives in respectively Herodotus and Diodorus (Hdt. 7.166; D.S. 11.24.1). Such synchronisms – and they are many – imply historical judgements. As Emma Dench has put it, 'it is a small step from the synchronization of battles to a sense of "common cause", and, indeed, of a common enemy' (Dench 1995: 11, 51);[39] indeed arguably the process should be seen in reverse, the synchronisation as the product of the idea.

It was then, I contend, second nature for Thucydides to write with such potential parallels in mind. Thucydides' echoes show the same reflex attraction to the idea of a (near-)circularity to history as the story of Artayctes and Protesilaus at the end of Herodotus' *Histories*, with its reference back to the Trojan hero, and forward – through the identity of Artayctes' nemesis, Xanthippus – to the Athenian empire of Xanthippus' son Pericles (9.116–121).[40] This is just one instance of the way in which, conversely, Herodotus' account of the Greek conflict with the Persian empire was shaped by the experience of the Peloponnesian War.[41]

# 8

# THE TYRANT'S MYTH

## Sian Lewis

SICILY HAS ALWAYS OFFERED an excellent arena for an examination of tyranny, especially in the fourth century. The tradition of Sicilian tyranny was strong, beginning in the seventh century with figures like Phalaris of Agrigentum, and continuing into the fifth with Anaxilas of Rhegium and the Deinomenids at Syracuse. In the fourth century, in common with many other areas, Sicily saw the emergence of new and powerful autocratic rulers, Dionysius the Elder and his successor Dionysius II at the beginning of the century, and Agathocles at its close. The prevalence of tyranny in the fourth century, in places across the Greek world, from Sicyon and Pherai to Heracleia and Halicarnassos, is often presented either as a peripheral phenomenon, unrelated to the development of the 'major' *poleis*, or as a sign of decline from the political sophistication of the fifth century. Neither view, in my opinion, does justice either to the significance of areas such as Sicily, or to the potential of tyranny as a political solution to the problems of the period. There is also a tendency to underestimate the sophistication of tyrannies in this period, in terms both of how tyrants presented themselves and of what they achieved, and this is the theme of my discussion.

There are several ways of thinking about the Sicilian tyrants. Some have presented them as distinctive, as does Andrewes in *The Greek Tyrants*, seeing them as significantly different from the tyrannies in mainland states, since the Sicilian leaders, from Gelon onwards, were primarily military. Andrewes refers to 'military monarchy' in the fifth century, and characterises the appearance of the fourth-century tyrants as a failure of political maturity, that is to say, a failure of the Syracusans to embrace democracy, rather than a positive development (though he admits that if the Dionysii had remained in power, Sicily might have rivalled Rome) (Andrewes 1956: ch. 11, 142). Some, such as Mossé, describe the Sicilian tyrants as a new phenomenon, making a sharp distinction between fifth and fourth century, and presenting Dionysius as the precursor of the hellenistic kings (Mossé 1989: 99–120). And some omit them from their explanation of tyranny altogether, considering them too late to be of any relevance to the stories created about early rulers (Ogden 1996).

It seems to me wrong to create divisions between eras and types of tyranny, either geographical or temporal; what should be emphasised is rather continuity, especially within Sicily itself. Aristotle, from his perspective in the 330s and 320s, presents tyrants as a seamless group, lining up Dionysius I alongside Cypselus of Corinth as 'demagogue tyrants', and the Pisistratids with Philip of Macedon (Arist. *Pol.* 1310b 16ff, 1311a 36ff). It is not the case that there is a period of archaic tyranny which dies away, and a distinctly new pattern of classical tyranny which replaces it; Aristotle's sources may be better on Dionysius or Clearchus than on Cypselus or Pheidon, but he quite explicitly places them as exempla of the same phenomenon. The question of periods is thrown into sharp relief by a consideration of Sicilian history: the tyranny of the Deinomenids at Syracuse did not end until 466, with a subsequent attempt by Tyndarides to seize power in 454/3, and Hermocrates' attempt to become tyrant took place in 408/7, an interlude brief enough by comparison with ancient times (D.S. 11.67–8, 11.86, 13.75). Yet the former rulers are seen as archaic, inhabiting the world of Pindar and Bacchylides, while the latter are classical, real figures whose actions can be understood in terms of political, military or economic necessity. My intention is to use the Sicilian tyrants as a case study of the differences our sources present between archaic and classical tyrants, especially as we possess so much information about the image and self-presentation of these rulers.

Of all Greek rulers, Dionysius comes through our sources as the most concerned with the manipulation of public opinion. Theatricality is a feature evident in the actions of most tyrants: Gelon, for instance, presented himself unarmed in the assembly at Syracuse after his victory over Carthage, laying down his tyranny and offering accounts to the people, only to be reinstated and hailed as saviour, benefactor and king (D.S. 11.26.5–7). Dionysius is an even stronger example of this: he is often referred to in a context of theatre and audience; at Diodorus 13.94, for instance, we are told that Dionysius, during the campaign against Carthage in which his tyranny was begun, arrived in Syracuse while a play was being performed, and as the people left the theatre, they rushed up to Dionysius, forming an audience for his deceptive speech. At Himera, according to Valerius Maximus (1.7.6), the population of the city formed an admiring audience on the walls as Dionysius entered the city. Our sources indicate his constant concern to make statements about his political role, and present himself in a particular way. He attempted to shape his own image in Greece, with an extravagant display of wealth at the Olympia of 384, in an embassy led by his brother Thearidas, and he communicated with Greece at large through his own poetry and plays, entering works in the pan-hellenic contests, and the Lenaia at Athens.[1] It is not an exaggeration to describe Dionysius as engaged in a continuous propaganda war: the level of conscious manipulation is most apparent in his family relationships; his three daughters were named Arete, Sophrosyne and Dikaiosyne, announcing his relationship with the cardinal virtues of the ruler, and, even more significantly, he underwent a double marriage ceremony and had two wives, one Italian and one Syracusan.[2]

This aspect of fourth-century tyranny has not received as much attention as it merits. For figures like Dionysius, the accounts of their rule have a strong explanatory thread, so that it is possible to trace the stages by which they took power and the events of their rule, in a way that is not possible for the archaic period. Later tyrannies are easier to explain in their political context, so the less factual material connected with the reigns is often ignored as irrelevant. There is, for instance, only one brief mention of the Dionysii in Ogden's *Crooked Kings*, to illustrate their similarity to archaic rulers (Ogden 1996: 91–2). Yet the Sicilian tyrants, from the Deinomenids through the Dionysii to Agathocles, are surrounded by stories very similar in kind to those surrounding archaic tyrants. For example, Gelon, the future tyrant, was preserved from an earthquake which destroyed his school by the intervention of a wolf, which rushed in and seized his writing-tablet; he chased it out of the building and so escaped death (D.S. 10.29). An omen was given to Dionysius' mother before his birth: according to Philistus, when she was pregnant with Dionysius, his mother dreamed that she gave birth to a little satyr. This was interpreted by the Galeotai as a sign that Dionysius would rise to greatness (Philistus *FGH* 556 fr. 57). Agathocles was cast out at birth by his father because of an oracle from Delphi, but was saved by his mother in secret, and later reconciled with his father; subsequently a statue of him dedicated by his mother was found to have had a honeycomb built around its hips by bees, presaging his future importance (D.S. 19.2).

These stories, plainly, are similar in type to the accounts of archaic tyrants, with elements like the theme of the 'lost child', and the warning to the tyrant's family. Cypselus of Corinth, Pisistratus at Athens and Orthagoras at Sicyon were all subjects of a warning oracle before their birth, while children exposed at birth but rescued and returned to power by supernatural agency appear in the legends of both tyrants and kings in myth (see Ogden 1996: *passim*).

It is not as surprising as it may seem if a contemporary description of Agathocles the military leader, with a fairly coherent account of his early life, could coexist with a story of exposure and rediscovery, or if the intelligent and ruthless Dionysius at the head of his mercenaries can also be the mythical figure who discovers bees nesting in his horse's mane. The creation of history along traditional lines is well documented at all periods in the ancient world: the Mamertini, for instance, were mercenaries installed in Messana at the time of Hieron II, yet by the time of Augustus an alternative version was current, which made them colonists of the Samnites sent out as a *ver sacrum*.[3] They lent aid to Messana and were rewarded by the grateful citizens with land. Even while people knew the origin of these settlers, the creation of history in line with mythic expectation went on, and the alternative explanation could gain currency as the more 'real'. It would be unexceptional if a successful tyrant should generate stories about his birth or accession to power along familiar lines: spontaneous rumours about the tyrants were in circulation among the citizens of Syracuse, as we shall see, and indeed a wider audience. It is always the case that flatterers will create stories about powerful rulers, and rumour spring up of its own accord. The creation of stories about living rulers, however, can be shaped by them to take a variety of forms; while rejecting praise in one form, a ruler can encourage it in a different guise, as did Augustus, who rejected outward manifestations of worship, but was happy to have the divine power of his countenance noticed: 'it greatly pleased him, whenever he looked keenly at anyone, if he let his face fall as if before the radiance of the sun' (Suet. *Aug*. 52–3, 79.2). My interest is in the role that such stories played in contemporary Sicilian society, alongside coherent and detailed analyses of the tyrants' success.

Of course, some of the anecdotes of the tyrants' early life are no more than historians' later fabrications, and if one could say that all the omens are later additions, this would make my enquiry otiose. There is, however, evidence that some of these stories were generated in the time of the tyrants themselves. Most of the stories appear to derive from Timaeus, who was (according to Plb. 12.24.5) interested in dreams and omens, and this may account for the presence in Diodorus of a set of omens or tales at the start of each tyrant's reign. Yet the anecdotes were not simply invented by the historian; they have an independent origin, and many of the traditional motifs appear to originate with the tyrants themselves. The clearest example of this is the omen associated with Dionysius I at Himera, foretelling his importance to Sicily, reported by Aeschines in the speech *On the Embassy* 2.10. Aeschines claims that Demosthenes compared him to Dionysius I, and related 'the dream of the priestess in Sicily'. The scholiast gives the story: a woman of Himera had a vision in which she was taken up to Olympus, where she saw a red man crouching in chains at the altar of Zeus, and asked who he was; her guide told her that he was to be the *alastôr* of Sicily and Italy. Later she encountered Dionysius and recognised him as the red man; she was subsequently done away with by Dionysius in order to protect his reputation (Schol. Aesch. 2.10). This version of events was widely enough known in the 340s for Aeschines to assume his audience's familiarity with it. Valerius Maximus also preserves an account of the event, with some variations (1.7.6): the woman is '*non obscuri generis*', she has her vision before Dionysius comes to power, and so is truly prophetic; she recognises Dionysius in his triumphal entry into Himera.[4] It is suggested by Sordi that the variations apparent in the two different versions of this story imply that it existed originally in a positive version, and was made less favourable by Timaeus.[5] Valerius' setting of the scene in Himera makes the scenario that of the refoundation of Himera, and the role of the woman as priestess more logical. Dionysius, in this version, would have been the liberator of Himera, standing at the altar of Zeus Eleutherios, as an omen of salvation and good fortune, the *alastôr* of Sicily and Italy against Carthage. Timaeus has taken the story and removed the positive aspects, making Dionysius an *alastôr* for his own country, and the woman an ordinary citizen, who subsequently disappears; Himera was, for Timaeus, the city which was to produce his *bête noire*, Agathocles.

The story that Dionysius' birth was heralded by an ominous dream also appears contemporary. It is attributed by Cicero to Philistus, a contemporary of the tyrant, and, in Cicero's phrase, *doctus et diligens* (Cic. *Div.* 1.39). The dream is part of a tradition in Greek thought, certainly: Pericles' mother Agariste in the fifth century was said to have dreamed that she gave birth to a lion before her son was born, and Hecuba to have dreamed of a firebrand before giving birth to Paris.[6] The simplest assumption is that the story was concocted by Philistus in his role as court historian after Dionysius came to power, to offer his rule divine support. Caven suggests that the story may actually have been believed by Dionysius, but it is easier to read the dream as entering into a debate, as propaganda (Caven 1990: 235–6). The image of the satyr not only gives Dionysius a sense of superhumanity, but also plays on his name to associate him with Dionysus and his followers, the significance of which will be discussed below. Also attributed to Philistus is a further omen of Dionysius' future greatness: Dionysius was hunting one day and lost his horse while crossing a river. He abandoned it, but suddenly heard it whinnying, and it emerged from the wood with a swarm of bees nesting in its mane.[7] Bees as an omen figure in stories of archaic tyrants, notably Cypselus (in one version hidden in a beehive to save him from his enemies), and Periander's wife Melissa (who was, of course, daughter of Procles, tyrant of Epidaurus).[8]

The creation of myths, as in the case of Dionysius, may underlie the presentation of Agathocles too, though in this case we have less contemporary information. Timaeus' account of Agathocles is wholly negative; indeed, Agathocles is the paradigm of the evil ruler, yet the story Timaeus presents about Agathocles' origins is clearly positive in outline (Agathocles is a 'lost child' rediscovered and reaching greatness), made negative by the application of the same oracle as in Timaeus' version of the Himera episode. Just as Dionysius shifts from being an *alastôr* of Carthage on behalf of Sicily to become the *alastôr* of Sicily, so Agathocles is predicted to be a cause of evil to Carthage and to all Sicily, making a generalised prediction from a specific (D.S. 19.2.3). A previous, positive version of both childhood and omen must have been current before Timaeus. The similarity between the oracle of the bees in Agathocles' story and that of Dionysius is also striking: by using the same imagery, Agathocles would inscribe himself in a hereditary relationship to previous tyrants.

McGlew has advanced a particularly interesting suggestion: that the archaic tyrants like Cypselus and Pisistratus in fact modelled themselves on legendary predecessors, adopting roles such as founder of cities in order to make their role explicable to the citizens (McGlew 1993: 8–9, 173–82). He makes a case for the Sicilian Deinomenids following this practice, founding cities and receiving worship after their deaths as founding heroes. Gelon is named as a founder of cities in Herodotus (7.155–6), and Hieron was buried and worshipped as founder in his city of Aetna (D.S.11.66.4). If sixth- and even seventh-century rulers looked to mythological paradigms in forming their self-presentation, it would indeed be reasonable for a fourth-century ruler to do the same. Dionysius, we can say, is creating himself in the form of these great rulers, using the same terms of reference to describe his power, even though its basis was in the more mundane form of mercenary force. Dionysius' own foundations at Pharos and Lissos (D.S. 15.13.4) are usually interpreted as a practical step in establishing his Adriatic power, but they also served to assimilate his actions to those of past tyrants. An explicit suggestion that Dionysius was consciously emulating Pisistratus is made by Diodorus at 13.94, where the gaining of a bodyguard from his fellow citizens by means of a ruse is made a specific parallel. The idea of conscious imitation on such an obvious level seems unlikely, but I do think that a purposeful link between Dionysius and Pisistratus deserves to be taken seriously. Gernet discusses Dionysius' marriages as an example of conscious archaism, and suggests a possible emulation of the Athenian tyrant in this way (interpreting Pisistratus' marriages as bigamous also; Gernet 1968: 344–59). While Pisistratid bigamy is hard to support from the sources, Dionysius does give the impression of aiming to weave archaic themes around himself.

Dionysius has been represented as the archetype of the hellenistic ruler, especially in his claiming of divine favour or patronage. But this too can be seen as a blend of archaic and modern ideas. The association of Dionysius with his namesake Dionysus can be traced in a number of incidents: the dream of the satyr, as I have said, plays on his name to establish a particular relationship with the god. The two marriages also have a strong similarity to religious ritual, with the Italian bride brought to Syracuse in an ornate quinquereme, and the Syracusan bride carried in a chariot drawn by white horses (D.S. 14. 44). The idea of procession followed by sacred marriage cannot have been far from the minds of onlookers, particularly if the story of secrecy over the consummation of the marriages can be taken as true (Plut. *Dion*. 3). Poetry is an obvious link, marking the tyrant as a devotee of Dionysus, and he entered the Lenaia (a Dionysiac festival) at Athens as well as the pan-hellenic contests. A later source, Dio Chrysostom, includes the tantalising claim – impossible to substantiate – that there were in Syracuse statues of Dionysius which gave him the appearance or attributes of Dionysus, which the citizens hesitated to destroy.[9] One has only to think of Pisistratus entering Athens in a chariot accompanied by the living image of Athena to see a continuity with the past rather than an entirely new departure.

An episode which has received little attention in the context of public show is the treatment of the Rhegian commander Phyton after Dionysius' successful siege of Rhegium in 387/6. The campaign was motivated, according to Diodorus, by the insult offered to Dionysus when he requested a marriage link with the city, perhaps in an attempt to mirror Hieron I's marriage to the daughter of Anaxilas of Rhegium; the Rhegians, however, offered him the daughter of the public executioner as wife.[10] The campaign thus again has a double motivation, practical and mythic. In due course, Dionysius launched a campaign to conquer the city, and when it was taken, treated its commander with extreme brutality. Phyton's son was drowned at sea, and Phyton himself first exposed before the city walls on one of Dionysius' siege engines, then led through the streets and beaten, before finally being himself drowned at sea with his family (D.S. 14.112). Many historians take this as either unexceptionable practice in war, or a story demonstrating the cruelty of the tyrant in the normal way, part of the 'black legend' of Dionysius. It is, however, a story with considerable resonance. Can it be accepted as historical? Diodorus comments in his account that many of the Greeks grieved for Phyton at the time, and that his courage became a subject for poets; this implies that stories were in circulation about Phyton's actions. Philostratus (*Vit. Apoll.* 7.3.2) records a variant account, in which the exposure of Phyton on a siege machine becomes Dionysius' battle tactic, but this version is clearly intended to carry a moral about democracy.

It is the theme of drowning which is significant, since it is so rare as a method of execution, and indeed so impractical to carry out. Drowning as a death had a peculiar horror for the Greeks, since it made burial impossible, and precluded recovery even of the bones. The exposure of Phyton on one of Dionysius' siege machines could be read as part of the tyrant's theatricality – Diodorus describes Phyton's punishment as *tragikê*, but drowning taps into a much longer and richer tradition. What statement is Dionysius making through his choice of drowning as a punishment? The quality of irrecoverability of drowning made the sinking of weights in the sea a feature of oath-taking ceremonies.[11] But the sea was also a prime site for the disposal of polluted objects or individuals, thrown out at sea after death. According to Plutarch, the families of both Dionysius II and Dion were cast into the sea after the tyrant's deposition; this is not a simple doublet, since Dionysius' family were murdered by the Locrians and their bodies put out to sea, while Dion's wife, sister and infant son were put on board ship by Hicetas the Syracusan and drowned by the sailors. Both episodes suggest a schema of revenge on a tyrant through drowning, borne out by Aratus and Antigonus' drowning of the tyrant Aristomachus of Argos in the sea at Cenchreae in 224 (Plut. *Tim.* 13, *Dion.* 58.8–10; Plb. 2.60). There is an element of ridding the city of pollution – compare Philip II's drowning of the followers of Onomarchus the Phocian as temple-robbers – but also a sense of a fitting end for tyranny. Drowning features in many myths of tyrants and founders, as both a danger to which they are exposed when young (Romulus and Remus, Tennes, Battus, Telephus) and one frequent in their deposition and punishment, as with Procles of Epidauros.[12] By drowning his enemy, was Dionysius trying to call on the imagery of an archetypal slayer of tyrants?

An episode from earlier in his reign lends weight to the idea: at Enna in 403 Dionysius was responsible for both the creation and deposition of a tyrant. While on campaign near Leontini, he encouraged one Aimnestos to stage a coup in the Sicel town of Enna. The coup was successful, but Aimnestos refused to hand the city over to Dionysius, so Dionysius changed sides, and urged the Ennaians to overthrow their tyrant. When he captured the city, Dionysius 'took Aimnestos and handed him over to the Ennaians for punishment', establishing himself as a liberator. He then left the city (D.S. 14.14; see Berger 1992: 78). A negative interpretation dwells on the duplicity of the tyrant, aiming to create trust among his enemies by apparent support of democracy; but the act of deposing a tyrant is one which the ruler could use to his credit. This too mirrors the acts of the Deinomenids: Hieron I, although himself tyrant of Syracuse, removed the tyrant Thrasydaeus from Acragas and Himera in the 470s, and allowed the cities their liberty, instead of taking them over, adopting the role of liberator of tyrannies (D.S.11.53.4–5; see McGlew 1993: 139–44). Thus as with Phyton, Dionysius was aware of the traditional roles of the ruler in myth (founder, liberator) and the ways in which these roles could be manipulated to create a positive image for himself.

What is the implication of this kind of 'image management'? First, it argues against the belief that Dionysius did his best to play down the interpretation of his rule as tyranny, using the title of archon, and allowing the institutions of the democracy to survive (Sanders 1987: 92). That is not to say that he was not attentive to appearances in this way, but that the image of rulership is more complex than a simple tyrant:democrat opposition. Through myth and omen, he projected himself as an autocrat within an existing tradition. But what is to be gained from assimilating oneself to groups of tyrants now overthrown? Clearly there were elements of Deinomenid rule which could usefully be tapped, such as military prowess against a great enemy. Continuity within Sicily was certainly very powerful: the success of the Deinomenids against Carthage was a feature to be emulated. But one should not underestimate the power of older archetypes too: assimilation with the divine does carry security in holding a tyranny. One can also consider the possible complicity of the demos in the acceptance of the omens surrounding their ruler, which might explain the coexistence of positive and negative versions of the Himera story. The factor of inevitability in the rise of the tyrant is one which appeals to the people's vision of themselves (relieving them of responsibility for the tyranny by weakness or passivity), and removing the necessity of asserting themselves against the tyranny, whether the tyrant is considered beneficial or harmful.

Of course, the most striking feature of this view of Dionysius' reign is the positive image itself, since the impression of Dionysius I left by later historians is unrelievedly bad. It is true, however, that much anti-tyrannical rhetoric originates in Athenian sources (Sanders is right in this respect), and it is doubtful whether the opposition between tyrant and democrat was as sharp in Syracuse as in Athens. The appeal to public opinion was one at which Dionysius was skilled: consider his working alongside his fellow citizens in the fortification of Epipolai (D.S. 14.18.7), or the affability which shines through Diodorus' description of his 'workshop of war': 'every day Dionysius would go around the workers, encouraging them with kind words, and he honoured the most enthusiastic of them with gifts and invitations to dine with him' (D.S. 14.42.1). One has to wonder how much the vocabulary of democracy meant to the Syracusans of the fourth century; to be a tyrant was not necessarily a totally negative role.

The desire to recreate and reimpose the myths of the past is detectable down to the third century, in the rule of Hieron II. Justin (23.1–6) relates an intriguing set of traditions about Hieron's origins and childhood, which includes elements from all his predecessors' stories. Hieron is at the same time offspring of the line of Gelon, and of a low-born mother; like Agathocles, he was exposed by his father at birth, but subsequently rescued; his miraculous escape from death was aided by a swarm of bees, which figure in Dionysius' and Agathocles' stories; like both, the sooth-sayers declare him marked out for future kingship. Like Gelon, he en-counters a wolf in the schoolroom, an episode undoubtedly borrowed out of context from Gelon's story. The point of origin of these stories can only be guessed, but Hieron certainly tried to establish his place in Syracusan tradition by naming his son Gelon and his daughter Damarete (Plb. 7.8; Liv. 24.22; Paus. 6.12.2–4). It would not be surprising if the myths of origin too were a conscious attempt to place himself in legendary continuity with his tyrannical predecessors.

A final contrast illustrates the rule behind the tyrant's use of myth: the striking absence of omens connected with Dionysius the Younger. Given that he ruled for ten years, there is no reason why he should not have established or collected omens concerning his birth too, or his eventual succession to (or loss of) power. Yet in Diodorus, and all other sources, the rule of Dionysius II has nothing ominous about it. Plutarch reports another wolf episode during his reign (*Dion.* 26, in which Dion is indirectly rescued by a wolf, which carries off letters from Timocrates warning Dionysius II of his arrival), and this may, as Pearson thinks, be connected with a dynastic theme (Dion is preserved by a wolf just as Gelon was), but this does not relate to Dionysius II himself, nor can it definitely be said to be contemporary (Pearson 1987: 199). It is not solely because Dionysius II was not faced with the same problem of legitimising his power as his father that no stories were generated for circulation, positive or (via distortion) negative, but rather because his birth, as son of one of the tyrant's wives, and his marriage to his half-sister Sophrosyne were distinctive enough. His eventual rule did not need to be predicted, as he was already part of the legend. The sole hint of myth-making comes from Plutarch *De Alexandri Fortuna* (*Mor.* 338b–c), which records a line of verse in which Dionysius referred his birth to Apollo; if true, it sits oddly with the elder Dionysius' links with Dionysus, and may perhaps represent an attempt to assert himself against his father's memory. But as well as referring to Apollo, the verse also puns on Dionysius' mother's name, Doris – his maternal status remaining as important as his paternal.

What I have tried to show through this examination of the classical Sicilian tyrannies is that just as we seek the reality behind the myth for archaic tyrants, trying to reconstruct the constitution of Corinth, or the status of Pheidon, so it might be salutary to look for the myth behind the reality of the Dionysii and their successors. Dionysius I is usually read as a practical, if not cynical, politician, with all the elements of myth filtered out, yet the layer of mysteriousness was an important part of the tyrant's success. Dionysius, and other classical tyrants, drew on a repertoire of traditional narratives in order to explain what they were doing; the process is not simply legitimation, but a method of explaining their position by assimilation to archetypal predecessors. Nor was the process one-way; the tyrant's subjects appropriated these myths and used then for their own ends. Myth does not end where history begins.

# Part III

# THE COMING OF THE ROMANS

# 9

# THE COMING OF THE ROMANS:

## Sicily from the fourth to the first centuries BC

## *John Serrati*

WHILE THE ECONOMY REMAINED steady the stability brought about by the reforms of Timoleon did not last much beyond his retirement. Fresh political anarchy ensued, with various individuals and groups vying for power, amongst them a soldier called Agathocles (316–289) from Sicily's most powerful city, Syracuse. He was initially exiled by the city's oligarchy, but this merely gave him time to acquire experience as a mercenary captain in Italy. He returned in 319 and was appointed *strategos autokrator*; a military coup that deposed the oligarchy and installed him as tyrant followed in short order. His first few years in power were spent reining in the Greek cities of eastern Sicily, which had broken away from Syracuse after Timoleon had stepped down. In 311, Agathocles felt powerful enough to disregard a three-year-old treaty and invade western Sicily, and to challenge Carthage for the hegemony of the island. But his *hubris* was abruptly repaid with a disastrous defeat at Himera.

Thereupon Carthage once again laid siege to Syracuse. Agathocles now pursued a radically different plan from previous Greek warlords, and promptly invaded Africa, in the hope that pressure on the Punic capital would force their army at Syracuse to withdraw. After an initial victory, his plan did not come to fruition; he was unable to take Carthage, and Syracuse remained under siege. He returned to Sicily, and in 308 in his absence his forces in Africa were almost completely destroyed. He returned there for a short while but conceded defeat and abandoned the remnants of his army, which were swiftly annihilated. He was forced into a peace with Carthage in 306 that left him with a free hand in eastern Sicily. Again he succeeded in reconquering most of the Greek half of the island.

Agathocles maintained good relations with the Greek rulers of the eastern Mediterranean, and he was perhaps seeking legitimacy and equality in their eyes when he crowned himself king in 305. Afterwards, he married Theoxene, a stepdaughter of Ptolemy I. Being unable to match Carthage, he turned his military attentions northwards, and twice invaded Italy. By 295 he ruled much of the extreme south of the peninsula, and even managed to extend his dominion to Corcyra. However, his growing unpopularity in Syracuse brought about his assassination in 289. Though a fair general, he achieved little that was of lasting importance. Militarily, his invasion of Africa was a bold move that would have earned him a significant place in history had it been successful. Nonetheless, his empire rested upon his person and melted away immediately after his downfall. Politically, he did next to nothing for Syracuse or Sicily, and his attempt to set up a dynasty failed miserably. The fact that he merely used Greek Sicily to further his own military career contributed to both his notoriety and his death. His only lasting impact came in his relations with the kings of the eastern Mediterranean. His assumption of the royal title and his connections with the successors of Alexander brought Sicily more firmly into the hellenistic world.

As usual, the individual states of Greek Sicily once again asserted themselves in the power vacuum and created political and military anarchy. Agathocles' former mercenaries, the Mamertines of Campania, seized Messana (Zankle) in the northeast, and through their plundering expeditions proceeded to become a thorn in the side of Syracuse. Carthage again threatened, but no champion arose to counter the danger. Therefore in 278 Syracuse appealed to King Pyrrhus of Epiros, cousin of Alexander the Great and related to Agathocles through marriage, who was campaigning in Italy against Rome at the time, to intervene on their behalf. He was stunningly successful against both the Mamertines and the Carthaginians, nearly driving the latter from the island, but his success made his Greek allies suspicious that he was a conqueror rather than a liberator. Sensing this discontent, he again turned his ambitions to Italy in 276.

After a number of years Hieron II (269–215) rose to power in Syracuse and eventually became tyrant. After an initial defeat, he scored a crushing victory over the Mamertines in 265 at the Longanos River. Then he followed Agathocles' lead and had himself acclaimed as king. The Mamertines, fearing a Syracusan siege, appealed to Carthage for aid. A small force was sent, and this was enough to deter Hieron until the following spring, but over the winter the Mamertines decided that Punic protection was not enough, and sent out an appeal to their fellow Italians in Rome. It was a momentous decision that would have lasting repercussions for all parties involved.

Rome accepted the Mamertine request, and thus began the First Punic War in 264. Messana was initially taken, and this forced Carthage and Syracuse, the oldest of enemies, into a military alliance. Both were swiftly defeated, and the following year Syracuse was threatened with a Roman siege. With no help from Carthage in sight, Hieron concluded a treaty with the Romans, allowing him to retain his kingdom. Rome now attempted to drive Carthage from Sicily. The war was long, and drawn out by the fact that, while Rome was unbeatable on land, it could never achieve decisive control of the sea. Agrigentum (Akragas) fell in 261 and Rome was successful in its first naval engagement at Mylae the following year. Rome now decided to take the war to Africa, and, after victory in a massive sea battle at Cape Economos, an attempt was made on Carthage itself, but the expedition met with failure and a relief fleet, ferrying the survivors home, was nearly destroyed in a storm.

Panormus was taken by the Romans in 254, and victory over a Punic force outside the city's walls three years later allowed the Romans to lay siege to the strongholds of Lilybaeum and Drepana (Drepanum). However, stalemate ensued, as Rome could not be defeated on land while Carthage could supply the besieged cities by sea. An effort to reassert Roman sea power ended in disaster at Drepana in 249. The next several years saw intermittent fighting as the Punic forces, under Hamilcar Barca, father of the great Hannibal, harangued the besiegers at every opportunity. At last, with a final supreme undertaking, Rome mustered together another fleet and defeated the Carthaginians at the Aegates Islands. Carthage sued for peace and Sicily belonged to Rome.

The kingdom of Hieron had remained untouched by the war after 263, and he had used this time of peace to bring Syracuse to an unprecedented level of prosperity. Through his tax on grain, he enriched the kingdom significantly, and he styled himself as an eastern Mediterranean monarch, complete with a royal family and a ruler-cult. He maintained strong relations with his counterparts in the east, to whom he sent many benevolent and large gifts. He was an astute politician and a realist, and he knew which way the military wind was blowing. His support for Rome was unwavering, and in 248 he was raised to the status of a full ally and his indemnity was cancelled. He continued to support Rome and to supply the Roman army with food until his death in 215. His court was home to intellectuals and artists from all over the Greek world, most notably the great scientist Archimedes. The latter achieved his most famous discoveries in Syracuse and was also responsible for greatly strengthening the defences of the city. With Rome as his protector, Hieron was able to turn his attention to the agricultural economy of his realm, and, as one of the longest-serving monarchs of the ancient world, his reign saw Syracuse become one of the richest states of the Mediterranean.

Sicily's role in the Second Punic War was much smaller than it had been in the First, but the battles there were in many ways decisive. After an abortive Carthaginian attempt on Sicily in 218, the island remained in relative peace until the death of Hieron in 215. His son and successor, Hieronymos (215), was persuaded to break with Rome and throw his lot in with Carthage, but he was soon assassinated. Hannibal, master of southern Italy by this time, did not underestimate the importance of Sicily as both a source of food and a major point on the supply route from Carthage. A Punic victory on the island would open up great new supply lines for his army in Italy, and would change the face of the entire war. Rome also did not fail to appreciate the importance of Sicily, and sent the man they considered their best general, Marcellus, to the theatre. After the assassination of Hieronymos, Hannibal had sent Punic ambassadors to Syracuse, who seized control of the city. After failing to persuade the Syracusans to return to their former alliance with Rome, Marcellus laid siege to the city in 213. His initial assaults met with disastrous reversals at the hands of Archimedes and his machines. Marcellus blockaded Syracuse, and over the next two years the defences were broken down by a combination of assault from without and betrayal from within. In 211 the city fell and was sacked. Sicily would serve as a supply base for the army of Scipio Africanus during his African campaign from 204 to 201, but with the fall of Syracuse the Second Punic War in Sicily was essentially over.

Over the course of the second half of the third century, the Romans, consciously or not, set about transforming Sicily into the first Roman *provincia*. The first praetor was installed in 227 and there came to be two quaestors in the province – one at Lilybaeum and the other at Syracuse, which after 211 served as the capital. The Romans adopted the old agricultural tithes on the island, including that of Hieron; the produce was now used to feed both the city of Rome and the army in the field. Sicilian grain played a tremendous logistical role in the Roman conquests of the second century, and Sicily enjoyed a period of peace and prosperity. The tithe system was known, by the first century at the latest, as the *lex Hieronica*, named after the last great king of Syracuse, who supposedly invented the system. By ancient standards it was highly regulated, and appears to have functioned efficiently. Cities on the island were in large part left to govern themselves, and several enjoyed special privileges for previous loyalties they had shown to Rome. This period also saw the abandonment of many hilltop towns in what has previously been seen as an urban decline. However, save for the damage caused by the eruption of Etna in 122, the archaeological record appears to show the opposite, and it is now thought that the abandonment of the hilltops is a symbol of economic prosperity taking precedence over defence (Wilson 1985b).

Grain production and exports reached an unprecedented scale in Sicily during the second century. While small farmers were still in abundance on the island, the *lex Hieronica* did favour the owners of large estates, and thus many such places sprang up. But the appalling conditions on these massive slave-run farms led to two large-scale slave revolts in Sicily, 135–132 and 104–100, both of which were put down with great difficulty.

After the second revolt, the Roman consul Rupilius spent a year with a special commission imposing a settlement upon Sicily. The *lex Rupilia* is seen as the first provincial constitution for Sicily. The law set down a series of regulations by which the province was to be administered. These dealt with agriculture, ports, imports and exports, poverty and the law courts. Unfortunately, the last section is the only reform on which we have any information. This section (elaborated on by Cic. *Verr*. 2. 2. 32–44) is specific and far-reaching. It lays down a system by which all courts on Sicily were to function, and makes clear distinctions about cases involving Romans and non-Romans. If it is any indication of what the rest of the law looked like, then the governor of Sicily would have been given strict guidelines in nearly every area of administration. The law also probably contained large sections on taxation and the tithes.

Yet the *lex Rupilia* does not appear to have stopped unscrupulous governors from exploiting the province, and the most infamous of such cases on Sicily came with the rule of Verres from 73 to 71. Upon his return to Rome he was prosecuted by Cicero in one of the most celebrated trials of the Roman republic. The case established Cicero both as a lawyer and as the patron of all Sicily. The province soon recovered from the deprivations of Verres, and it continued to be a major provider of grain for Rome. This aspect, together with its position between Italy and Africa, made it much coveted by the strongmen who vied for power in the civil wars of the late Roman republic. Upon seizing Italy, Caesar conferred Latin rights on Sicilians, a significant concession that illustrated not just the importance of Sicily but also its proximity to Italy and its status as the first Roman province, but it was not long before the island once again became the centre of a major war.

In 42 Pompey's son Sextus took control of Sicily and blockaded the gain supply to Rome. As ruler, the islanders largely co-operated with him; an action for which they would pay a price. The island was retaken by Octavian and Lepidus, with some of Antony's forces alongside. During the campaign, Octavian managed to subvert the loyalty of Lepidus' forces, and this set the scene for his elimination from the Triumvirate. The fighting against Sextus, although short, was heavy and very destructive to certain parts of Sicily, on a scale not seen since the third century. Octavian was ruthless in his vengeance; those who surrendered to him immediately were pardoned, while others were stripped of their Latin rights and charged large indemnities. The entire population of Tauromenium was deported. After 27, Augustus forced several veteran colonies on the island, and conferred municipal status on a few cities. However, by this time the importance of Sicily to the Roman empire, though still significant, was beginning to wane, as the vast grain fields of Egypt had now been incorporated into the Roman borders.

In the last three centuries before Christ, Sicily underwent a transformation from an island of political anarchy to one of economic prosperity. The onset of the third century brought little change for the Sicilians; Carthage would still make various attempts at domination and tyrants would emerge in the Greek half of the island to combat them. Once the tyrant died, the Greek cities squabbled amongst themselves and the whole process started all over again. For all of their three centuries of bitter fighting, the Greeks and Carthaginians achieved little; both sides came close on several occasions, but always fell short of delivering the *coup de grâce*. In the end they only served to weaken their own positions, and it was left to Rome to put a stop to the fighting by defeating both parties. This gave Sicily the lasting settlement that it needed. Long periods of peace brought unprecedented prosperity to the island, and preserved the distinctive mixture of Greek, Punic and Roman culture that made Sicily unique.

# 10

# GARRISONS AND GRAIN:
## Sicily between the Punic Wars

### *John Serrati*

THIS CHAPTER WILL EXAMINE the role of the Romans in Sicily between the First and Second Punic Wars, and will illustrate the island's role in the development of Roman *provinciae*, demonstrating that early administrative structures were put in place because of military needs which preceded them. As Sicily was the first overseas territory acquired by the Romans, no administrative structure as yet existed by which Rome could govern a province. However, an analysis of the sources indicates that some sort of structure did exist before the installation of the first praetor to govern Sicily in 227.

The purpose of the Roman occupation of the island was first and foremost security, but the exploitation of local resources demanded the gradual imposition of greater administrative and bureaucratic structures. The Romans used these resources both to safeguard Sicily and later on to feed the Roman army, and the first elements of a Roman *provincia* emerged as a by-product of this exploitation. Certainly, the Romans could and did apply their experience of administration in Italy to the island's cities. This can be seen in the individual treaties that were signed with various *poleis* in Sicily; these agreements, as with some of their Italian counterparts, made city states liable for military service through the provision of ships for the Roman navy and for general coastal defence. There is also evidence to show that Sicily was garrisoned during this period.

In the realm of taxation, it is generally assumed that the Sicilian agricultural tax under the Roman republic, what Cicero calls the *lex Hieronica*, was instituted by the consul Laevinus in 210. However, it will be demonstrated that an agricultural tax was established much earlier, and that on conquering Sicily, the Romans did not have to invent a tax structure, as it made more sense merely to continue to use agricultural tithes that had existed in Sicily from at least the fifth century. This tithe was taken over from the Punic western half of the island, and then instituted across all Sicily.

Any examination of Sicily during this period would not be complete without first exploring the independent kingdom of Syracuse. King Hieron II, while very much a Roman client king, can be seen as acting in his own self-interest. His economic and foreign policy permitted Syracuse, under the protection of Rome, to experience a period of economic prosperity, and allowed him to act as an equal to the hellenistic monarchs of the eastern Mediterranean.

## THE KINGDOM OF HIERON

Upon their arrival in Sicily in 264, the Romans would have found the island dominated by King Hieron II of Syracuse. He began his ascent to power with his election as a Syracusan general in 275. He sided with a popular faction and in 271 was made *strategos autokrator*, or general plenipotentiary, a position traditionally occupied by Syracusan strongmen before they became tyrants (Caven 1990: 56; Davies 1993: 195, 249). He then entered into a war with some former Syracusan mercenaries known as the Mamertines; defeated in 269, he won a resounding victory four years later, and was afterwards declared king. The Mamertines then appealed for protection to Rome and Carthage; both responded, and thus began the First Punic War in 264. Originally siding with Carthage, Hieron received little aid from them, and, facing a Roman siege, switched sides and concluded a treaty with Rome a year after the war started. He remained a steadfast ally to the Romans, and gave them aid and supplies on several occasions. As a sign of gratitude, his treaty was renewed for life in 248. He ruled Syracuse in relative peace for the next three decades. At some point he appointed his son Gelon as co-ruler (D.S. 26.15.1).[1] According to Livy (23.30.10–12), after the battle of Cannae, Gelon sided against his father and espoused the Punic cause. Punic raids on the Syracusan coast in this year can be seen as a show of support for Gelon (Liv. 22.56.6–8). While the young co-ruler may have been bribed with promises of power by pro-Carthaginian forces within Syracuse, the fact that he found backing from some of the lower classes may show a degree of discontent with the rule of Hieron, but the coup came to nothing, as Gelon died in mysterious circumstances within a short time. A year later Hieron was dead as well, and the Syracusan throne was left to Gelon's son, Hieronymos. The young king promptly allied himself with Carthage but was assassinated before coming to blows with Rome. Syracuse, still allied with Carthage, was subjected to a two-year siege by Marcus Claudius Marcellus. The city fell and was sacked in 211.

An analysis of the kingdom of Syracuse is beneficial both for understanding the political geography of Sicily of these years, and for illustrating just how successful its tithe system was, and why the Romans may have adopted it. King Hieron II used both the Roman protection over his realm and the lengthy peace to bring Syracuse to unprecedented levels of prosperity. Excellent farming conditions and the royal tax on crops combined to allow Syracuse to export grain on an extraordinary scale. This point has been demonstrated by the discovery of two massive grain stores in the city of Morgantina. The site has been dated to the third century and there is little doubt that it lay within the realm of Hieron.[2] So great was the Syracusan kingdom's agricultural influence that even a year after its capture and sack by Rome in 211, the Sicilian *medimnos* was still the standard measurement for grain in Italy (Plb.9.11a.3). Hieron tried his best to style himself as a benevolent hellenistic monarch and to show that Sicily was indeed still very much part of the Greek world. When in 269, according to Polybius (1.9.8), Hieron was acclaimed king, it was 'by all the allies'; this implies that, while Syracuse was the seat of his power, Hieron ruled a kingdom of which the city was merely a part. This is further demonstrated by the coins which were minted in his name or in those of the royal family. All treaties were made with Hieron personally, not with the city of Syracuse, exactly in the style of an eastern Greek king. And when he died, according to Livy (24.6.4) and Polybius (7.3.1) Rome had to attempt to negotiate a new treaty with his successor, Hieronymos. The young king also sent a delegation to renew his predecessor's treaty with Egypt. These two incidents imply that the treaties concluded with his grandfather Hieron were now invalidated by latter's death.[3] Then in 214, the city of Leontini, part of the Hieronic hegemony, protested at being included in a treaty made with Rome by the city of Syracuse; Leontini claimed that Syracuse by itself had no right to make a treaty for it (Liv. 24.29.7–12). This again would imply that Syracuse as a city had no power over others, while the king acted on behalf of his entire territory (Karlsson 1993: 37; Pritchard 1970: 368). Yet Polybius (7.8) is explicit is his statements about how the king's authority was derived from the citizens, and that on several occasions, Hieron magnanimously tried to step down, but was prevented from doing so by the people of Syracuse. Just as Pergamon was for the Attalid kings, so Syracuse, although to all appearances treated as any other part of Hieron's kingdom, was in fact the base and source of his power.[4]

Some sources refer to Hieron as the most powerful monarch in Sicily, or even by the actual title of 'king of the Sicilians', and it has been argued that this was not an exaggeration, as Hieron not only controlled Syracusan territory but may have also had a general alliance (*symmachia*) with the free Greek states of Sicily.[5] If he did adopt the title 'king of Sicily', he would have been immersing himself in the political rhetoric of his predecessors. Gelon in 481 is called king of Sicily by Herodotus (7.157), and Dionysius is referred to as the '*archon Sikelias*' by three Athenian decrees from the first half of the fourth century (*IG* II[2] 18; 103 = Tod II,

133; 105 = Tod II, 136). Agathokles, Hieron's immediate predecessor, had assumed the royal title; and according to Diodorus (20.54.1) this was in deliberate imitation of Alexander's successors in the east. Even triumphal records from 263 speak of Hieron as 'king of Sicily', though this may reflect Rome's perception of the political situation at the time.[6] Hieron's battles at the Cyamosauos (269) and the Longanus (265) show that the mercenary army of the kingdom was under his personal command, again in the style of a hellenistic monarch.[7] And there are even strong indications that Syracuse itself was not under his direct rule, but was run by a council like any other city in his hegemony.[8] As a final attestation to the hellenistic nature of the monarchy, evidence exists that points to the beginnings of a royal cult at Syracuse.[9] From this we may conclude that King Hieron did not want his contemporaries to perceive him as merely a Syracusan monarch; he made deliberate attempts to style himself as a great Greek king whose monarchy was on a par with the Successors in the eastern Mediterranean.

Hieron sought friendly relations in particular with Egypt, bestowing many gifts on the Ptolemies and donating grain in times of famine (Mosch. *ap*. Ath. 5.209b). His benevolence may serve too as an attestation of the wealth the king generated for himself and his kingdom through the skilful use of his tithe system.[10] He also engaged in the competitive philanthropy that often characterised Greek diplomacy at this time, and made a point of sending offerings and aid to many of the cities of Greece; he even competed in the Olympic games (D.S. 26.8; Plb. 1.16.10, 5.88. 5–8, 7.8.6), and was invited to a pan-hellenic festival in honour of Asclepius on Cos, an island under Ptolemaic protection (*SEG* XII. 370, 378–80; Lampela 1998: 54). Although in essence Hieron was a Roman client king, that he could act in his own interests is demonstrated by the assistance he gave to Carthage during the mercenary revolt (240–237) which broke out immediately after the First Punic War. The king knew full well that he was sandwiched between the empires of Rome and Carthage, and Polybius (1.83.2–4; see Schmitt 1988: 81–2) claims that he gave aid to the latter with the express purpose of maintaining an equilibrium between the two. It was in his interest to keep both powers strong, and to maintain the belief, real or illusory, that he could tip the balance of power, thus making alliance with Syracuse a valuable commodity.

Yet it does not follow that he was his own man; his existence was allowed, and guaranteed, by the Roman government. He may have acted in his own best interests, but he never overtly opposed Rome. In many ways he was the ideal client king, and, much to his advantage, he was unswerving in his loyalty to Rome; his praises were sung by the senate in 216 and by several ancient authors.[11] In 237 Hieron visited Rome for the first and only time so that he could view the games. There he donated

200,000 bushels of grain to the people of the city (Eutrop. 3. 1–2). It is highly probable that he was invited for an official state visit in order to receive thanks for his support in the First Punic War. Years later, Diodorus (25.14) tells us that during the Celtic War (225–222) Hieron gave aid to Rome again in the form of food and was later compensated for the donation. So strong was his relationship with Rome that it could almost have the appearance of being between equals, since the Romans could have simply demanded these provisions, yet they chose, in this instance at least, to pay Hieron for his help. The latter point would seem to refute the notion that Hieron's aid to Rome was given as part of some sort of formal treaty.[12] This argument would imply that in effect the Romans were still exacting an indemnity from the king twenty-five years after his monetary payments were cancelled in 248 (Naev. *Poen.* 6. fr. 43Bl; Zonar. 8.16). In the light of the Roman payment, the economic relationship between Rome and Hieron appears more one of merchant and consumer rather than of master and servant. Lastly, at some point during this period, the king greatly strengthened the defences of his territory, especially those of Syracuse (Karlsson 1993: 38–41, 45), and he also employed the mathematician Archimedes to build some very ingenious counter-siege engines (Liv. 24.34.13; Plb. 8.7.2; Plut. *Marc.* 14.9). These were applied in 213, much to the bewilderment of the attacking Romans.

From the moment they set foot in Sicily in 264, the Romans had to work around, and later with, King Hieron. Although reduced in status to that of an allied monarch, he was still a powerful force, and the Romans never underestimated his influence over the Sicilians and his ability to safeguard the eastern half of the island. As such he is given special mention in the treaty that ended the First Punic War.

## THE TREATY OF 241

'There shall be friendship between the Carthaginians and the Romans on the following conditions, subject to ratification by the people of Rome. Carthage to vacate all of Sicily and to not make war upon Hieron or to take up arms against the Syracusans or their allies. Carthage to return all prisoners to the Romans without ransom. Carthage to pay Rome an indemnity of 2200 Euboic talents in instalments over twenty years.' But when these conditions were communicated to Rome, the people did not approve of the treaty, and sent ten commissioners to oversee the negotiations. On arrival they made no major modifications to the terms, but they increased the burden for Carthage: they reduced the condition on payment of the indemnity by a half, added on 1,000 talents, and demanded the evacuation by Carthage of all the islands between Sicily and Italy.

(Plb. 1.62.8–63.3)

In addition to the above text, Polybius (3.27.3–4) later states that the allies of Carthage and Rome were not to make war with each other; neither side could exact tribute from or form alliances with the other's allies; and neither side could erect public buildings or recruit mercenaries in the other's domain. Zonaras (8.17) adds the clause that Carthaginian warships were forbidden to sail along the coasts of Italy or along the coasts of Rome's allies abroad. The islands that lay between Sicily and Italy were certainly the Lipari, and perhaps also the Aegates groups.[13]

Certain cities also had separate treaties signed with Rome which granted them special privileges. Messana, the city at whose behest Rome invaded Sicily twenty-three years earlier, was given the status of a full ally, a *civitas foederata*, with rights outlined in a full treaty.[14] Four other places were declared to be free states which were immune from taxes (called *civitates sine foedere immunes ac liberae* by Cicero in the *Verrines*).[15] These were Halaisa (Halaesa), Halicyai (Halicyae), Centuripe and Segesta (Cic. *Verr.* 2.3.13). Halaisa and Halicyai both surrendered to Rome in 263, while the other two were accorded these privileges because they claimed a kinship with the Romans through Aeneas.[16] This was the framework within which the Romans would administer their first extra-Italian possession, and it illustrates that at least some form of Roman control was present on the island from the initial treaty of 241. That the Roman presence was a permanent one is evident in the garrisons set in place immediately after the First Punic War.

## SICILY AS A ROMAN PROVINCE

Roman practice involved individual cities being left to govern themselves, but the foremost purpose of the conquest of Sicily and the later installation of a bureaucracy to run the island was for security; Sicily represented a bridge between Carthage and Italy, and its control would be vital for either side should one decide to strike at the other. So, based on the fact that Sicily was a recently conquered land, and that the island was meant to serve as a major source of grain for the Romans, it is unlikely that there would have been no Roman supervision. In the context of Sicily, both security and grain supply were interrelated; the primary purpose of the *lex Hieronica* was to feed the Roman garrisons on the island, and in the second century to feed Roman armies overseas. Roman government structure appeared on Sicily not as a result but as a by-product of this process. It cannot be overstated that Sicily was the very first extra-Italian possession, and in 241 the senate had no model upon which to base any kind of lasting settlement. Administration and taxation of conquered lands in the third century therefore either continued native practices already in place, or 'developed in response to conditions on the spot, rather than being imposed from the centre'.[17] In this sense, many institutions which modern scholars associate with provincial governments – tithes, tributes, large bureaucracies and such – evolved out of a series of *ad hoc* measures designed to meet immediate needs.

Furthermore, the Roman concept of a *provincia* developed in tandem with government structures on Sicily. From 241, the Romans were in firm control of the island, and as a result we may assign to it the modern term of 'province'. But *provincia* could mean a number of different things to the Romans, and judging by the fact that the Romans before 241 had not conquered any place outside of Italy, the late republican concept of a province as delineating an area of Roman military and administrative control, often within fixed borders, is not likely to have been among the word's mid-third-century definitions. From the works of Plautus we can see that the word was in common use in the third century, and it referred to any area of responsibility or control, be it personal, military or governmental (*Capt.* 474, *Mil.* 1159, *Trin.* 190). In this sense, from 214 until 211 Marcus Claudius Marcellus was assigned the Syracusan kingdom as his *provincia*, even though the place was not yet in Roman hands (Liv. 25.3.6). The definition of a *provincia* in its late republican territorial sense developed alongside Roman imperialism.

When the Romans conquered Sicily after the First Punic War, the place became a Roman *provincia* as a centre of Roman responsibility and as a place where Roman *imperium* was recognised and obeyed. In this sense the kingdom of Hieron, in theory independent, was very much part of the Sicilian *provincia*. This is further demonstrated by the war against Syracuse during the Hannibalic conflict, which was regarded by the Romans as a rebellion, since the city had to be brought back into the Roman sphere. Modern scholarship has sought to define when an area under Roman control evolved from being a province, in which the Romans exercised their authority, to a *provincia* with definitive governmental, administrative and tax structures (Lintott 1981: 54–61, 1993: 22–32). One major step in this direction came with the *lex Porcia* of 101, which stated that under normal circumstances, provincial governors were not to leave their assigned areas; thus this law helped to give *provinciae* greater geographical structure (Lintott 1981: 54, 1993: 23; see also Cic. *Pis.* 50). But it is irrelevant to speak of borders when dealing with an island, and therefore we should look to the assignment of a *lex provinciae*, a provincial constitution, as one of the major points in the transition of Sicily from an area of Roman administration and control to a *provincia* in the late republican and imperial sense. This came about with the imposition of the *lex Rupilia* in 132 (Cic. *Verr.* 2.2.32–44, 59, 90, 125; see also *MRR* 1: 498); but we should not discount the settlement of 241 altogether. In 132 the *lex Rupilia* was put together with the help of a senatorial commission, just as in 241 Polybius (1.63.1–3) informs us that such a commission was present for the island's first settlement. Similarly, the decisions to occupy Sicily militarily, to allot special status to some cities, to continue any existing tithes, and to impose a rudimentary amount of Roman bureaucracy must be seen as the beginnings of a *provincia* in every sense of the word, regardless of the fact that the process was begun unconsciously, and in order to equip the Romans with the means to wage war. Accordingly, the structure of the Roman *provincia* of Sicily should not be seen as something that came about through any one specific event, but as an evolving process, from the first structures of 241 to the final settlement of 132.

## ADMINISTRATION AND TAXATION

There must have been at least some government structure in place at Lilybaeum to oversee the garrison and to supervise taxes. Military tribunes could command the Roman troops in their garrisons; a magistrate with *imperium* was necessary to lead them in combat. The creation of a *praetor peregrinus* in 242 fulfilled this role (Liv. *Per.* 19). Badian has recently argued that this praetor was indirectly responsible for the Sicilian theatre, which would fit well since it was within the praetor's capacity to deal with foreigners.[18] Moreover, we have also been recently reminded of the true meaning of the word *peregrinus*; it did not simply denote any foreigner, but it could have negative connotations, as it referred specifically to foreigners who had been conquered by Rome (Stewart 1998: 184, 198). *Peregrini* were people who lived under Roman domination; as such, they could not go to war with Rome, they could only rebel (Rich 1976: 15), as some of the Sicilians did in the Second Punic War. Finally, we are informed by Varro (*L.* 5.53) that *ager peregrinus* was called such because it was land that had been conquered by Rome. If the *praetor peregrinus* had jurisdiction over these lands in Italy (as is argued by Stewart 1998: 195), then it would be reasonable to assume that his jurisdiction should have included Sicily as well, as the island was conquered land occupied by conquered peoples.

Although we are informed about his judicial functions, we also know that the *praetor peregrinus* had the duty of calling out both infantry and naval contingents from the allies (Liv. 40.26.7, 42.27.3), and therefore he did indeed have a military function. It will be demonstrated below that the Sicilians were required to provide Rome with military assitance between the Punic wars if it was necessary. Before the institution of a praetor in 227, the only official in Rome with *imperium* whose function it was to deal with foreign troops was the *praetor peregrinus*. Therefore, there is no reason *a priori* to believe that he, like other praetors, did not also exercise military powers.[19] However, he was certainly not a provincial governor, since the sources are explicit that this office only came into being in 227 (Liv. *Per*. 20; Sol. 5.1; see also *MRR* 1: 229). He does not appear to have resided in the province, and his sole function, in relation to Sicily, may have been to travel down from Rome when his *imperium* was required for military purposes.

Several sources attest to the fact that in the later republic there was indeed a quaestor in Lilybaeum, and it is this office which was most probably in place prior to 227.[20] A quaestor was best suited for this purpose, since he not only had the financial powers necessary to run the province, but could also on occasion command a fleet (Plb. 1.52.7). Finally, it has been convincingly argued that Rome actually increased the number of quaestorships to accommodate Sicily and later Sardinia after the First Punic War.[21] Nevertheless, the Roman taxation system in Sicily which will now be illustrated could not be operated without at least some supervision, and prior to 227, a quaestor is the most logical choice. From 227 onwards Sicily was ruled by a praetor, who was elected annually at Rome. The possible motivations behind this decision will be discussed below.

The standard view concerning the implementation of a tax or tithe on crops in Sicily is that it was instituted across the entire island by Valerius Laevinus in 210.[22] At this point in the Hannibalic war, Rome was desperate for grain to feed both its population and its massive army. We are aware that the war in Italy was strongly affecting grain production in some areas. Laevinus, the proconsul of Sicily in 210, gave great encouragement to the Sicilians, many of whom had been driven from their land by the war, to restart their farms so that their grain could come to the aid of the Romans in Italy (Liv. 26.40.15–16; see also Cornell 1996: 97–117).

As described by Cicero in the *Verrines*, the *lex Hieronica* was a system by which each individual farmer owed roughly one-tenth of his yield as a tithe. The tenth was determined between the farmer and the tithe collector while the grain was on the threshing floor. The grain was then taken to granaries for use by Hieron or his army, or for straight sale. It was a strictly regulated system, with heavy fines imposed on both tithe collectors and farmers for violations. In the following section it will be demonstrated that by this method Hieron greatly enriched himself and his kingdom, and was able to play the altruistic monarch, making expensive gifts, often in the form of grain, to various states including Rome. In Roman times, the system was administered by the governor. Individual Sicilians, along with a few Italians, bid for the right to collect the tax. The grain was then transported to the nearest port, where it was shipped by *mancipes* (transport contractors), bound for private sale in the city of Rome. Sicily was so productive that a second tithe was often requisitioned by the Roman government to feed its legions.[23] In honour of its creator the scheme was referred to as the *lex Hieronica*, though it was not a *lex* in the traditional sense of a Roman law or statute. It may have been an actual law in the kingdom of Syracuse, though perhaps 'custom', 'method' or 'system' is best understood. Cicero was the first to use this name for the Sicilian tax structure, though it seems likely that it had been in place long before this, as his writings assume a certain familiarity with the term on the part on his audience. The scholars who date the imposition of the *lex Hieronica* to 210 propose that the fall of Syracuse brought Rome into contact with the tithe scheme of Hieron, and the Romans decided to implement his rules all over the island. However, evidence may point in another direction.

First, Appian (*Sic.* 2.2) claims that in the settlement of Sicily in 241 the Sicilians, under Roman authority, were given naval responsibilities and were charged an agricultural tithe. Although the passage also says that a praetor was installed in this year, a statement we know to be false, as evidence already cited clearly states a praetor was not present until 227, that does not mean Appian should be discounted entirely; Livy (23.48.7) states that prior to the Second Punic War, the Sicilians had paid taxes to Rome in kind. Furthermore, upon becoming a *civitas foederata* in 213, Tauromenium was given a treaty which contained a clause that forced it to sell grain to the Romans.[24] Finally, in 211 we are told that the Romans sent an embassy to Alexandria to secure grain imports from Ptolemy IV Philopater (Liv. 27.4.10; Plb. 9.11a). This was due to a severe shortage in Italy, which had resulted in a significant rise in price for Sicilian grain. This proves that Sicilian grain was indeed present at Rome in 211, and it has been subsequently argued that the shortage in Italy was due both to the depredations of Hannibal and to the fact that very little tithe grain had come to Rome from Sicily since 214 (Lampela 1998: 60–1). Taken as a whole, the evidence strongly suggests that an agricultural tithe did indeed exist in Sicily in between the Punic Wars.

The treaties signed with individual states after the First Punic War also provide a clue. Shortly after 241, Segesta, one of the four cities declared to be free and immune from taxes, began to mint coins which depicted Aeneas and Anchises in order to further its claim of kinship with Rome (Gardner 1876: 137; Hill 1903: 213). Since Cicero says the city was treated specially because of this, we can conclude that its privileged position goes back to 241. Therefore, a tax must have been in place in at least some parts of Sicily between the wars, since it would have been superfluous to declare a city free from a tax which did not exist. We also know that for centuries the Carthaginians had been charging their subjects in Sicily an agricultural tithe (D.S. 13.59.3, 114.1, 14.65.2). Surely, when the Romans conquered the western half of the island they would have left this tithe in place; for Polybius (1.58.9) relates how the previous war with

Carthage had left Rome exhausted, both physically and financially. If the senate could have recouped part of their losses by means of an existing agricultural tithe, then it seems likely that they would have done so (Scramuzza 1938: 231). What is more, Cicero (*Verr*. 2.3.12–13, 15) states that when the Romans conquered Sicily, they made no changes to the existing local structures. While this is surely an exaggeration, it does indicate that taxes were probably not changed, since if the Romans had removed any financial burdens from the Sicilians, Cicero would have made use of this as an example of Roman magnanimity (Badian 1972: 28).

The farmers of western Sicily continued to pay a tithe as they always had, only now it went to Rome. However, the question still remains as to whether this tithe did in fact follow the rules of Hieron. It is widely assumed that the Hieronic taxation system was based upon those of the hellenistic monarchies of the eastern Mediterranean, and especially on the tax structure of Ptolemaic Egypt.[25] The fundamental difference was that in the east, the king was in theory the owner of all the land, while in Syracuse the system was put in place very late in the area's history, and there are numerous examples of private land tenure.[26] It is likely that Carthage was influenced to some extent by the governments of the eastern monarchies, and it was heavily involved in trade with the eastern Mediterranean. The same was true of Hieron, and it is possible that both were influenced by Ptolemaic practices, and would have had many basic similarities.

At some point the Romans adopted a system of taxation which had been in place in the domain of Hieron, and they proceeded to spread its use to the whole of Sicily. This system was effective and it suited their purposes. We cannot say with confidence when Hieron's tithe structure was either adopted by the Romans, or applied to the whole of the island, but we can suggest that the system of Hieron as used by the Romans, the *lex Hieronica*, although probably more efficient than anything which had preceded it on Sicily, may have had similar features to the Greek or Punic system it replaced.

The Romans retained other taxes in the former Carthaginian realm. Since they now controlled the lucrative port city of Lilybaeum, they left in place harbour taxes, customs dues and general tariffs, which had been imposed by the Carthaginians (Liv. 33.47.1) and were present in the first century (Cic. *Verr*. 2.2.171, 185, 3.167); it is very likely therefore that in the third century the Romans continued sources of revenue that predated their conquest.

Finally, the question remains over how the settlement of 241 affected what was the formerly free part of Sicily which lay in between the Syracusan kingdom and the old Punic west. This area had changed hands several times, usually coming under the hegemony of either Syracuse or

Carthage. But in 264 the area just east of the river Himera was held by neither side, and therefore would not have paid any type of tithe to an overlord. Conceivably, the purpose of instituting a praetor in 227 was to expand the tithe system to the rest of Roman territory on Sicily. There seems to be little other reason for this; Sicily was not threatened by invasion, since the military energies of Carthage were concentrated in Spain while those of Rome were focused on northern Italy. However, something changed between the wars. As has already been noted, Livy claimed that before 218, all Sicily paid a tithe, and of the four cities declared to be free of tax, only Halicyai and Segesta lay within the former Punic territory. The other two, Halaisa and Centuripe, lay between the Syracusan and Carthaginian domains, and would therefore have had no need of a special exemption from tax. With the imposition of a praetor, Rome may have sought to increase its grain supply and therefore took the decision to implement the tithe system in the central part of the island. So they instituted a governor to oversee the operation, since now the tithe may have been too large for the quaestor to handle. It would be at this point that Halaisa and Centuripe were declared tax-free zones.

While it is not possible to determine exactly when the *lex Hieronica* was adopted, we can conclude that some sort of tithe existed in the western half of the island. And this agricultural tax probably shared basic principles with the tax structure of Hieron. The Roman tithe may have been spread to the interior in 227, the year of the implementation of a praetor to govern Sicily, and he may have brought an expanded bureaucracy with him. It is certain that by 218 the Sicilians were paying a tithe to Rome, and this demonstrates that the Romans did exploit the resources of Sicily in the interwar years. The exploitation of these agricultural resources was designed, consciously or unconsciously, to further Roman imperialism and conquest, and the aforementioned state structure appeared because of this. As a result, the primary purpose of the grain tithe would have been to feed the Romans upon whom the security of the island against Carthage depended.

## MILITARY FORCES ON THE ISLAND

*Garrisoning the province*

The Roman settlement of Sicily began many years before the actual war with Carthage was won. The construction of a road between Panormos and Agrigentum by the consul Gaius Aurelius Cotta in 252 suggests that the Romans intended to incorporate the island permanently into their authority.[27] The route was designed originally to serve a military function, and it would have consolidated Rome's holdings in central and eastern Sicily. The construction of roads was a well-used Roman method of control, and had been practised in Italy since the construction of the Via Appia in 312.[28]

The evidence suggests that Roman troops were installed in Sicily immediately after the First Punic War. According to Polybius (2.23.9), when Italy was invaded by Gallic tribes in 225 the senate demanded lists of men ready for service from their allied and subject towns, and they also took stock of their own forces. At this time, Sicily had been at peace for more than a decade. Later in the same book we learn that 'In Sicily and Tarentum, two legions were kept in reserve, each consisting of about 4,200 infantry and 200 cavalry.' There is no reason why the Romans would have put in a garrison at this point in time; their troops must have been positioned in Sicily earlier.

Unfortunately, prior to the installation of a praetor in 227, there was no Roman official present on the island who held *imperium*, the prerequisite of command. As argued earlier, it is possible that the troops on the island fell under the jurisdiction of the *praetor peregrinus*, yet even if this was not the case, it does not refute the notion that there were Roman troops present in Sicily from 241 onwards. This is an *ad hoc* use of troops, and it is doubtful that a lack of *imperium* holder would have stopped them from defending Sicily. The western half of the island had only recently come into the hands of Rome; Carthage was still a strong power that was physically near to Sicily and had the naval capability to ferry an invasion force over at any time. A substantial Punic population is likely still to have inhabited the west, and collusion between them and Carthage must have been a realistic possibility. It would not make sense for Rome to expend twenty-three bloody years subduing the place only to abandon it because Rome lacked a precedent of how to administer and garrison conquered lands outside of Italy. Furthermore, the presence of an *imperium* holder and troops under his exclusive command only became part of the definition of the word *provincia* in its fully developed sense in the first century. While it remains true that *imperium* was in theory necessary to command, and no *imperium* holder was present on Sicily in any permanent capacity before 227, it seems highly dubious that the Romans would not have taken measures to safeguard Sicily from a Carthaginian invasion or an insurrection in the west. Rome had fought for too long over Sicily, and the island was too strategically important, to leave it without a military presence. *Imperium* holder or no, its defence was essential.

That this garrison remained in place after 225 is shown by Livy (21.49.6–7). During the failed Carthaginian attempt on Sicily in 218, he states that the governor already had garrisons at his disposal to guard the Roman possessions on Sicily. That these were legionaries is certain, since in 217 we know that legionaries were transported from Sicily to Italy (Liv. 23.31.4, 32.2, 32.16). As there is no attestation of troops assigned to Sicily from 218 to 215, this must have been the Sicilian garrison which was in place all along (Brunt 1971: 417–20; Clark 1994; Marchetti 1972: 5).

As to the whereabouts of the garrison, several potential locations emerge. It is likely that the garrison was split between several sites, the main body being at Lilybaeum while smaller contingents manned various hilltop forts in the western half of Sicily. As the Romans were relatively new to Sicily, it would make sense for them to continue to control the island as the Carthaginians had, and to occupy the various strongholds built by their predecessors in the west. This would also allow them to patrol more territory and to exert greater control over the interior, which was on the whole devoid of urban centres in which garrisons were often quartered.

It was common Republican military practice to quarter at least part of a province's garrison in a city (Cic. *Man.* 38), and the speed with which the praetor was able to safeguard Lilybaeum in 218, especially with a Punic fleet nearby, might suggest that the Sicilian legion was based there. The old Carthaginian city would have served a multiple purpose. Because of its geographic location, it was the most probable landing point for an invasion from Africa. If the Punic government was expelled along with the military, then the establishment of a garrison at Lilybaeum, the former Carthaginian capital of Sicily, would have served to fill any administrative void left behind. This would be especially important if the Carthaginian grain tithe remained in place. Furthermore, the city was the probable home to a Roman quaestor. The place also had an excellent harbour, which the Roman or allied navy could have used as a base, with the legionaries of the garrison as marines. Finally, besides being less likely to revolt, the eastern half of Sicily could easily have been policed by Rome's ally Hieron.[29]

Based on the evidence of Polybius 1.56–58.2, it has been argued that the Romans established a permanent camp around 247 at the foot of Mount Heirkte, near the city of Drepana, on which sat the main Carthaginian force under Hamilcar Barca (Pottino 1994: 5–16). It is possible that this housed the Roman garrison after the war was over, but the location seems to be one more of necessity. The camp in question was purpose-built for the siege, and as such does not provide much command of the countryside beyond the surrounding area. However, another site in western Sicily appears as a likely candidate for a division of the Roman garrison in the interwar years. Approximately seventy kilometres west of Lilybaeum is the hilltop fortress of Monte Adranone. Situated in what Thucydides (6.2.3) described as the Elymian area of western Sicily, the site was characterised by Greek and Punic architecture in the sixth century and appears to have been under the direct control of Carthage by the 400s. Archaeological remains show that the place was heavily fortified, and a

*Fig. 10.1* Monte Adranone; possible remains of Carthaginian
military barracks (photo: author)

building close to the south gate has been identified as a block of Punic
barracks (Fiorentini 1995; fig. 10.1). Diodorus (23.4.1–2) mentions that
two places called Hadranon were assaulted by the Romans in 263, and
only the first attack met with success. This has been passed off as an error
on the part of Diodorus (Lazenby 1996: 52–3), but it may be correct. First,
at 23.4.1 Diodorus calls the place 'city of the Hadranites' (*tên hadranitôn
polin*), while in the following passage he says the 'village of Hadranon'
(*hadranôna kômên*). The former is the city of Adranon founded by
Dionysius I in 400 near Mount Etna in the east of Sicily, and called
*Adranon* by Diodorus at 14.37.5.[30] This would make sense, as the Romans
were campaigning vigorously in this part of Sicily in 263. As for the latter
village of Hadranon, this should be identified with Monte Adranone in the
west of the island. Diodorus made no mistake in distinguishing the two,
as he makes the Romans attack both the village of Hadranon and a place
called Makella, the latter being equated with the modern Macellaro,
approximately twenty-five kilometres north of Monte Adranone (*RE*
14.772–3). Furthermore, Makella is mentioned as an enemy of Rome on
the *columna rostrata* of Duilius commemorating his victory at Mylae in
260 (*CIL* I²: 25). By this time the Romans controlled the eastern half of
Sicily, and therefore it is highly unlikely that Makella, and by association
the village of Hadranon, could have been in the east and still under the
control of Carthage. This still leaves the question of what the Romans

were doing so deep in Punic territory so early in the war. Diodorus perhaps provides an answer when he tells us at 23.5 that Segesta, as mentioned above, at this time came over to the Romans. It is possible that a small force was sent to garrison the latter city and on the way made attempts on both Makella and the village of Hadranon.

At Monte Adranone a destruction layer characterised by burning and the presence of lead missiles has been dated to the mid-third century (Fiorentini 1988–9: 18). Therefore it is likely that the place was violently taken by the Romans when they started their western campaigns in 250. However, the fortress continued to be occupied afterwards, only this time the inhabitants were Roman. This is attested by a Roman *denarius* found in the destruction layer, indicating that the site had at least some residents in the late third century.[31] The place is an ideal location for a garrison; it is a high point marked by steep sides, which has a commanding view of much of the surrounding territory. It is little wonder the Carthaginians fortified the site. The presence of a Punic garrison in such a strong position meant that the taking of Monte Adranone was crucial if the Romans wished to campaign in and eventually occupy the western half of Sicily. It would be logical to assume that once the Romans had taken the place, they would have left a garrison to exercise control over the area just as the Carthaginians had done. After the war was over, a number of garrisons would have been placed in the west for reasons already stated. Monte Adranone presented itself as an ideal spot, already fortified by Carthage. The Romans could simply have taken over the place around 250 and set up more temporary structures on top of the Punic buildings which had been destroyed. The *denarius* makes it likely that Romans were present in the late third century; the site could have been reoccupied by Rome during the Second Punic War, but it is likely that Monte Adranone served as the home of at least part of the Roman garrison left behind in the settlement of 241.

The legion may indeed have been subdivided further, but the absence of Roman remains precludes any firm conclusions about any place outside the village of Hadranon. On the basis of the evidence it would be reasonable to conclude that there was indeed a Roman garrison placed in the western half of Sicily. In accordance with the Roman practice of quartering garrisons in cities, the most logical location for the bulk of this garrison would have been in Lilybaeum; this was the former Punic capital, home of a Roman quaestor, and the most likely point of invasion from Carthage in the event of another Punic war. However, if the Romans wanted to control the interior more directly, this would have necessitated the sending out of smaller detachments to exercise Roman authority. This system would have allowed for military supervision of both the coastline and the interior of the former Punic west.[32]

*The Sicilian allies*

Sicilians themselves served in the Roman navy. During the initial Carthaginian attack on Sicily in 218, the Sicilian cities were ordered to produce their full contingents of ships and crews, with ten days' rations. Livy (21.49.7–8) refers to these states as *socii navales*, which means that, as in Italy, they were places bound by treaty obligations to furnish Rome with military support. These *socii navales* had to bear the cost of paying for the ships, provisions and crews, including marines.[33] This system could have originated with the settlement of Sicily in 241. While the Romans used an analogous system of alliances in Italy and Sicily, it is worth noting that the Sicilians were not treated in the same manner as the majority of the allies in Italy, since a *socius navalis* was seen as a lower status of ally than those who served on land (Badian 1958: 292; Thiel 1954: 32–6). Perhaps we might infer that, from the island's incorporation into the Roman sphere, Sicily was still not seen as forming part of greater Italy, and therefore the Sicilians themselves did not merit the status of full *socii*. Yet at the same time, the geographical nature of Sicily cannot be discounted, and the status of *socii navales* reflects the island's strong naval traditions.

As we have already seen, individual treaties were signed with states outlining their relationship with Rome and their duties towards the Roman military. We are aware that it was through one of these treaties that Messana had to furnish one ship, while Tauromenium had the special right of being exempt from service altogether. The fact that we know of no other place with such a privilege suggests that Tauromenium was the exception. As governor of Sicily in the first century, Verres called out allied naval contingents from twelve different Sicilian cities (Cic. *Verr.* 2.5.49–50, 76, 83–4, 90, 133). This service is further attested by an inscription which shows the Sicilian cities of Halaisa, Kaleakte, Herbita and Amestratos (Amestratus) all serving in a sea battle under the command of an otherwise unknown Roman named Caninius Niger (*AE* 1973: 265; see also Scibona 1971: 5–9, pl. 2). The date of the stone is unclear, yet it illustrates that Sicilians did provide ships for the Roman navy. Significantly, it should be noted that Herbita and Amestratos, as well as three of the twelve cities called into service by Verres, are all inland sites, which may lead to the conclusion that all cities, regardless of their geographical position, still had to furnish a naval contingent. The allied fleet would usually have been under the command of the praetor, or perhaps his quaestor, although Cicero (*Verr.* 2.5.82–3) does tell us that at times an allied Sicilian admiral could command. Furthermore, Cicero (*Verr.* 2.4.21, 5.51) tells us that certain cities were also bound to furnish both garrisons and marines. The only place he names specifically is Messana, and it seems likely that the garrisons supplied by the allied cities were for local defence only, and when called away from home it would be for service aboard one of their native vessels. During the Carthaginian attack in 218, the praetor did arrange for individual cities in the west to be garrisoned, and we should perhaps assume that this entailed a call-up of local soldiers under treaty obligations.

### The Venerii

The Venerii were a corps of slaves who formed a 200-man guard at the temple of Venus Erycina. The Roman settlement of 241 included the adoption of the temple of as an official Roman cult, for the goddess was closely associated with Aeneas (Galinsky 1969: 63–4; Gruen 1992: 46–7). To maintain the temple, the Romans charged seventeen cities a tax in gold; the names of these cities are not preserved, but in his description of these events, Diodorus (4.83.4–7) does tell us that they were all places that had been loyal to Rome. This tax paid for the Venerii. Epigraphic evidence shows that they were under the command of a *tribunus militum*, who in all known cases was a native Sicilian (*CIL* X. 7258; *IG* XIV. 282, 355). Although their primary duty was to guard the temple, at some stage, perhaps with the implementation of a governor in 227, they appear to have become a police force for use by the Roman provincial government. They acted as the praetor's personal bodyguard and enforced his orders, and we also find them making arrests, seizing goods that were to be confiscated, acting as bodyguards to members of the praetor's staff, collecting the temple tax and any offerings to the goddess, and carrying out the general orders of the governor.[34]

On the basis of the above evidence, it is possible that Sicily had a significant military presence in the years between the First and Second Punic Wars. There is testimony of a Roman garrison on the island, which should be seen as an aspect of the settlement of 241. This settlement established a system of alliances by which the Sicilians themselves maintained garrisons as well as a reserve navy.

## CONCLUSION

Referring to Sicily, Cicero states clearly that, 'Prima omnium, id quod ornamentum imperii est, provincia est appallata' ('It was the first jewel in our imperial crown, the first place to be called a province') (*Verr*. 2.2.2). As both Sicily and Sardinia received praetors at the same time, in order to call the former the first province, Cicero would have to be referring to a time before 227. Therefore, it is likely that in 241 Sicily was organised as the first Roman province. Many of the structures which come to be associated with late republican *provinciae* were first experimented with in Sicily. Upon taking the island, the Romans decided to leave the existing institutions in place, while at the same time adding elements of Roman rule – conscription for the Roman navy and perhaps an administration run by a quaestor and supervised by the *praetor peregrinus*. They may have installed a garrison and signed treaties with individual Sicilian states, granting some special privileges. The major institution they left in place was the Punic agricultural tithe in the western half of the island. Through this the Romans saw a way by which to compensate themselves financially for the twenty-three-year war they had just fought over the island. While this tithe may not have been the *lex Hieronica* by name, it did have many of the same principles. Using this tax in Syracuse, King Hieron II, though ultimately under the suzerainty of Rome, had enriched his tiny empire and used his position to play the strengths of Carthage and Rome off against each other, ultimately to his own benefit.

After fourteen years the Romans decided to install a praetor to govern the province; this perhaps also heralded the expansion of the tithe system to the central part of Sicily. The island was now taxed all over, and at this point the tithes imposed by the Romans may all have been brought into organisational conformity with the system of Hieron. Although the Roman management of Sicily is characterised by experimentation, at the same time the conquerors often found it useful to continue using existing systems of government and administration. The best example of this can be found in the maintenance of the old grain tithes, and their eventual expansion over the entire island. It is significant that Roman administration in Sicily appears to have grown out of Roman military need; the legions required Sicilian grain and therefore the Romans gradually instituted more government in the province to facilitate the harvesting, transportation and distribution of the yearly agricultural yield to forces operating around the Mediterranean. Put more simply, 'State structure appeared chiefly as a by-product of rulers' efforts to acquire the means of war' (Tilly 1990: 14).

# 11

# CICERONIAN SICILY:
## an archaeological perspective

### R. J. A. Wilson

## INTRODUCTION

OF ALL THE POLITICAL speeches delivered by Marcus Tullius Cicero, it was his *Orationes in Caium Verrem* that marked an important turning point in the orator's career. His prosecution of Verres after the latter's turbulent governorship of Sicily in 73–71 BC was significant not because of Verres' outrageous behaviour as such – other ex-governors before him had been prosecuted for provincial misdemeanours – but because its triumphant success marked Cicero out as the most brilliant of the younger advocates of his day, his influence increasing at the expense of his rival Hortensius.[1] The trial was also important because of the powerful connections of Verres, and the political context of the year that it took place, 70 BC, the year in which Pompey and Crassus were consuls for the first time, when they presided over the dismantling of Sulla's political settlement. The *Verrines* have, therefore, been extensively quarried for generations by classical scholars interested in Cicero's career and in the political nuances of the late 70s BC; the speeches have been studied for the important light that they throw on the judicial system and the legal procedures of the extortion court;[2] and the *Verrines* have been scrutinised and judged for the subtleties and polish of their oratorical style. They have also been extensively used as a sourcebook for understanding Roman provincial administration at a comparatively early stage in its development, and, more generally, for the social and economic history of Sicily during the late republic.[3]

But how far can they be pressed into service as evidence for the condition of Sicily in the 70s BC? When Cicero is presenting background information as a scene-setting exercise to further the understanding of his audience for what follows, he gives reliable factual information which is often not available from any other source. Thus it is from Cicero that we learn that a version of the Hieronian tithe system continued to function in Sicily after 241 BC; it is due to Cicero that we know that Noto, Messina (Messana) and Taormina were *civitates foederatae*, linked by treaty with

Rome, and also *immunes*, tax-free, and that the five communities of Centuripe, Halaesa, Segesta, Halicyae (Salemi), and Panhormus (Palermo) were both free communities and also tax-exempt (*liberae et immunes*), even though not linked by treaty with Rome (*sine foedere*); all the rest of the Sicilian cities were tax-paying communities (*civitates decumanae*).[4] Yet despite the value of this and much other basic factual information, the *Verrines* as a historical source are patently and fatally flawed. Quite apart from the fact that it is in the nature of a legal speech to highlight the defendant's alleged villainy with as many colourful details as possible, Cicero was so successful in his devastating attack on Verres in his first *Actio* that, as is well known, the ex-governor of Sicily was impelled to flee into exile at Marseilles. The second *Actio*, more than three-quarters of the whole, was nevertheless published by Cicero in the interests of his own political advancement, and so that the damning evidence collected in his fact-finding tour of Sicily (which he tells us lasted just under two months, fifty days to be precise: *Verr.* 1.1.2.6) would not be entirely wasted. Of course he claimed that the speeches were ready and that he published them as they would have been delivered; but clearly there was still scope, before publication of the second *Actio*, for deliberate distortion or even substantial falsification of the evidence, in the clear knowledge that both Verres and his advocate would not be there to respond.

What we need, and what of course we normally do not have, is corroborative evidence from other sources to substantiate Cicero's principal claims. There is some help from the slightly later work of the Sicilian-born Diodorus, especially for our picture of the countryside; he started work on his *Bibliotheke* about 60 BC, a decade after the *Verrines*, but it was not completed until the early years of Augustus' reign.[5] One example where we do have an alternative viewpoint concerns Cicero's presentation of M. Claudius Marcellus' capture in 211 BC of Syracuse, an *urbs ornamentissima* as Cicero calls it (*Verr.* 2.1.21.55). To quote the *Verrines*:

> When the noble city of Syracuse, strongly fortified by art, and defended by nature against assault by land and sea, nevertheless fell before his strong arm and military skill, he [Marcellus] left it not merely unharmed, but so richly adorned it that it was a memorial alike to his victory, to his clemency and to his self-control.
>
> (*Verr.* 2.2.2.4)

Compare this image of impeccable restraint and good behaviour with the more conventional picture of Marcellus, such as in Plutarch's life, where he is said to have exported to Rome great numbers of Greek works of art from Syracuse, and in response to criticism of such action pronounced 'that he had taught the Romans, who previously understood nothing, to respect and marvel at the beautiful and wondrous works of Greece' (Plut.

*Marc.* 4). There seems little doubt that the latter image of Marcellus is closer to the truth: but this is simply turned on its head by Cicero, who cannot present Marcellus as a looter of statues, since such a picture would undermine the case he was to make later in his oration against Verres as the arch-robber and despoiler of Greek art in Sicily on an unprecedented scale.

On the purely historical level, therefore, the details provided by Cicero to flesh out the general picture of Verres' corruption and insatiable greed are probably wholly unreliable. Can we, for example, really trust any of the figures which Cicero gives us? Did the numbers of farmers registered in the territory of Agyrium really decline from 250 in Verres' first year as governor (73 BC) to a mere eighty two years later, as Cicero claims,[6] or is he deliberately falsifying the figures? Even if they did drop so drastically, does this represent permanent abandonment of the terrain, as Cicero implies (one, furthermore, not reversed by Verres' successor as *praetor*, L. Metellus, or so Cicero alleges: *Verr.* 2.3.53.122–55.128)? Can we really take on trust the grain figures that Cicero gives us for various cities, and then use these as a basis to estimate Sicilian grain production as a whole – a total of 30 million *modii* annually, according to Carcopino's mathematics? Or should the total rather be the 60.5 million *modii* in line with Holm's calculations over a century ago, or is Beloch's grand estimate of 48 million *modii* nearer the truth?[7] There is undoubtedly room for fresh research estimating wheat yields, using new approaches based on modern yield figures and estimates for the size of ancient territories, the percentage of farmable land, and suggested ancient population densities, even though all such exercises on the ancient economy are bedevilled by statistical uncertainties;[8] but the basic figures supplied by Cicero should be set aside in any such approach, rather than being imbued, as they have been in the past, with a degree of historical accuracy which they simply do not deserve.

It is not, however, my purpose here to re-examine the historicity of Cicero's *Verrines*, on which there is a huge literature. Rather my aim is to set the picture of first-century BC Sicily in its wider archaeological context, as far as we are able to on present evidence; for although a crude tool chronologically, in that we can rarely if ever be confident of connecting the archaeological record with so narrow a period as the three-year governorship of Verres in the late 70s BC, the archaeology of first-century BC Sicily has recently come into sharper focus than ever before, and so we can begin to use it as a general control on the picture of the island provided by Cicero. Certainly until recently a review of this kind would not have been possible, but such has been the explosion of archaeological research in Sicily since the late 1970s that much more information is becoming available about both Sicilian urbanism during the period of the late republic and also to a lesser extent the state of the countryside. Let us consider first the state of the towns around the time of Verres' governorship.

## SICILIAN URBANISM IN THE FIRST HALF OF THE FIRST CENTURY BC

This was a time when some cities in the island were in terminal decline, and the gradual abandonment of many of the hill cities of the interior during the whole of the hellenistic era (from the late fourth to the late first century BC) is one I have documented in some detail elsewhere (Wilson 1985a). It is also true that at some places, like Iaitas (Monte Iato) and Soluntum, the decline set in somewhat later than the time of Cicero's visit: for the process of urban abandonment was a gradual one which continued into the period of the middle empire. The phenomenon of the gradual decay of the hill towns is not one of absolute decline as such in the economic fortunes of Sicily, but essentially one of practicality: it does not make sense to live on a largely waterless hilltop 1,000 metres or so above sea level when there are no longer Carthaginian armies marching up and down below, nor does it make sense to drag grain and other agricultural produce up to the top of a hilltop town for market if the Roman taxation system demanded not only that it be taken down again, but also transported to the nearest port for shipment to Italy. In that connection, incidentally, Cicero's claim for Henna (Enna) is surely open to question:

> No Sicilian town lies further from the coast than Henna: yet compel the people of Henna to deliver so much corn at the coast, at places so widely apart as Phintias [Licata, on the south coast], Halaesa [on the north coast] and Catina [Catania, on the east coast], and they will transport it there within the day.

> (*Verr.* 2.3.83.192)

Before the arrival of the motorway but after the introduction of the internal combustion engine it took several long hours to drive across the Madonie mountains from Enna to Halaesa, but with an ox-cart for transport it must surely have taken more than a day; this is no doubt another case of Ciceronian exaggeration. So it is perhaps not surprising that many of the places perched on top of hills were slowly decaying around the time that Cicero was writing. The great advantage of such decline, archaeologically speaking, is that there is a large number of urban centres available for research and excavation which were not subsequently built over, and of which the last phases belong to precisely the period that concerns us, around the late second and the first century BC – places like Camarina, Soluntum and Acrae,[9] which have little or no Roman imperial, medieval or later overlay.

It is, however, hardly remarkable that the decay of many of the hill towns, which Cicero must surely have witnessed for himself, is not a phenomenon reported in the *Verrines*, simply because Cicero had a vested interest in representing Sicily as a highly prosperous province before Verres got his hands on it. One of the cites demonstrably in decline in the first century BC on the basis of the archaeological evidence, Leontini, is in fact described by Cicero as a *civitas misera atque inanis* (*Verr.* 2.2.66.150), but this is very much the exception to the general rule (*BTCGI* VIII: 524–55). Other places in decline at this period on archaeological grounds include Megara Hyblaea – mentioned once by Cicero in connection with an episode about pirate activity, but with no comment on the state of its fortunes[10] – and Morgantina, which I take to be the same as the Murgentia of Cicero.[11] This is a town he mentions twice in passing, in a list of places 'where the cornlands were so completely abandoned that we looked in vain not only for cattle but for the proprietors who were once so numerous',[12] and we hear too of a certain Polemarchus, 'a good, respectable inhabitant of Murgentia', whom Verres forced to pay a tithe at over the odds for his 50-*iugera* farm (*Verr.* 2.3.23.56). There is no hint in Cicero of urban decline; yet the careful and very extensive American excavations at Morgantina for over forty years have shown conclusively that there was very little new public or even private building activity after the city's heyday in the second half of the third century BC.[13] Then it formed part of Hieron's independent kingdom of Syracuse, and so fell outside Rome's jurisdiction during the first thirty years of the fledgling Roman province. The only major new public building in the last two centuries BC was the meat market (*macellum*), erected *c*.120 BC (fig. 11.1). Although the grand third-century residences of Morgantina continued for the most part to be occupied during the second century BC, by the first century BC many were becoming subdivided into smaller apartments, such as the House of the Arched Cistern and the House of the Ganymede; only one house shows signs of major redecoration with frescoes of the Second Style of the type current in first-century BC Italy, the so-called House of the Tuscan Capitals.[14] But decline in the first century BC at Morgantina was a gradual one; excavators have not found, here or anywhere else, any evidence of a sudden lurch for the worse as a result of Verres' alleged Sicilian depredations. By the time of Augustus, Morgantina was already pronounced a dead city by Strabo (6.2.4), and some of the precious *emblemata* mosaic pavements had probably been ripped out from floors for resale and reuse elsewhere.[15]

Another town demonstrably in decline during the first century BC is Heraclea Minoa, mentioned in passing several times by Cicero (who calls it just Heracleia),[16] but again without any adverse comments as to its fortunes. The city limits had been redefined here with new walls enclosing

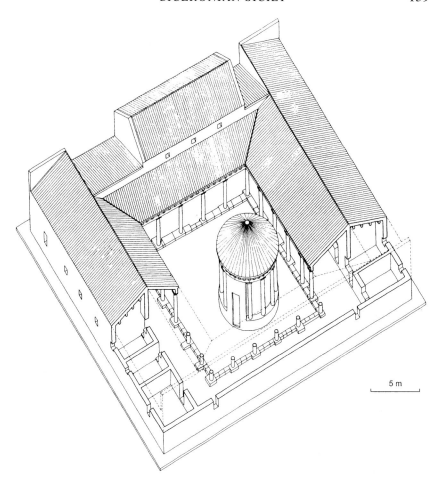

*Fig. 11.1* Morgantina, reconstruction drawing of the *macellum*
(meat market), built *c*.120 BC (after Sposito 1995: 73)

a smaller circuit during the second century BC, and already by then or early
in the first century BC the theatre must have been disused, because structures were built in the area of its scene building, and houses were built
over part of the *cavea* (fig. 11.2).[17] There can be no more telling indication
of urban decline than when major public buildings such as the theatre
fall into disuse. In one of the houses currently under excavation, arranged
around a central light well with plain unfluted columns standing on
strange conical bases, evidence for destruction or abandonment lies
around on the ground still awaiting detailed examination, including
Dressel 1C amphorae of a type which went out of production around the
middle of the first century BC.[18] Heracleia was totally deserted at the latest
by the end of the third quarter of the first century BC, within a generation

*Fig. 11.2* Heraclea Minoa, Greek theatre (*c.*300 BC?), showing buildings encroaching on the *cavea* (seen in the background), and in the area of the stage building (right), probably in the late second/early first century BC (photo: author)

of Cicero's visit, because no scrap of Italian red-gloss sigillata pottery, which reached Sicily around 25 BC, has been found there.

Heracleia and Morgantina had their heydays earlier than the first century BC; so for a better idea of towns which can be demonstrated archaeologically to have been flourishing at the time of Cicero's Sicilian fact-finding mission, we have to turn elsewhere. The best examples are Soluntum, situated in a splendid position on a hill 10 miles east of Palermo, a site excavated from the late 1950s to 1970 but never properly published;[19] Monte Iato (Iaitas/Ietas), a hill town south of Palermo 850 m above sea level, where the Swiss have been excavating for over a quarter of a century;[20] Segesta, a site long famous for its Greek temple and its theatre, which has seen an explosion of archaeological research since the late 1980s;[21] Tyndaris (Tindari), where an *insula* of the town was excavated in the 1960s;[22] and Halaesa, just inland from the north coast, where a substantial part of a *stoa* lining the *agora* was excavated in 1970 and again in 1998.[23] All these are places mentioned by Cicero in the *Verrines*,[24] and most were probably visited by him in the course of his investigations. Furthermore, all with the exception of Tindari went into decline during the empire and saw little substantial rebuilding after the first century BC, although at Monte Iato and Segesta the picture is complicated by reoccupation in the early medieval period. Let us look briefly at some of these sites in turn.

Despite being the least well published, Soluntum gives us in many ways the clearest idea of what a late hellenistic town in Sicily actually looked like (fig. 11.3). Recent work has now established beyond doubt that the hill town was the successor to the original Phoenician foundation, Thucydides' Soloeis (6.2.4), which lay on the bay of Solanto below, and that transfer to the new site on the hill occurred for reasons of security in the second half of the fourth century BC.[25] Virtually nothing as early as that, however, is now visible on the hill, and it is certain that Soluntum was totally restructured in the second and early first centuries BC. This has become clear from more recent study of some of the public buildings and also the decoration of the private houses. The *agora*, for example, is not well preserved (fig. 11.4), but it belongs to a type paralleled elsewhere in second-century BC Sicily, lined with a long *stoa* with rooms opening off the back and a portico of columns along the front.[26] Fallen architectural pieces, such as a *sima* cornice with lion heads (fig. 11.5), have been dated to the late second century BC; indeed the substantial nature of the cornice makes it certain that the *stoa* was designed as a two-storey building (von Sydow 1984: 276 and 356). The columns fronting the *stoa* have almost entirely disappeared; but they must have been of stone rather than of timber to support such a *sima* and a two-storey superstructure. The poor-quality shelly tufo stone would of course originally have been stuccoed and the architectural details brightly painted in contrasting colours.

Above the *agora* there is the council chamber, where the city *boule* met; it was originally identified as an *odeion*, but its proximity to the agora makes its identification as a *bouleuterion* certain (V. Tusa and L. Natoli in Adriani et al. 1971: 91–2, 111; 377–8 and 385 in English). This is a structure often mentioned in connection with the deliberations of city communities in the *Verrines*, a structure called by Cicero the *curia*; but in the case of Syracuse's council chamber Cicero specifically tells his audience that the Syracusans themselves call it the *bouleuterion* (*Verr.* 2.2.21.50) – a reminder that Greek terminology and the Greek language were ubiquitous in first-century BC Sicily. Half a dozen examples of Sicilian *bouleuteria* are known in addition to this one at Soluntum. That at Acrae was excavated in the nineteenth century, and Morgantina's was discovered (like that at Soluntum) in the 1960s; but they have now been joined by an example at Agrigento, by not just one but two *bouleuteria* at Monte Iato (see below), and most recently by what is suspected to be the site of the council chamber at Segesta, on the terrace just above the agora there, although the structure is very poorly preserved.[27] All these buildings are of the same shape, basically square with the seating arranged in a semi-circle, and it seems likely that this was everywhere the preferred Sicilian type – as opposed to the pi-shaped, rectangular version well known from examples at Priene in Asia Minor, or in the west at Glanon in the south of France.[28]

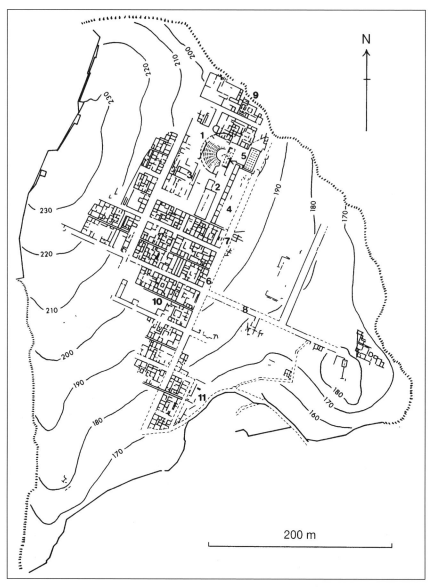

*Fig. 11.3* Soluntum, plan of the late hellenistic town
*Key:* 1 theatre; 2 *bouleuterion*; 3 Punic-style double sanctuary; 4 *agora* with
*stoa*; 5 public cistern; 6 *decumanus maximus*; 7 open-air altar with altar of
Punic type; 8 *cardo maximus*; 9 modern edge of escarpment (part of the town
has been lost over the cliff here); 10 'House of the Harpocrates'; 11 public baths
Contours in metres above sea level

*Fig. 11.4* Soluntum, rear rooms at the back of the *agora*'s *stoa*, second century BC, from south (photo: author)

Next to the *bouleuterion* at Soluntum is the theatre, not a well-preserved example of its type (fig. 11.6), but the subject of a recent meticulous monograph by Armin Wiegand (Wiegand 1997). This structure is now firmly set in the context of other Sicilian theatres of similar date, including those of Iaitas, Tyndaris and Segesta: the scene building of all of them is characterised by its U- or pi- shape, and three of them incorporate details of telamon figures. The date of all of them is, I believe, firmly established as belonging in the second century BC (although such a chronology for the Monte Iato theatre is, as we shall see, controversial): Wiegand, for example, on the basis of architectural details and other considerations, places the Soluntum theatre in the second century BC (fig. 11.7; Wiegand 1997: 52–5). In other words some of the so-called 'Greek' theatres of Sicily, of which Segesta's is one of the most famous, do not belong to the late fourth century BC, the date usually ascribed to them in the archaeological literature, but were constructed up to two centuries later when Sicily was already a Roman province. The scene building of the theatre of Tindari, for example, which displays a characteristic late hellenistic Sicilian irreverence for the standard rules of Greek architecture by mixing Ionic dentils with a Doric frieze, has been dated to about 100 BC, and it is clear that the original theatre was completely restructured around then (Bernabò Brea 1964–5; Buckler 1992: 289–93). This down-dating of some of the Sicilian theatres, and

*Fig. 11.5* Soluntum, *agora*, Ionic *sima* block, with dentil, astragal and
lion-head decoration, *c*.130 BC (photo: author)
Length of block: 1.15 m

indeed of other hellenistic structures in the island, started with the
meticulous research by von Sydow on architectural details from a number
of Sicilian sites (von Sydow 1979, 1984); and now this lower chronology
has been supported by the latest archaeological research in Sicily itself.
One example is recent excavation at the theatre of Segesta (fig. 11.8),
where a second-century BC date is now established both on archaeological
grounds and by a fresh study of the architectural ornament from the
building.[29]

The implications of all this for our knowledge of Sicily under the late
republic are profound. Until very recently the whole of the Roman period
in Sicily has been seen by Italian scholars as one of slow and inexorable
decline. As recently as 1981, Filippo Coarelli wrote eloquently about the
total absence of building work during the late republic, and presented a
generally gloomy picture of decline in the province during the second
and first centuries BC, the result (as he saw it) of Roman oppression and
exploitation of the island.[30] Now with further excavation year by year the
evidence is growing to substantiate the view that the second century BC in
particular saw massive investment in building programmes in many of the
Sicilian cities, both public and private. Cicero reminded his audience
of Cato's remark that the island was the Italian nation's storehouse, 'the
nurse at whose breast the Roman people is fed' (*Verr.* 2.2.2.5); and when
both Livy and Diodorus, writing a little later than Cicero, state that Roman
rule brought prosperity to the Sicilians as well as benefits to Rome, they
are reflecting what I believe to have been the truth.[31] Second-century
building programmes, both public and private, at Soluntum and else-

*Fig. 11.6* Soluntum, theatre, second century BC, looking south (photo: author)

where, are symptomatic of a buoyant economy and a sign that the local urban elites, even after paying their tithe to Rome, still had money to spare to invest in new construction. The re-emergence of city coinages soon after the middle of the second century BC, after an absence everywhere except at Syracuse since the end of the Second Punic War, is another clear sign of urban self-confidence.[32] Agricultural production, stimulated rather than depressed by the need to produce more grain for export to Rome, is likely to have been booming in many parts of Sicily in the course of the second and early first centuries BC; and although, as we have seen, some hill cities were being abandoned then, there were plenty more that were not. So when Cicero describes a place like Centuripe as 'one of the largest and richest cities in Sicily' (*totius Siciliae multo maxima et locupletissima*: *Verr.* 2.4.23.50), he need not have been stretching the truth very far with regard to its prosperity, even if it is an exaggeration to rank Centuripe as being among the largest Sicilian cities.[33] Centuripe, incidentally, in addition to its agricultural prosperity derived from its control of a substantial part of the fertile plain of Catania, also had a sideline in the form of a flourishing terracotta industry, which seems to have continued in production throughout most of the first century BC.[34]

What about public buildings at other places which Cicero mentions, buildings which are likely to have been constructed not all that long before his visit to the island in 71/70 BC? Further east along the north coast lies Halaesa, 'among the foremost of the many Sicilian cities of fame and high repute', as Cicero describes it (*Verr.* 2.3.73.170). Here is a well preserved

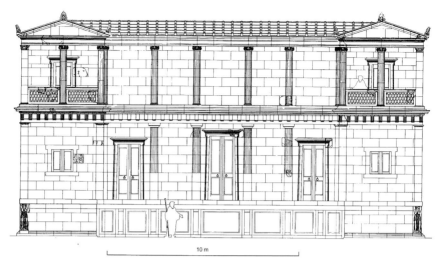

*Fig. 11.7* Soluntum, a suggested reconstruction of the *scaenae frons*, second
century BC. The use of caryatids here is seen in small-scale examples, on the
lowest storey (bottom left and right) (after Wiegand 1997; Beilage 20)

if incompletely published example of an *agora* and adjacent *stoa* dating
to the second century BC of the type we have already seen at Soluntum
(fig. 11.9). Only part of the *agora* paving has been uncovered. It includes
five statue bases, the largest of which (probably designed to carry an
equestrian statue) is faced in neat *opus reticulatum* and so is later in date
than Cicero's time (cf. n. 23). One wonders whether any of these bases
ever held statues of Verres himself, who (if Cicero is to be believed)[35]
courted such honours from as many Sicilian communities as possible. The
column bases at the front of the *stoa* originally bore a Doric entablature,
and the floor of the *stoa* was largely of brick, with an intermediate row of
columns, and at the back a series of small rooms. One or two of these may
have been offices, and others shops, but some, perhaps most, may have
had a religious role as little shrines. This is suggested by the circular
pedestals (?altars) in two of them, and by the finding in the *stoa* of three
inscriptions of the second/first century BC dedicated 'to all the gods'.[36]
The use of such rooms at the rear of *stoai* as shrines is also attested at
Soluntum, where one chamber still contains a block at eye-level with two
inscriptions of *c*.100 BC dedicated to 'Zeus Olympios and all the gods'.[37]
If the slightly later inscription found in the *stoa* at Halaesa and referring
to a 'basilica' does indeed imply a basilical use for the *stoa* there (a
conclusion, however, which cannot be taken as certain, although such a
use is in line with practice in the Greek east),[38] then many of the hearings
that are reported in Cicero's *Verrines* in various different towns may well
have been conducted in such buildings. These Sicilian *agorai* of the

*Fig. 11.8* Segesta, the theatre, second half of the second century BC,
looking northwest (photo: author)

second century BC, of which Halaesa's is the best preserved, were clearly
the focal point of the religious and perhaps juridical activities, as well as
the political and commercial life, of the *polis/civitas*. This is the sort of
physical setting one has to imagine when Cicero talks, as he often does,
about events taking place *in foro* of a Sicilian town.[39]

South of Palermo lies the hill town of Monte Iato, the ancient Ietas
or Iaitas, mentioned only once in the *Verrines* in passing, in a list of
communities allegedly brought to ruin by Verres.[40] Here three buildings
are of particular interest, the *agora*, the theatre and a peristyle house
('Peristylhaus I'). Excavations in the *agora* since the late 1970s have
revealed some details of the paving of the open piazza as well as the
buildings which lined it; the main layout seems to belong to the late third
or early second century BC, when *stoai* were laid out on the north, west and
probably east sides of the square. Interestingly the north *stoa* has a raised
platform or *tribunal* at the northwest corner (fig. 11.10), and its excavator
has suggested that the presiding magistrate might have sat there during
hearings[41] – in other words that the *stoa* was used for legal proceedings
and other petitions, as might also have been the *stoa* at Halaesa.

Opening off the west *stoa* at Monte Iato is a *bouleuterion* with characteristic semi-circular rows of seats; it was built about 130 BC and was
capable of holding up to 200 people (fig. 11.11; Daehn 1991). But of even
greater interest is the more recent discovery of a second *bouleuterion*,
with a capacity of about seventy seats, constructed around the middle of

*Fig. 11.9* Halaesa, the *agora* and *stoa*, seen before the 1998 excavations (which have uncovered more of the complex at the far end), probably second century BC (photo: author)

the second century BC.[42] The replacement of one *bouleuterion* by another, much larger one, only twenty or so years after the first is intriguing. It is presumably a reflection of the expanding population (which desired greater representation in the city's affairs), and of the increasing general prosperity of Iaetas, during that period: perhaps there was an influx of new settlers after the Slave War of 135–132 BC.

Immediately adjacent to the earlier *bouleuterion* is the theatre of Iaetas, not a well-preserved structure as it suffered heavily during early medieval occupation of the hilltop. The whole layout and the type of stage building are in line with what are now taken to be other second-century theatres in Sicily, and Isler has indeed proposed that the Monte Iato theatre went through a major refurbishment and reconstruction around about 200 BC; but in his view the original theatre, including the highly decorated stage building with its female telamons and satyrs, dates to around 300 BC.[43] If this is correct, this little Sicilian theatre in the back of beyond would be the earliest example of a Greek theatre anywhere in the Greek world with elaborate sculpture in its scene building, and it would be earlier too than the great Hieronian theatre at Syracuse of post-238 BC, which is far more likely to have been the trend-setter for decorated stage buildings in Sicily than distant Monte Iato. I have suggested elsewhere (Wilson 1990b: 69–71) that the Monte Iato sculptures belongs to the early second-century reconstruction of the theatre, and Wiegand, in his recent publication of

*Fig. 11.10* Monte Iato, reconstruction drawing of the northwest corner of the *agora*, with *tribunal* base in the north *stoa* (background) (after P. Omahen, in Isler 1997a: tav. CXCIV.2)

the Solunto theatre, also disputes Isler's dating of the Monte Iato theatre (Wiegand 1997: 50–1, 53). If accepted as a second-century building in its visible form, Monte Iato's theatre falls into place as another example of a public building erected in the Sicilian Greek hellenistic idiom at a time when Sicily was politically already a Roman province.

Similar controversy surrounds Isler's dating of the splendid two-storey peristyle house at Monte Iato, with superimposed columns in its peristyle of the Doric order (at the lower level) with Ionic above. There are some twenty-five rooms in all in this house on the ground floor alone, which occupies some 830 m$^2$ (fig. 11.12); if there was a full upper story the floor space of the house must have been double that. Pavements were of *opus signinum* and, in two cases, mosaic (both were very fragmentary, having collapsed from first-floor rooms; one had a rosette design). There was also a private bath-installation on the west side of the house, added according to the excavator about fifty years after the main house was built. Isler has dated that original period of construction to *c*.300 BC and has suggested that the house was directly influenced by Macedonian palatial architec-

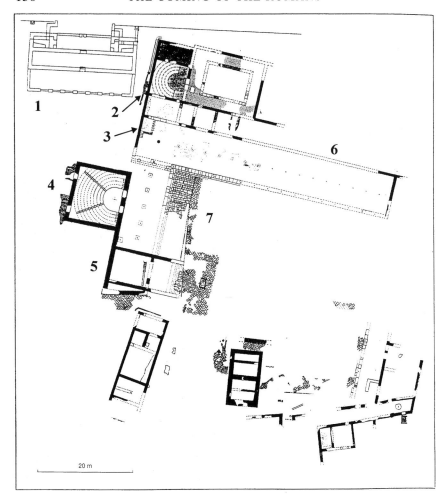

*Fig. 11.11* Monte Iato, plan of the *agora*
*Key:* 1 stage building of theatre; 2 earlier *bouleuterion*, *c*.150 BC; 3 *tribunal*;
4 later *bouleuterion*, *c*.130 BC, with west *stoa* in front of it; 5 temple;
6 north *stoa*; 7 paving of the *agora* itself (H. P. Isler (Zürich))

ture.[44] Yet the Ionic diagonal capitals used in the house, an original Sicilian invention with the further addition of palmettes at oblique angles between the volutes, are likely to have been a creation of the third century, and probably of Hieronian Syracuse after 260 BC, like its counterpart the Sicilian Corinthian capital;[45] and other architectural ornament from the house, as well as the mosaics, suggest a date sometime in the first half of the second century BC for the main phase of the visible mansion.[46] The house was occupied throughout the first century BC until it collapsed in the mid-first century AD, possibly as a result of earthquake.

*Fig. 11.12* Monte Iato, peristyle house 1 seen from the north (photo: author)

## PRIVATE HOUSES IN THE *VERRINES*

We have strayed rather far from Cicero's *Verrines*, where theatres (for example) are not mentioned, but at least we have had a glimpse of the sorts of building, both public and private, which Cicero and his contemporaries would have seen in Sicily in the 70s BC. Of course we cannot connect any of the surviving remains with the names of specific individuals in Cicero, and the temptation does not in fact often present itself. One such occasion occurred in 1993 when a unique pair of stone consoles in the form of ships' prows were discovered during the excavation of a later second-century BC house at Segesta: on the basis of the naval allusion of the consoles, the structure was tentatively claimed as the home of Heraclius, the *navarchus* of that city mentioned in the fifth book of the *actio secunda* of the *Verrines*, and who died in 72 or 71 BC.[47] There is, needless to say, no epigraphic proof from the excavations that Heraclius ever lived in the house where the consoles were found; but no doubt the label given to the house by its excavators, the 'Casa del Navarcha', will stick, however tenuous the hypothesis of its owner's real identity.

Cicero nowhere gives us a detailed description of the private house of any one of his Sicilian hosts, but one can imagine a man like Sthenius of Termini Imerese living in a dwelling of the same level of pretension as the Monte Iato mansion. Sthenius was clearly a man of some substance, a member of the local Sicilian aristocratic elite in his town: Cicero describes him as a:

man who at his own cost adorned his little town by erecting public
buildings and works of art, whose services to the state of Thermae and to
the Sicilians in general are attested by a bronze tablet set up in the senate
house (*curia*) at Thermae, engraved with an inscription officially recording
his benefactions.

(Verr. 2.2.46.112)

His house was clearly impressive enough for the provincial governor to
stay there (for Verres had been a friend before he became an enemy,
according to Cicero: *Verr.* 2.2.34.83), and status symbols of his wealth
were on display: Sthenius is described as having been a 'collector' all his
life, so that his house was packed with 'Delian and Corinthian bronze
of special elegance, pictures, and even finely wrought silver, of which he
had, considering what the means of a man of Thermae would allow, a
good collection' (*Verr.* 2.2.34.83). Verres of course is alleged to have made
off with the lot. These are the sorts of item which archaeology either
cannot yield, or produces only very rarely. Late republican silverware has
not to my knowledge ever been found in Sicily; inevitably one wonders
how much has been looted illegally by the clandestine excavators.[48] Certainly the frequency with which silver tableware is mentioned by Cicero
as the principal object of Verres' cupidity (along with tapestries, which of
course do not under normal conditions survive)[49] suggests that both were
a commonplace on the tables and the walls of the Sicilian wealthy in the
first century BC; their total loss is all the more regrettable. So too is that of
Corinthian bronze (*aes Corinthium*), the term used by Cicero and later
Pliny to denote silver and gold inlay work on a copper alloy background,
of the type found occasionally in small boxes and in couch-end decor-
ations elsewhere in the Roman world.[50] Again examples of secure Sicilian
provenance are, as far as I am aware, unknown.

   No Sicilian private house of the second or first centuries BC elsewhere
quite matches that at Monte Iato in terms of size, except for one at
Marsala; but there are good examples of the type at Soluntum, where there
are a little under a dozen examples of medium-sized houses with central
peristyled courtyard: the House of the Harpocrates, with an *opus signinum*
decorated pavement in its principal room, is a good example.[51] Some of
these houses were being decorated or redecorated around the 80s or 70s
BC, as suggested by examples of early Second Style wall frescoes, with
imitation marble panels and garlands and masks (fig. 11.13); and some of
the mosaic pavements of the Sicilian houses were being laid at this time,
such as a splendid rosette 'mat' in a house at Tindari (fig. 11.14), or the
figured mosaic with a hunt scene in a grand mansion at Palermo, both of
them dating to around 100 BC.[52] No Sicilian wall painting or mosaic is
striking enough to warrant mention by Cicero. The 'paintings' of Sthenius
coveted by Verres (*tabulae pictae*: *Verr.* 2.2.34.83) were clearly portable

*Fig. 11.13* Soluntum, detail of a fresco showing theatrical mask, sashes and festoon of fruit and flowers, *c*.80/60 BC (Museo archeologico regionale, Palermo) (photo: author)

*Fig. 11.14* Tyndaris, polychrome mosaic threshold 'mat' (a doorway to the
right was subsequently blocked up), *c*.100 BC (photo: author)
Ranging pole: 3 ft (0.92 m)

frescoed panels on a wooden backing, items which have not of course
(with rare exceptions) survived from antiquity; and although, as we have
seen from a likely example at Morgantina,[53] there was clearly a market
for second-hand mosaic *emblemata*, stealing mosaic floors is not listed
among the wide range of Verres' peccadilloes.

## STATUES AND SANCTUARIES

Stealing statues was another matter, however, and even if we believe only
a quarter of what Cicero claims to have been Verres' wrongdoings in the
shady world of art pilfering, with the governor allegedly hiring gangs of
thugs to acquire his ill-gotten gains for him, it is clear from Cicero's long
catalogue of items in the fourth book of the *actio secunda* that Sicily in the
first century BC (as indeed in most parts of the Roman world then and later)
was packed with statuary of all sizes and in a variety of media.[54] It is an
aspect of the physical appearance of Roman buildings which it is easy to
forget today, conditioned as we are to seeing our ancient sites largely
statueless, the vast majority of the survivors having been transferred to
museums. Sadly very little survives of late hellenistic sculpture in Sicily,
which renders Cicero's inventory of works that once were there all the
more valuable.[55] Examples include a marble Victory from Tindari (or

*Fig. 11.15* Soluntum, statue of Zeus in local tufo stone, *c*.150/100 BC
Height (excluding foot-stool): 1.65 m (Deutsches Archäologisches Institut,
Rom, InstNeg 96.337)

1                              2                              3

*Fig. 11.16* Henna (Enna), bronze coins issued by the municipal mint, 44/36 BC
*Key:* 1 obverse, female head, almost certainly Proserpina; 2 reverse of same
issue, standing male figure, very probably Triptolemus; 3 different issue,
obverse, head of Ceres

rather the lower part of it), which has been dated stylistically to the late
second century BC and probably formed part of a temple *acroterion*; some
damaged limestone statues, not of particularly high quality, recently uncovered at Segesta; and the massive seated statue of Zeus from Soluntum,
1.65 m high, usually dated to the second half of the second century BC, a
rugged and provincial but not incompetent work carved out of the local
tufo (fig. 11.15).[56] What this last statue in particular clearly demonstrates
is not only that there was a school of local sculptors (if not at Soluntum
itself, then presumably at nearby Palermo) who were capable of executing
such a piece, but also that there was money around in later second-century
BC Soluntum actually to pay for it. But the inventory provided by Cicero
of statues from one of the great sanctuaries of Roman Sicily, the sacred
precinct of Ceres at Henna (Enna), makes one acutely aware of just how
much has vanished – the 'marble image of Ceres', the 'image of Libera
(= Proserpina) in the other shrine', a bronze torchbearer (probably Libera
again), and two statues in the open air before the temples, 'one of Ceres,
the other of Triptolemus, both of great size and very beautiful'; the former
had 'a large and exquisite statuette of Victory in her hand' (Cic. *Verr.*
2.4.49.109–10). None of this nor even the architectural remains of the
temples survive today: the structures must surely lie buried or destroyed
under the Lombard castle of the thirteenth century, and not on the much
lower, and smaller, bare rock known today traditionally as the Rocca di
Cerere, which is far too small to have accommodated the great shrine.[57]
Although cult images in such a major and popular religious sanctuary
might well have spawned copies elsewhere, no 'Enna type' has been
recognised among the many statues of the goddesses known; indeed the
only clue as to the appearance of the statues comes from the coinage of
Henna, such as on the issues struck after 44 BC. It seems very likely that
the types chosen here by the municipal mint represent the statues in the

town's famous sanctuary, but the coin images are too small and indistinct to provide much information (fig. 11.16; Burnett et al. 1992: nos 661–2).

## THE COUNTRYSIDE

One further aspect of the *Verrines* on which modern archaeology can throw a little light is the countryside, although it is much less abundant than it should be, because of the comparative lack of fieldwork and research in rural Sicily at this period. In the third book of the *actio secunda* we hear a great deal about the plight of individual farmers, living on their *fundi*, who were hassled by Verres' agents and tricked into handing over more than their fair share of the corn tithe. It would be good if plans were available of *villae* and *fundi* in the Sicilian countryside of the type where men like Nympho of Centuripa (*Verr.* 2.3.3.21) or Q. Lollius of Aetna (*Verr.* 2.3.25.61) actually lived; but although a few sites of the late second/early first century BC have been investigated in recent years, the excavations have always been very partial, and intelligible ground-plans of buildings have simply not been forthcoming.[58] The picture obtained from excavations in the late 1960s of a farm near Acrae in southeast Sicily remains one of the clearest, although still fragmentary: here there are rooms arranged about a central court, and agricultural implements, dry measures (possibly for corn) and wine amphorae among the finds (fig. 11.17(1); Pelagatti 1970). Excavations at Campanaio near Montallegro (Agrigento province) have also produced a fairly coherent plan of a large rural L-shaped structure, a maximum of 8.40 m wide and at least 17m long (its north end is lost to the plough), but this belongs to the second half of the first century BC and so is a generation or so later than Verres' governorship (fig. 11.17(2); Wilson forthcoming). The building had earth floors and drystone walls (fig.11.18) which took a superstructure of either pisé or mud brick, exactly as in urban houses of rather earlier date at nearby Heraclea Minoa; mud brick in fact continued to be used in the countryside of Roman Sicily down into the fifth century AD. Quite when the villa proper (i.e. the substantial, well-appointed rural mansion with peristyle and mosaic-paved rooms or at least *opus signinum* floors) was introduced in Sicily must await future research, but it seems already to have made an appearance before the end of the second century BC, not long after the earliest examples on the Italian mainland. The very partially excavated peristyle villa in the hinterland of Lilybaeum, for example, appears to belong to the second century BC: it had at least one mosaic-paved room and another with an *opus signinum* paved floor (Fentress et al. 1986). Pottery from the villa at Castroreale San Biagio on the north coast in Messina province also goes back to the second century BC, and walling from what is probably the earliest villa here can be seen incor-

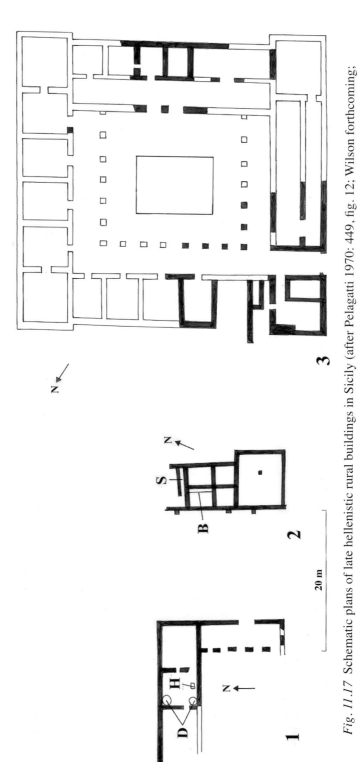

*Fig. 11.17* Schematic plans of late hellenistic rural buildings in Sicily (after Pelagatti 1970: 449, fig. 12; Wilson forthcoming; Fentress et al. 1986: fig. 1)

*Key*: 1 Aguglia near Acrae (Syracuse province), second/first century BC; 2 Campanaio (Agrigento province), c.50 BC; 3 Timpone Rasta (Trapani province), late second century BC. Walls found: solid; walls conjectural: open line

B = bench; D = *dolia*; H = hearth; S = staircase

*Fig. 11.18* Campanaio, a multi-phase rural building, *c*.200 BC–AD mid-fifth century, looking north. The southern- and easternmost rooms of the phase-3 building of *c*.50 BC, shown in fig. 11.17(2), are those containing the 2-m ranging poles (photo: author)

porated in the later building alterations. Certainly other substantial villas were being built in the island in the first century BC, such as the seaside villa of Borgellusa near Avola in Syracuse province.[59]

Archaeologically, however, there is much still to learn of the first-century BC countryside in Sicily, and there is currently little to place beside the information to be gleaned from the *Verrines*. One thing which is strikingly clear from Cicero's accusations is the apparent prevalence of farmers with small- to medium-sized estates, and this provides a striking contrast to the picture provided by Diodorus and others of the Sicilian countryside being dominated by vast estates (*latifundia*) with huge slave-run ranches.[60] There must have been plenty of examples of the latter in Sicily – otherwise the island would never have experienced two slave wars at the end of the second century BC – but that they coexisted with small- and medium-sized estates at the time of Verres' governorship (and no doubt before) seems certain. We do not hear in the *Verrines* of the really big and powerful landowners, precisely because Verres was too astute (or too scared) to have tangled with them: rather he sets his sights on the smaller landowner and the tenant farmer, who were softer targets than the big *domini*. Certainly the limited amount of field survey evidence availble now from Sicily suggests the presence in the countryside of plentiful smallholdings in the first half of the first century BC: they are documented archaeologically in the hinterland of Heraclea Minoa, where several farms of about 150 *iugera* in extent have been identified, and a similar picture of scattered farms in the late republic has also been forthcoming from survey work in the territory of Himera.[61] In both areas many of the small farms gave way in the early empire to larger estates. By contrast, recent work in the neighbourhood of Alcamo in western Sicily has suggested that the density of rural population was greater in the empire than it was in the late republic (Filippi 1996: 62–71), and a similar picture comes from the nearby Monreale survey, where a decline in the number of sites occupied in the Roman republic can be detected by comparison with the fourth and early third centuries BC.[62] Here one can perhaps suggest the earlier formation of large estates, perhaps in the style of those described by Diodorus, at the expense of smaller properties. Clearly the pattern of landholdings is likely to have varied immensely from one part of Sicily to another at any one time, so making unreliable the sorts of sweeping generalisations on the basis of the written texts (or indeed of only a handful of surveys) which have generally dominated discussions of the state of Sicilian agriculture in the first century BC.

## CONCLUSION

Thanks to archaeological research since the late 1960s, there is now a reasonable body of archaeological evidence, especially from the towns, to set beside the Ciceronian speeches. What it suggests is that much of Sicily was flourishing at the time of Verres' governorship, and whatever the latter's extravagances there is absolutely nothing from the archaeological record to suggest that Sicily's fortunes took a nose-dive around the time of Verres' depredations – whether temporarily or permanently, or whether due to Verres or for socio-economic reasons. On the contrary, everything points to a burgeoning Sicily at this time, with its grain and other agricultural produce much in demand in Italy, and Sicilian farmers reaping the profits of the increased productivity of their land in response to the demands of Roman taxation. Verres was clearly more corrupt than most, and his behaviour sufficiently out of order to lead to his prosecution and downfall; but his actions did not ruin Sicily. Cicero's *tour de force* is a good and colourful 'read', but it is not, and was never intended to be, history.

# 12

# BETWEEN GREECE AND ITALY:

## an external perspective on culture in
## Roman Sicily

### *Kathryn Lomas*

THE STUDY OF ACCULTURATION – the processes of cultural change within a society and its relationship to surrounding cultural groups – is an increasingly important strand in scholarship on the ancient world, and one which is vital to our understanding of its history. Most regions of the ancient Mediterranean contained a multiplicity of cultural groups, and therefore questions of ethnicity, definitions of identity, and definitions of shifting cultural boundaries are essential to our understanding of how these societies developed. One of the crucial factors in evaluating cultural identities and cultural change is the heterogeneous nature both of the expression of these identities, and of the viewpoints which they represent. Communities (or indeed individuals) do not, by and large, have a single, monolithic identity. They prioritise different identities (or facets of identity) depending on context, on the cultures they are interacting with, and the audiences they are presenting themselves to. Thus a community in the Roman empire may wish to stress its *Romanitas* in some aspects of activity, but may also wish to acknowledge other cultural affiliations, or to present itself as having its own distinctive local identity, in other fields of civic behaviour. Similarly, it may wish to emphasise its assimilation to one particular audience, and its difference to another. This cultural pluralism can be viewed as an essential tool in reconciling the various loyalties and levels of identity inherent in a world where cities were at one and the same time individual communities, part of a local culture (which might in itself be composed of a number of ethnic and cultural strands), and part of the Roman world. The identity of cities in the later republic and early empire is therefore a shifting construct balancing numerous competing forces.

This is always a complex set of intertwined problems, but in studying Sicily, it becomes particularly convoluted and also completely central to our understanding of the development of the island. The complexity lies in a combination of the diversity of Sicily's cultural heritage and the process of colonisation to which the island was exposed – itself an ill-understood process which is currently the subject of much-needed research (Malkin 1994; Osborne 1998; Bradley and Wilson forthcoming). An examination of acculturation in Sicily involves evaluating not only relations between three main indigenous ethnic groups – Sikans, Sikels and Elymnians, all of them known principally from archaeological evidence – and two different colonising groups – the Greeks and the Phoenicians – as well as incorporating later incomers to the island. In addition there are numerous different sub-groups within these categories, and a vast variety of models of the processes of colonisation and acculturation. Much of the recent archaeological research on acculturation in Sicily has indeed focused on the issues raised by the colonisation period and the archaic history of the island, the point at which the relations between incomers and indigenous populations are probably most difficult to entangle, and which must of necessity be approached by archaeological means because of the lack of literary evidence (Leighton 1996a; cf. Leighton (chapter 3), Hodos (chapter 4) and Shepherd (chapter 5), this volume). However, acculturation does not cease to be an important issue in the later history of Sicily. Following the disruptions of the fourth century BC caused by the wars between Greeks and Carthaginians, and the Roman conquest of the island in the third century, a number of important new factors come into play. Two important new ethnic groups – Campanians and Romans – appear on the island, and any analysis of acculturation in the Hellenistic period and the early empire must take these into account.

The relationship between Roman culture and the pre-existing cultures of Sicily was a highly complex one, to a large extent because of the pre-existing cultural diversity of the island, but also because of its relationship with Rome and the circumstances of its conquest. Lying only a few kilometres off the coast of Calabria, it was open to much Italian influence, and the history and culture of southwest Italy indicates that this region, vice versa, had long maintained close links with Sicily.[1] Furthermore, sources for Sicily in the period after the Second Punic War stress the large numbers of Romans and Italians resident on the island, and the long-standing connections between Sicily and Rome. Nevertheless, the people of the island were not directly incorporated by Rome either as Roman citizens or as allies, as those of the cities of Italy had been; Sicily was instead ruled as a province, something which inevitably coloured the processes of cultural transmission. There is also the fact that in Roman eyes, some indigenous cultures were more equal than others. Although the predominant culture in southern and eastern Sicily was Greek, which had a fairly high cultural status for the Romans, there were areas of western Sicily where this was not the case. Punic influence remained strong there, and in the aftermath of the wars against Carthage would have had a very different cultural value; and the Campanian enclaves in the north of the island would have been different again. However, given the enormous range of this subject, this chapter will only attempt to assess cultural identity in terms of hellenism and its interaction with Roman influence.[2] A complete review of the cultural history of Sicily after the Roman conquest is well beyond the scope of a single chapter, so for present purposes, the main focus will be on the relationship between Greek and Roman culture in hellenistic and early imperial Sicily, and its place in the context of the wider pattern of hellenism in the western Mediterranean.

The question of who was setting the agenda in defining what it was to be a Sicilian in the Roman world is also problematic. A juxtaposition of literary, epigraphic and archaeological material is vital as a means of providing a way into the debate on 'emic' versus 'etic' definitions of identity[3] – that is, identities which are defined and imposed by groups external to a community, as opposed to definitions of identity which are generated internally. Only a relatively small number of viewpoints can be established from the frequently incomplete ancient evidence, but a spectrum of viewpoints is vital, nevertheless. The surviving literary sources are, for the most part, generated from outside the communities they describe, and tell us more about identities constructed for a community by outsiders – whether Greek or Roman – than about a community's own view of itself.[4] Epigraphic and archaeological evidence, on the other hand, can give an insight into the internally generated self-perception of a community.[5] Since this chapter is concerned with establishing the communal identity of cities as defined internally, the emphasis will be on examining the public manifestations of elite culture and the actions of the city as a community. The principal forms of evidence under consideration are programmes of public building carried out by the state or by individual benefactors, and the form and language of inscriptions which record the actions of the state or of prominent individuals, both areas of activity which can be powerful statements of the cultural identity of cities and their inhabitants.[6] The underlying assumption here is that in a culturally pluralist society, these represent active choices about cultural identity which are entirely separate from questions of demography and actual ethnic background of the inhabitants, and which can therefore be used to examine variations in patterns of representations of identity according to social, geographical and chronological context. The overriding necessity, however, is to construct a model for cultural change and interaction which reflects the fact that this process is an active dialogue between Sicilians and Rome, not a passive process of romanisation.

At first glance, the urban environment of Greek Sicily, as represented by its public and monumental building programmes, seems to have remained very obviously hellenic in its cultural affiliations. Having said this, the difficulties of being prescriptive on this point are legion, because of both the methodological constraints of Sicilian archaeology and the varied relationships between the communities in question and Rome. As emphasised in a recent major work on Roman Sicily (Wilson 1990a), many of the cities which were significant in the province in the late republic and early empire are still inhabited and, even within the restrictions imposed by urban archaeology, have not been fully explored or recorded. There were undoubtedly far more romanised structures than have been found or recorded, so the impact of Rome on the urban environment is difficult to quantify.[7] Dating of structures is also a major problem, and many of the buildings discussed below are either difficult to date accurately, or have a large number of building phases which complicate the issue.

The record is skewed still further by the fact that many cities which did not have Latin or colonial status struggled to survive beyond the first century AD. Syracuse, Tyndaris, Tauromenium, Catania and Thermae, which became Roman colonies in 21 BC (Panormus, in the west of the island, may also have received colonial status in 14 BC), and Segesta, Centuripe and Noto, which had Latin status, all have evidence of significant public building activity, and an obvious motive for adopting Roman norms, but it is clear that there is no simple correlation between the extent and nature of public building programmes and the status of each individual city.

In many cities, the first major building phase after the Roman conquest coincided (as it did in many parts of Italy) with the economic boom of the second century BC,[8] with successive phases coinciding with the reign of Augustus, the later first century AD and the Antonine period. This was in most cases clearly directed at monumentalising and enhancing the public areas of the city. Structures attested are of typically hellenistic type and include monumentalised *bouleuteria* and *stoai* in and around the *agora* of many of these cities. Typical examples include Soluntum, where a *bouleuterion* and *stoa* was constructed, and a monumental complex at Monte Iato, consisting of *stoai*, temples and a *bouleuterion* (Wilson 1990a: 46–56). In some of the smaller communities such as Soluntum, Monte Iato, Halaisa and Centuripe, and also some of the larger cities with Latin or colonial status – for instance Tyndaris and Agrigentum – this remained the basic physical form of the centre of the city until the second century AD.[9] As one might expect, there is evidence of a greater degree of public building in the period after the Augustan settlement of 21 BC, particularly in those cities which became Roman colonies as a result of this. At Tauromenium the *forum* was repaved and monumentalised. The boundary wall has been dated to the first century BC, and there is evidence

of Augustan repairs to a square structure which may have been the
*bouleuterion*, although the identification is still uncertain (Wilson 1990a:
50–1; Bacci 1980–1: 737–48). At Catania, an Italic-style *forum* was built,
using *opus reticulatum* (rare in Sicily) and consisting of colonnades fronting rows of shops on all four sides, and there was also extensive rebuilding
of the theatre. Syracuse is a more problematic case because of the incom-
pleteness of the data and the chronic difficulties of dating the structures
which have been excavated. The main *forum* seems to have undergone
major rebuilding in the second century AD, although only a small portion
of it survives, but a small triangular *forum* dates to the first century AD, and
a monumental *palaestra* abutting the Altar of Hieron is likely to date
to the Augustan period. Most of the fabric of the theatre dates to the late
third century BC, but with additions and renovations which may date to
the first century AD. Other evidence of monumental public building of the
Augustan period includes a fragmentary monumental arch and an amphitheatre (Wilson 1990a: 51–2).

However, this is slender evidence on which to argue for a policy of
'italicisation' as a result of the Augustan settlement of the island, despite
the sizeable programme of colonisation and reorganisation initiated in the
years after the civil wars and the defeat of Sextus Pompeius (Wilson
1990a: 44–5; for Augustus' own comments, see *Res Gestae* 28.1). The
Augustan settlement clearly did have a large impact, but the testimony
of Augustus himself must surely remain suspect, and ambiguities of
recording and dating many of these monuments alone make this difficult
to argue conclusively. A good number of them may just as easily fall
anywhere within the Julio-Claudian era.

The other difficulty is in determining who provided the impetus for
these building programmes, and why, given that there are relatively few
inscriptions to give a social context to these structures. Augustus himself,
notoriously, boasted in the *Res Gestae* that he had endowed his veteran
colonies in Italy with all possible public amenities (*RG* 3.3, 10.2, 28; Suet.
*Aug*. 46), but the archaeological and epigraphic evidence hardly bears
this out (Keppie 1983: 113–22; Jouffroy 1986: 105–8). The high level of
public building in the Augustan period was by no means restricted to
colonies, and most of the motivation and finance appear to have come
from within communities rather than being the product of an imperial
benefactor (Jouffroy 1986; Millar 1986: 295–318). Given Augustus' well-
known preoccupation with Italy (Zanker 1988; Galinsky 1997), it seems
unlikely that Sicilian cities would have received greater levels of support
and euergetism. The type of building activity which was the subject of this
investment is also significant. Imperial benefactions tended to involve
specific forms of activity (Millar 1986: 295–318), and most of the Sicilian
examples fall into Millar's categories of typical imperial activities.

Caligula, for instance, restored the city walls of Syracuse along with an unspecified number of temples, apparently implementing a project planned by Tiberius, because they had fallen into disrepair (Suet. *Cal*. 21).

The aqueduct constructed by Domitian at Lilybaeum in AD 84 (*CIL* X.7227) is another example of a project which involved major capital investment and fell into a category of building which was frequently associated with imperial activity.[10] The restoration of a temple at the sanctuary of Venus Erycina by Tiberius on behalf of the citizens of Segesta, and later rebuilding at the sanctuary by Claudius, are a similar case, since the sanctuary was one of more than purely local significance.[11] It enjoyed prominence as a sanctuary in the Greek world, and the cult of Venus Erycina was also popular in Rome, where there were several temples dedicated to it. It is very possible that, as in Italy, the cultural and political changes of the Augustan period prompted a phase of urban development and renewal, but the impetus from this is as likely to have come from within the province and the individual communities as from the emperor. There is no specific reason to see these programmes of urban renewal as the result of imperial intervention or the colonisation programme.

Some of the public building taking place in imperial Sicily does indeed seem to be a graphic representation of a cultural shift to Roman norms, but much of this is either difficult to date, or likely to have taken place later in the principate. At Centuripe, for instance, one of the few cities to adopt Roman concrete construction techniques on a large scale, the most substantial remains – baths, a *nymphaeum* and a temple complex – date to the second century AD (Wilson 1990a: 94–104). At Catania and Tauromenium, the rebuilding and substantial romanisation of the theatres was not a single act but an on-going process, with building phases and additions at several points in the first and second centuries AD (notably Augustan/Julio-Claudian, Flavian and Antonine/Hadrianic).[12] Whatever the exact dating, it is undeniable that the substantial romanisation of some of the theatres in Sicily would have been a powerful cultural symbol (Bejor 1979; Frézouls 1983; Rawson 1987; Gros 1994). The physical shift from a specifically Greek form of building to a Roman one makes this particularly striking, and the point is reinforced by the identification of theatres with the Augustan social order. The popularity of the theatre as a building type soars during the Augustan and Julio-Claudian era, a time which coincided with legislation to use theatre seating as a means of physically mapping out social divisions within the community (Jouffroy 1986: 320–32; Rawson 1987). The advent of the amphitheatre was an equally graphic symbol, since it was a structure which was not indigenous to the Greek world, and which was associated particularly with both imperial activity and veteran colonisation (Welch 1994: 59–79; Coleman forthcoming). Here again, however, the patterns are ambiguous. The three extant examples – Syracuse, Catania and Termini Imerese – have dating problems: Syracuse may be Augustan, which would make it an early example of its type,[13] while Termini may date to later in the first century and Catania to the second century AD. Lilybaeum and Panhormus probably had amphitheatres by the second century, but these are attested only in inscriptions.[14] Elsewhere, adaptations to theatres suggest that they were used for games, spectacles and water-battles, but whether the decision not to construct a purpose-built amphitheatre was due to cultural factors or to economic imperatives is impossible to say.

The evidence of public buildings is, therefore, difficult to assess. The underlying signal sent out is that the trend was to more romanised structures, but this has to be set against the fact that the most active cities in terms of construction of public buildings were the Roman colonies, and that there remained important local variations in decoration and construc-ion technique which indicate that these structures were by no means a wholesale acceptance of a Roman or Italic norm. This is in sharp contract to the pattern in southern Italy, where the material culture of the Greek colonies is substantially italicised by the early empire, and where the majority of the archaeologically attested public buildings of this date are very similar to those of the rest of Italy (Jouffroy 1986: 320–32). Strabo makes it clear that characteristically Greek structures – such as the gymnasia at Naples and Tarentum (Str. 5.4.7, 6.4.3) – were still in use and were part of the hellenised character of these cities, but new structures mostly corresponded to the Italic norm.

There is, however, one aspect of the urban landscape which did come to reflect rather graphically the changing political circumstances and cultural affiliations of Sicilian cities. Many urban centres – not just the colonies and other major cities, but also the smaller settlements – made prodigious use of statuary to give emperors and other Roman dignitaries a very visible presence in the public space of the city. This is a trend which started much earlier than the adoption of Roman and Italic aspects in monumental building. Cicero makes copious reference in the Verrines to statues and monuments in honour of the Roman generals who were based in Sicily in the Second Punic War, most notably Marcellus and Scipio Africanus (Cic. Verr. 2.2.3–4). The spin which he places on this is that these were set up to commemorate honoured benefactors and patrons. The fact that they were the conquerors of the island and that the actions of the cities may therefore have been less than entirely voluntary is obscured. Whatever the motivation in each specific case (and this is likely to have varied significantly according to context), these visible reminders of Roman power quickly became a ubiquitous part of the urban landscape, in a way that romanised public buildings did not.

The other category of evidence for urban cultural identity – that of the inscriptions – seems to show a clearer pattern, with a trend towards romanisation of form, content and language in public or elite inscriptions, and the strong persistence of Greek in non-elite epigraphy. On the figures collected by Wilson (Wilson 1990a: 313–20), the actual proportion of Greek inscriptions to Latin ones varies considerably across the island. The balance is fairly even for eastern Sicily, dividing approximately 50:50 at Catania and Messina, although with a less clear-cut pattern at Syracuse and Tauromenium. In the west of the island, at Lilybaeum, Panormus and Thermae, there is a much clearer preponderance in favour of Latin (Panormus: 17 per cent Greek, Thermae: 15 per cent Greek).[15] However, the pattern is far more complex than suggested by the raw statistics. When different fields of epigraphic activity are examined, the balance of hellenism and Roman influence starts to look much more significant. In the west of the island, the obvious answer to the question of why Latin became much more readily established is that Greek was not the only (or even the principal) pre-Roman language in use. Punic was a significant presence in this area and may have continued to be spoken (Apul. *Met.* 11.5). However, this does not explain the relatively low survival of Greek texts at non-Punic Thermae. Similarly, eastern Sicily, an area where Greek was the predominant pre-Roman culture in most cities but which was exposed to a much higher concentration of Roman personnel and Roman influence (e.g. Cic. *Verr.* 2.2.68–73, 4.43, 5.115, 5.140; Liv. 39.1.15–17), shows a much higher survival rate of Greek as an epigraphic language. As with the west of the island, the difficulties of drawing conclusions are pointed up by the example of Messana. Although originally a Greek colony, its development had always been coloured by its proximity to the Italian mainland (Strab. 6.1.6, 6.2.3; Thuc. 6.4). More to the point, it had been recolonised by Dionysios I's Campanian mercenaries in the fourth century BC, and Greek may no longer have been the primary cultural and ethnic identity of the city by the time Rome came onto the scene.[16] Certainly its Italic connections were a politically significant factor in Rome's first involvement in Sicily in the 260s BC, and Cicero makes great play with its non-Greek nature in the *Verrines*. He consistently refers to it by its Italic rather than its Greek name, emphasising its cultural difference and 'otherness' to reinforce its isolation in being the only city to support Verres and, by implication, to share in the infamy of his criminal behaviour.[17]

The typology of Greek and Latin texts is as distinctive as their distribution. Even in the areas where Greek remains a significant statistical presence, the forms of inscription which relate to elite activity and to the identity of communities are mostly, and in some cases exclusively, Latin. At Catania, for instance, where there is still a significant quantity of Greek epigraphy, Latin is adopted for the vast majority of official inscriptions from the Augustan period onwards (Wilson 1990a: 315). A similar pattern is found at Syracuse and Tauromenium, while at Lilybaeum a number of Greek official inscriptions have been found, but Latin quickly becomes universal in high-status inscriptions in the early empire. Greek texts, by contrast, are predominantly funerary inscriptions and are generated to a large extent by the non-elite at all of these sites. The early and middle empire is therefore characterised by a predominantly romanised civic identity in most cities. Even away from the major centres with their colonial or Latin status, epigraphic evidence indicates a level of romanisation in the ways in which communities presented themselves. Many magistrates are referred to by the Latin title of *duumvir* rather than by Greek magistral titles (e.g. *CIL* X.7353; *AE* 1945: 64; for numismatic evidence, see Wilson 1990a: 40–2), although Greek titles do not die out entirely. Inscriptions found in the territory of Lilybaeum, for instance, honoured a number of prominent men, including both a *duumvir* and a member of the local senate who is referred to by the Greek term *bouleutes* (*IG* XIV.273, 276, 277, 296).

The really curious *volte face*, however, occurs in the late empire, when Greek civic identity undergoes a resurgence. Greek texts increase in number, and Greek language and epigraphic forms are used again for precisely the sort of public elite text which is an indicator of perception of civic identity (*IG* XIV.273, 276, 277, 296, 1091; *AE* 1966: 167). At Lilybaeum, for example, official dedications in Latin are the norm from the Augustan period but Greek reasserts itself in the fourth century AD, and there is a similar pattern at Catania (*IG* XIV.273, 276, 277, 296; *AE* 1966: 167; Wilson 1990a: 317–18). Greek magistral titles and administrative terminology also reappear, but this need not be a reflection of an erosion and disappearance of *Romanitas*, as Wilson argues. Comparison with some of the Greek colonies of southern Italy indicates that revival of Greek elements of civic government within the framework of a Roman colony or *municipium* was not at all impossible.

The telling fact is that these manifestations of hellenism coexist with Roman features. Their apparent disappearance and reappearance are actually the result of a change of emphasis in what is promoted, and in some cases the accident of survival of the particular categories of epigraphic evidence in which they are attested.[18] The most striking example of this phenomenon in a Sicilian context dates to the third century AD and was found in Rome. It was a Greek inscription set up by the city of Tauromenium in honour of Iallia Bassiana (*IG* XIV.1091): 'The *boule* and the *demos* of the renowned city of the Tauromenitans wish this to be set up in honour of Iallia Bassiana, distinguished in all virtue, goodness and wisdom.' The striking thing about it is that although it was set up in Rome itself and by a Roman colony, the city of Tauromenium chose to commission a Greek inscription using Greek terminology, describing the dedicators as *boule kai demos*, and the language of a Greek honorific decree. As such, this is a striking example of a city making a very striking and specific cultural choice, and consequently a very public statement of renewed Greek identity. The late date strongly militates against its being a simple continuation of Greek language or forms of government, as do parallels from elsewhere in the western Mediterranean (Lomas 1993: 174–8), and its chronology makes it all the more notable.

What we seem to have in Sicily is, therefore, a pattern of cultural choice and identity which is strikingly dissimilar from those of both southern Italy and most other culturally Greek provinces. The Sicilian elite is sending out culturally ambiguous signals via the built environment, con-structing hellenistic-type buildings in some contexts and retaining the overall form of the hellenistic *agora* for the main public areas of many cities, but at the same time romanising theatres, and adopting some characteristic features of the Roman city, such as amphitheatres. In con-trast, epigraphic records of civic life are much more strongly romanised. There is also a dichotomy between elite and non-elite responses to cultural change, with a much greater openness to Roman culture amongst the elite, but Greek influence remaining strong in other social contexts. This pattern would not be remarkable taken in isolation, but when set against the wider context of hellenism in the Roman world, it begins to look rather anomalous.

In southern Italy, the nearest comparison in terms of geography and historical development, the behaviour of the elites of the Greek cities is very different. Of the communities which continued to flourish after the Hannibalic war, a number seem to have acculturated completely, using Roman titles and civic forms, adopting Latin and incorporating Roman cults (Lomas 1993: 174–8), and after the Social War, the Roman *tria nomina* became the standard form of personal name (Mello 1974; Costabile 1978; Lomas 1993: 172–5; Leiwo 1994). Nevertheless, hellen-ism remained an important part of the civic identity of many communities and underwent an important resurgence in the early empire. Cicero stresses the Greekness of communities in this region, and includes testimony to the hellenic elements in cities in which there is little trace of Greek culture in inscriptions or material culture (Cic. *Arch.* 5–11; cf. also Cic. *Balb.* 21). Similarly, Strabo stresses that a number of cities continued to value elements of their Greek heritage – the *ephebia*, *gymnasia*, cults, titles of magistracies, etc. (Strab. 5.4.7, 6.1.2, 6.3.4).

Nor is this a construct imposed by outsiders viewing these cities through their own preconceptions. A number of Greek cities in Italy make very striking statements in their own right about their Greek identity in certain fields of civic life, most notably in honorific inscriptions and in the perpetuation of Greek institutions such as games and *gymnasia*. Epigraphic evidence attests an important resurgence of hellenism in these fields of activity, but only in certain contexts (Miranda 1990; Lomas 1993: 174–87; Leiwo 1994). Public building programmes were very Roman in character, and material culture was almost entirely italicised, particularly at the non-elite levels of society.[19] In many cities, therefore, the hellenism of the early empire appears to be a conscious cultural choice. It is also very much an elite construct and choice, confined to specific fields of civic activity, and differs sharply from the choices of the non-elite. Chronologically, it is also a phenomenon of the early empire. By the end of the second century AD, hellenism is beginning to fade markedly into the background. In contrast, Sicilian hellenism seems to fade from civic life during the period at which Italian interest in Greek culture was at its strongest, but undergo a resurgence at a time when Greek culture in Italy had substantially faded away.

The underlying processes of this response to Rome are by no means obvious, but there are clearly very different processes of assimilation and very different cultural choices at work even within a relatively small area of the western Mediterranean. One point which emerges quite strongly is that this is a process of cultural choice and construction of fluctuating identities. It is not a function of demography or ethnic background, as has been recently (and in my view wrongly) argued in a study of Roman Naples (Leiwo 1994: 167–72). One of the most striking features of the epigraphy of Roman Sicily is the fact that there is very little correlation between the language of the text and the ethnic/cultural origin and legal status of the individuals named. More specifically, forms of names also vary widely, from the full Roman *tria nomina* through *nomen + cognomen* (also Roman) to name + patronymic (Greek).[20] Inevitably, there is also a high preponderance of single names which give little information about cultural affiliations. However, it is clear from this eclectic mix of names, language and onomastic forms that there was little relation between perceived ethnic origin and cultural choice.

In the cities which gain colonial status, and amongst other groups of enfranchised Sicilians, there is an even mix of conventions. Some individuals follow the practice common in the Greek east of adopting a Roman *praenomen* and *nomen* but retaining a Greek name as a *cognomen*; for example, M. Valerius Chorton, a decurion of Lilybaeum who was the subject of an honorific decree in Greek, or of the *gymnasiarch* Tiberius L.F. Diognetos (*IG* XIV.276, 277). A Latin example is provided by a *sportula* inscription from Thermae in honour of Antia M.F. Cleopatra (*CIL* X.7352). Equally, there are numerous other examples from both Greek and Roman texts of individuals of high status who had completely romanised, or italicised, names. In non-elite (and primarily funerary) epigraphy, there is similarly little correspondence between personal names and language. Names of Greek origin are found in Latin texts and Latin names in Greek ones.[21] Greek names in Latin texts are harder to interpret socially, as the frequent assumption underlying much of the research on Greek *cognomina* is that they indicate servile origin. Although this seems to be borne out by evidence from Italy and the Latin-speaking west, it cannot be assumed to hold good for Sicily. Many of the examples of Greek cognomina found here seem more analogous to the patterns of the eastern provinces, where they are derived from Greek proper names incorporated into the Roman onomastic structure.[22] The Sicilian examples are less clear cut, but Greek names of any form are by no means automatic signs of low social status, and the lack of correlation between language, name-form and apparent ethnic background seems to indicate that choice of language was a signal of the cultural identity and affiliations of the individual, not his or her ethnic origin.

The difficulty of assessing evidence for cultural identity in Sicily lies partly in deciding whether this was a case of Roman influence which never penetrated the culture of the island to a significant extent, and was in the end simply eroded by the indigenous level of hellenism, or one of active resurgence or deliberate reinvention of Greek culture in the third–fifth centuries AD. I would argue, on the basis of parallels with some parts of Italy, that this should be viewed as a case of active reinvention of culture, represented by evidence such as the Iallia Bassiana decree. Cultural change always includes a large measure of cultural choice by a population, or its most powerful members, and Roman Sicily is no exception. The choice of the Sicilian elite in the early empire was to romanise in many aspects of their civic life, but by the late empire, the cultural priorities had clearly shifed.

The real problem is not that this resurgence of hellenism happened, but why it took so long, and why Greek aspects of civic culture make so little impact in the first and second centuries AD. This move away from Greek culture (or at least ambivalence to it) means that the Sicilian elite was in many ways deliberately turning its back on the philhellenic discourse of the early/mid-empire, which many other Greek cities in both Italy and the eastern Mediterranean used as a means of enhancing civic status and of communicating with the Roman elite and with the emperor (Bowersock 1965; Bowie 1974; Spawforth and Walker 1985; Lomas 1993: 174–87; Swain 1996: 65–100). Even Hadrian, the arch-philhellene, who is named on coinage as '*restitutor Siciliae*'.[23] seems to have left relatively few traces in the epigraphic and archaeological record. Similarly, the vast number of honorific statues and inscriptions dedicated to emperors and their relatives indicate that there was serious investment in maintaining good relations with central power, but there was little attempt to mobilise the Greek culture and history of the island to useful effect, even in the era of the Panhellenion and the Second Sophistic (Spawforth and Walker 1985; Swain 1997: 65–100). It is possible that the extension of the Roman citizenship to Sicily, along with the rest of the empire, by Caracalla somehow rendered overt demonstrations of *Romanitas* unnecessary and allowed Sicily to revert to its underlying Greek identity, but this is not borne out by examples of enfranchisement elsewhere. Comparative evidence of both individual enfranchisement and other group enfranchisments suggest that a more usual response to the acquisition of citizenship was to stress Roman characteristics, whether in representations of individual identity or those of group identity.[24]

This anomalous pattern of behaviour may reflect the position of Sicily between Italy and the eastern Mediterranean, leaving the island isolated and not very strongly influenced by the pattern of either, but there is ample evidence of reciprocal contacts between Sicilian and Italian cities, and also epigraphic evidence for individual contacts with the eastern empire.[25] However, the phenomenon could also be a reflection of a strongly regional identity. The question of regionalism in Greek culture and the Greek world is increasingly being recognised as a powerful factor, and as already noted, Greek cities in Sicily and in Italy differ from each other, from the cities of the Greek mainland and Aegean, and from those of the Greek east in significant ways well before Roman period. Hence it should not be surprising that the cultural choices made by the Sicilians after the Roman conquest show a considerable amount of diversity, and that the ways in which the Sicilian elite interacted with Roman culture differed from the behaviour of elites on the Italian mainland. It is possible, although probably not the whole story, that the ambivalent cultural history of Roman Sicily reflects an on-going regional difference in sense of identity and ways of constructing this, and also the extent to which colonial identities were modified by isolation from the centre and interaction with non-Greek neighbours. Thus the complex pattern may reveal an underlying pattern of cultural differentiation between Italy and Sicily which predates the Roman conquest.[26] External sources also observe Sicilian identity as distinctive, even from a much earlier period of history. Authors as various as Thucydides and Cicero,[27] writing in very different contexts and for very different purposes, stress that Sicilian culture was somewhat separate from mainstream hellenism. At the moment, this field raises more questions than it provides coherent answers, but it opens up important areas for the study of Greek culture in the Roman world. Specifically, it highlights strikingly the way in which the cultural dynamics operating in Sicilian society were quite distinctive and differed from those of other parts of the Greek world.

# 13

# THE CHARM OF THE SIREN:

## the place of classical Sicily in historiography

*Giovanna Ceserani*

IN 1957, SICILIAN AUTHOR Giuseppe Tomas di Lampedusa, more famous for his novel *The Leopard*, wrote a short story entitled 'The Professor and the Siren' (Tomasi di Lampedusa: 1986b). Set in 1938, it is about a retired professor of classics in his seventies, originally from Sicily but living in Turin. He is the most illustrious hellenist of his times, having been honoured by being nominated as senator and by doctorates *honoris causa* around the world. His work is distinguished not only by infinite erudition but also by a lively, almost carnal, sense of classical antiquity. Besides his profound culture, the main characteristic of the Professor is a terrible misanthropy and misogyny: he refers to other human beings as 'you people' and shows immense disdain for them. The reason for both aspects of his personality is revealed to the reader in an episode from many years earlier which left an indelible mark on the Professor. One summer in his youth, as he was preparing to compete for a chair of Greek literature and was declaiming Greek verses in the sun and solitude along the shore of the sea near Augusta, he met a Siren. With her he discovered love and spoke Greek. She, with a smile that expressed nothing but itself and an almost divine delight in existence, dissipated and uprooted false beliefs by her mere immortal presence. After loving her the Professor could not love anything else except images of archaic Greek art, and least of all the ignorant mortal race of humans.

What is relevant to this chapter is not the character of the Professor, even if some have attempted an identification of him with the archaeologist Paolo Orsi, and even if it is true that the story would seem if not to do justice to the famous humanity of the archaeologist, then to offer a perfect answer to Momigliano, who wrote about Orsi: 'no one will ever be able to reveal the intimate inspiration concealed behind his marvellous and tireless activity' as explorer of prehistoric, Greek and Christian Sicily (Momigliano 1978: 131).[1] For this chapter the figure of the Siren is of more interest. She is characterised as somehow more than Greek: she is eternal, one of the pre-Olympic deities, expressing in herself a synthesis between bestiality and immortality that cannot be articulated:

> She was a beast but at the same instant also an Immortal, and it is a pity that no speech can express this synthesis continually, with such utter simplicity, as she expressed it in her own body ... She belonged to the fountainhead of all culture, of all wisdom, of all ethics, and could express this primogenial superiority of hers in terms of rugged beauty. 'I am immortal because in me every death meets, from that of the fish to that of Zeus.'
>
> (Lampedusa 1986b: 280)

After encountering the Siren the Professor thinks of the temples of Agrigentum as 'modern'; he can find comfort only in the images of archaic and early classical Greek art. The Siren has an eternal and therefore historically undefined quality. She has had a succession of mortal lovers, whom she describes as Greek, Sicilian and Arab. She had one with fair skin and red hair who could perhaps be a Norman. The Siren's historically undefined quality, combined with her multicultural succession of lovers, works very well as a symbol of the dominant model in the historiography of Sicily, which is the subject of this chapter.

In two essays on Sicilian historiography, Momigliano identifies this model as one which presents the history of the island as a series of invasions (Momigliano 1978, 1979). Foreign dominations follow each other – the Siculi, the Sicani, the Phoenicians, the Greeks, the Romans, the Vandals, the Goths, the Byzantines, the Saracens, the Normans, the Spaniards, the French, the Austrians all invade, dominate and leave. The consequence of this view, Momigliano further argues, is that the identity of the Sicilians themselves remains most elusive and undefined; 'Sicilianity' is presented as a quality which is characterised by its continuity through history, but which is actually defined only by the absence of identification with any of the invaders.

Momigliano identifies the origin of this historiographical model in the work of the Dominican friar Tommaso Fazello, who published *De rebus Siculis decades duo* in 1558. Momigliano sees the shadow of this work operating continuously throughout the centuries to today. I want to argue that this interpretation might fall victim to its own projection of continuity. His thesis – that the lack of definition of identity provides a constant framework within which histories of Sicily are written – requires refinement. This interpretation perpetuates a false image of a stable model of historiography running from Fazello to the present day. Models do not enjoy a life of their own to such a degree as to constitute authority capable of influencing interpretation over the course of time. The use of models is bound to be different in different historical contexts; the same must be true of their meaning, and probably the two change in interaction. The model of successive invasions was consciously challenged, for example, at the end of the eighteenth century by Enlightenment Sicilian scholars themselves. But my questioning goes beyond taking into account these challenges. The usage of the concept of identity has certainly changed significantly between the sixteenth century and the present day. This is also the case with history itself: what history is, the shape it should take, its role and its methodologies have undergone radical change over this time. The historiographical model of undefined representation of the Sicilian people through lack of identification with any of the invasions can be questioned through its own historicisation. This means examining its different meanings in the intersection of different concepts of identity and different developments in the ways of approaching and narrating the past.

Momigliano's focus is the classical past of Sicily, especially the Greek past of the island. This will be my main focus as well. Momigliano uses Fazello's model to account for the fact that 'before, during, and after the eighteenth century, the Sicilians refused to identify themselves with the Greeks' (Momigliano 1979: 145). I will argue that an historicisation of the model of continuity allows a deeper insight and accounts for a more complex relationship with the Sicilian Greek past. To this end I will first examine the model of Fazello's work in its own terms. Subsequently I will highlight the critique and problematisation of Fazello as a 'model' by the Sicilian Enlightenment at the end of the eighteenth century. I will then argue that Fazello reappeared as a valuable model in the nineteenth century, but this phenomenon must be read as a reappropriation of it in a very different cultural context and with very different purposes from its construction in the sixteenth century. This interpretation of the history of the model intersects intimately, in my exposition, with the history of classical scholarship. This means taking into account the methodologies and approaches developed by scholars for the study of the past and the position of classical Sicily in this picture. The result is an outline of the shift in the conceptualisation of Sicily from Fazello's work, focusing on Sicily for its own sake, to the pivotal role played by Sicily in the crucial times of the Grand Tour and the rediscovery of the Greeks, to a progress-ive marginalisation of Sicily as provincial Greece by classical scholarship since the early nineteenth century. Taking into account European develop-ments and the interaction between Sicilian antiquarians and foreign travellers, the eighteenth-century Sicilian relationship with the Greek past will appear more complex than a mere denial of identification. The story of Fazello's model thus provides not a lingering shadow but a narrative of use and reuse, shedding new light on the modern historiography on classical Sicily and its relationship to Sicilian identity.[2]

The work by Fazello, *De rebus Siculis decades duo*, is the first in which Sicily as a whole is the object of research, in contrast with the earlier works of local antiquarians. The first decade is dedicated to an historical topography of Sicily and the second to an account of the history of the island. Fazello writes in the introduction that when he sat down to this work his intention was solely to provide a description of the island, but history stemmed naturally from the research on geography. In his own words:

> In the course of my work I came across various topics of which I could foresee that, if I left them neglected, my entire description would be bare and useless. Therefore, having undertaken to complete my work with such care, without realising or wanting it, I slipped into history. Following this unexpected event I conceived a great desire to collect into a single bundle everything that has been handed down by memory about Sicily and its history; and I conceived a desire to compose a not unprofitable work of history, to which I did not neglect to dedicate all the free time that, in the last twenty years, I came almost to steal from my great and numerous occupations.
>
> (Fazello 1558: 1)

The topography provided by Fazello has been much admired subsequently. The Dutch geographer Cluverius in the seventeenth century and the others who tested it in the following centuries proved that it was, for the most part, very accurate. Moreover it has an added value today as evidence of information available in the sixteenth century and since lost. In order to inspect the sites that he was writing about, Fazello himself walked around the island four times, or so he claims in the preface. In this respect he was similar to what Alain Schnapp has characterised as typical of English antiquarianism in the sixteenth century, when William Camden initiated the British 'periegetic tradition' in exploring the antiquity of his country. Camden shaped the study of the past in the form of regional history, investigated through a combination of literary information and description of the landscape, and close observation of toponymic and numismatic sources. Schnapp sees the origin of Camden's antiquarianism in the influence of humanistic continental works: he defines Camden as the 'Flavio Biondo of the kingdom of England' (Schnapp 1996: 139). Flavio Biondo's works, *Roma Instaurata* and *Italia Illustrata*, were also the models for Fazello's project (Momigliano 1978: 115). Fazello describes his methodology and the almost sacral pride he takes in it:

> And so that it did not seem that I was putting forward hurried statements on questions of geography and chronology that rest on antiquity, I surveyed the whole of Sicily four times or more and investigated everything most carefully. Then I compared the details with the authors until I gained complete satisfaction in certain facts. With this diligence (not without merit) I claim to have recalled to life, as if I saved them from Hades, many towns and huge cities buried under ruins, brushwood and ploughed fields. So, like the legendary Asclepius I think I have recomposed so many dismembered Hippolytuses; namely the many cities and places I recalled to light and renewed knowledge of antiquity.
>
> (Fazello 1558: 1–2)

Selinus is the site in whose resurrection Fazello takes most pride (Fazello 1558: 146–9). In his times it was common opinion that the town of Mazara was the ancient Selinus, while the material remains of the actual Selinus were unidentified and called 'Terra di Pulci'. Fazello describes the view of the three temples standing on the coast, their magnificent construction and Doric style, which have no equal, he writes, in the whole of Europe. In the surrounding area, he continues, ruins are everywhere and one walks on foundations, structures and wrecks of houses. Fazello explains that he could not bring himself to believe that so great a town as those remains attested to could disappear without leaving any trace in any ancient source. Once in Mazara he sets out on the case. First, he investigates accurately the whole town, the walls, the buildings and the surrounding countryside, searching for traces of antiquity, and does not find any. Then, he asks the local notables on what material evidence of antiquity, or on the authority of which source, they claim that Mazara is the ancient Selinus; the only evidence they can put forward is their forefathers' statements. Finally, after three years of doubt, Fazello finds the solution. Reading into the late hours of the night, he comes across a passage in which Diodoros, writing about Hannibal in Sicily, mentions a site on the mouth of the river Mazara near Selinus. From this passage Fazello is able to conclude that modern Mazara is merely the heir of the small city on the river, and to restore Selinus to its ancient glory. A further proof of the identification of the magnificent ruins with ancient Selinus is the golden and silver coins found everywhere in the surroundings with the script 'selinontion' [sic].[3]

Apart from the extraordinary problem of the identification of Selinus, the use of material evidence is scarce in Fazello's topography. He works mainly by means of toponyms: he relates modern names, which have changed in the course of time, to ancient sites mentioned in the sources. This methodology is best revealed in one of the cases of mistaken identification. Fazello identifies three different Motyas, none of which is the actual settlement of Motya on the island of S. Pantaleo near Marsala. His error results from an assonance amongst modern names. Fazello recognises one Motya in the modern village of Motica in the southwest of Sicily on the basis of Pausanias 5.25.5 – 'at the headland of Sicily, that looks towards Libya and the south, called Pachynum, there stands the city of Motya, inhabited by Libyans and Phoenicians' (Fazello 1558: 114–16). He further connects the Thucydidean passage 6.2.6 – 'but when the Hellenes also began to come in by sea in large numbers, the Phoenicians left most of these places and settling together lived in Motya, Soloeis and Panormus' – with a Motya on an island in the bay of Mondello (no one has been able to explain this association) (Fazello 1558: 153). Finally Fazello writes of a Motya in the hinterland of Agrigentum, probably misidentifying a small village in the area called Motion (Fazello 1558: 231).

The limited nature of the interest and the understanding of material remains is further illustrated by some of the names we still use today for Sicilian antiquities. The Temple of Concordia in Agrigentum was so named by Fazello. He recounts that the inhabitants of Agrigentum say the temple was constructed by the Lilybaeans after being defeated in a war. The proof for this, Fazello writes, is an inscription displayed in the town square, which reads: 'sacred to the Concordia of the Agrigentini; the republic of the Lilybaeans, for dedication by the proconsul M. Atterius Candidus and the propraetor L. Cornelius Quintus'.[4] Fazello does not even explain the supposed relationship between the inscription and the temple, for which there seems to be no independent justification.

The second decade is the one dedicated to history. As the story runs from the Cyclopes, first inhabitants of the island, to the reign of Charles V, it is here that the model of successive invasions for the history of Sicily discussed above is deployed. But much as it is true that the structure of Fazello's narrative follows the line of one invasion after the other, one kingdom after the other, I do not think that this structure reflects Fazello's failure to define Sicilian identity as such. His historiography must be understood in terms of its historical context. Just as the practice of historiography has altered since, so the conceptualisation of identity has also changed enormously.

Fazello's definition and defence of his historical work are deeply different from what we would expect today. He defines history as 'the light of truth' and 'magistra vitae' and preoccupies himself with defending the theological dignity of such aims (Fazello 1558: 2). The fathers of the church, from Eusebius to Orosius, have written historical works, proving, Fazello argues, that history is no danger to Christian religion or theology. Fazello is also preoccupied with defending himself from the critique of exploiting the work of others and not being original. However, he claims, evidence for such ancient events cannot be guessed by conjecture, but only learned from the ancient authors. Moreover, his work has the merit of having grouped together and ordered information on Sicily which otherwise would have to be collected from more than 100 different authors.

Today Fazello's work is mostly appreciated as the first history of Sicily, in comparison with previous chronicles. The latter were 'lacking any organic structure, the events being mechanically lined up one after the other, void of any message' (Ganci 1992: 11). Fazello, on the other hand, displays 'an attempt at a global interpretation, integrating Sicily into the context of Mediterranean history' (Ganci 1992: 11). At the same time scholars regret the monotonous structure of this history and blame it on the influence on Fazello of humanist and classical historiography:

'History is reduced to an uninterrupted series of wars, power struggles, sieges, battles, ambushes and consequent devastations and carnage' (De Rosalia 1992: 21).

Surely Fazello's history needs to be historicised as very different from the one dominant since the end of the eighteenth century. From such a position one can gain a new insight into the work of Fazello and formulate differently the problem of the lack of definition of Sicilian identity. Identities of peoples have been a main concern in the narrative of history as it was shaped at the beginning of the modern age in the late eighteenth century. Fazello was writing in a very different time, an age in which the vision of the world was informed by religious community and dynastic realms. To quote Benedict Anderson:

> these days it is -perhaps difficult to put oneself empathetically into a world in which the dynastic realm appeared for most men as the only imaginable 'political' system. For in fundamental ways 'serious' monarchy lies transverse to all modern conceptions of political life. Kingship organises everything around a high centre. Its legitimacy derives from divinity, not from populations, who, after all, are subjects, not citizens.
>
> (Anderson 1991: 19)

Peoples – and so the Sicilian people – were simply not historical characters in Fazello's day. He devotes a chapter to the customs of the Sicilians – *de moribus Siculorum* (Fazello 1558: 28–9). Here he quotes *topoi* from the ancient authors: the Sicilians are very good as orators, storytellers and deceivers (Cicero, Apuleius, Ausonius, Plautus); they invented bucolic poetry (Aristotle), the clock (Pliny the Elder) and so on. The only qualification added by Fazello to this list is that the Sicilians are 'most loyal to their kings'. This is as far as characterisation of Sicilians by Fazello can go. He claims to be writing out of compassion for his homeland – *commiseratio patriae* – but it certainly is a very different country from modern homelands. And the processes of identification seem accordingly to be following very different paths.

Identity as identity of people is a modern concern. Anderson links it with the rise of nationalism at the end of the eighteenth century. The seventeenth and eighteenth were the centuries of dynastic crisis, and by the end, Anderson argues, monarchies had to reshape their authority and image around the concept of the nation-state. The American and French revolutions did not put an end to monarchic states but transformed subjects into citizens: consensus had to be reorganised on this new basis (Anderson 1991: 21–2). Definitions of 'nation' and 'peoples' became major issues of discussions in the eighteenth-century debates of the Enlightenment.

The dynastic wars of the eighteenth century set a record of sudden change in dominion quite extraordinary even for Sicily, the land of successive invasions. Sicily, which had been under Spain since the fifteenth century, was under the control of Savoy (1713–18), Spain again (1718–20), Austria (1720) and finally the Bourbons, as part of the independent Kingdom of the Two Sicilies, with its capital in Naples, from 1735. These revolutions in government provided an exciting time of reforms, as the issue was to transform Sicily from a feudal land of aristocratic privileges to a part of a modern state. The Sicilian cultural history of the eighteenth century has been explored only in recent decades. This research has revealed a sophisticated Enlightenment culture engaged in the discussion of the reform of Sicilian political and economic structures (Giarrizzo 1992). The concept of 'nation' was also discussed by the Enlightenment Sicilians, and this gave rise to a new interest in the past. Fazello's history was discussed and constituted as a 'model' in terms of continuity. Interpretations of Fazello had an immediate political tinge. His history was republished and updated to include events up to 1750 (Fazello 1753). Continuity through dynastic change implied the legitimisation of inalienable baronial rights. Conservative members of the aristocracy defended the continuity model. More progressive minds criticised it and invoked new kinds of history to break the continuity (Giarrizzo 1992: 13, 18–27, 33, 98, 147–54; Momigliano 1978: 127–8).

The second half of the eighteenth century was also a crucial time for the development of the study of the ancient past. The origins of the discrete disciplines of 'archaeology' and 'ancient history' can be traced back to then. But in the eighteenth century there were no ancient historians and archaeologists: the study of the past was the prerogative of the antiquarians. Scholars of the history of the disciplines have stressed more and more the central role of the antiquarians in the formative process of both archaeology and ancient history. The antiquarians had declared their preference for material over written evidence since the seventeenth century, as in the work of Jacques Spon and Ezechiel Spanheim, founders of numismatics and epigraphy.[5] Because of their focus on evidence different from the literary sources, they created the need for new histories (Momigliano 1966: 9). Schnapp highlights further contributions made by the eighteenth-century antiquarians to the study of the past by means of objects. He stresses the importance for the development of archaeology of the systematic antiquarian projects of the Enlightenment period. Then the description of objects became the basis for the elaboration of the principle of typology; and types, revealed by shared traits, hinted at new histories concealed within the objects themselves. The French Comte de Caylus, in his *Recueil des Antiquités Egyptiennes, Romaines, Grecques et Gauloises* (1752), was able to organise objects in series and types, to identify which culture produced them and to establish a recognisable 'character of a nation' (Schnapp 1996: 238–42). The German Winckelmann (1968) constructed a stylistic chronology through typology: his *History of Ancient Art* of 1764 replaced previous iconographic commentaries on single objects.

These methodological novelties were accompanied by a change in taste: it was the age of the Grand Tour. Sicily can be seen as a privileged case study of this period. It was an essential destination of the tour. Travellers would sail from Naples after having seen the temples at Paestum. Once on the island they would be accompanied by various nobles and antiquarians acting as hosts and guides. Momigliano claims that the Sicilian antiquarians' attitude to the classical past in the eighteenth century was lukewarm: while the travellers went to look for the Greeks, they kept considering Sicilian history in terms of successive invasions (Momigliano 1978: 121–2). I would like to offer a different reading of their attitude by examining their works in the context of European antiquarian studies. The prince of Biscari (1719–1786) from Catania and the prince of Torremuzza (1727–1792) from Palermo are the most famous antiquarians of Sicily in the eighteenth century, recognised officially as such with their nomination as Royal Superintendents of Antiquities in 1779. Their works addressed explicitly the antiquarians of Europe, and furthermore they became characters in the works of the travellers they acted as host to. I will examine some of the writings of the princes and the works of Philippe D'Orville and the Baron Riedesel. The first travelled to Sicily as early as 1725, but his *Sicula* was published only posthumously in 1764; Riedesel travelled in 1766 and met both Torremuzza and Biscari. Reading the two sides of the story as a dialogue allows us to put the question of identity differently and casts new light on the relationship of the Sicilians with their classical past.

The prince of Torremuzza left a detailed account of his activities, both as an active participant in Sicilian political life and as an antiquarian, in his autobiography (which was published posthumously by Giovanni D'Angelo in 1804). The self-fashioned image put forward in this work is very revealing of the way Torremuzza perceived the study of antiquity in his times and of his own position in this picture. He tells of how his interest in antiquity originated by chance during the years of his youth, which he spent on his family lands around Tusa. One of his farmers found in the fields a vase full of copper coins and brought it over to the young Torremuzza, who then began to take an interest in antiquity. On the lands of the Torremuzza family lay the remains of the ancient town of Halaesa. The first works written by Torremuzza were a dissertation on a marble statue of a Roman praetor from Halaesa and a history of this town (Torremuzza 1745). In the autobiography Torremuzza discusses these works critically. He writes that they display 'every kind of erudition, and of acquaintance with the practice of Roman history; the footnotes which illustrate the subject-matter are longer than the subject-matter itself' (Torremuzza 1804: 14). This judgement is part of the trajectory that Torremuzza presents of his own apprenticeship and of his shift from mere erudition to antiquarianism. He is introduced to antiquarianism when he moves back to Palermo and joins the academy of 'Buon Gusto'. He also then meets the prince of Biscari – 'gifted with the deepest taste [*gusto*] and love for the study and specifically that of Greek and Roman antiquities' (Torremuzza 1804: 21); this was the beginning of their lifelong friendship. The shift from erudition to antiquarianism means in Torremuzza's account moving from an exclusively literary-based interest in the past – the piecing together of passages of history – to the appreciation and knowledge of ancient monuments.

Torremuzza became the most prominent eighteenth-century Sicilian expert on ancient coins and inscriptions. He first published a collection of the inscriptions of Palermo and then proceeded to publish the collections of all Sicilian inscriptions and coins (Torremuzza 1769, 1784). About his first epigraphic work he writes that it displays 'pedantry and erudition, at places not even strictly related to the subject-matter, making use of any opportunity to address the major secrets of antiquarianism'; 'this was not by chance', he continues, 'my aim was to inform the foreign *letterati* that the taste for antiquarianism had taken root in Sicily and that the most modern books on its various branches were readily known' (Torremuzza 1804: 28). The preoccupation with European antiquarian scholars is a constant in Torremuzza's autobiography. He reports names and provenances of the new *letterati* friends with whom he enters into correspondence through the years. He reports proudly the reviews in European journals of his works, and his admission to the Paris Academy and the London Society of Antiquaries (Torremuzza 1804: 36).

The works of Torremuzza do not represent major novelties in terms of methodologies and approach. He proceeds in the tradition of numismatics and epigraphy well established since the seventeenth century by Spon and others. His works do not carry the innovative drive of Caylus' or Winckelmann's. But it is by reading Torremuzza's works in the larger context of European scholarship that their characteristics can be best highlighted. This insight, furthermore, allows a better understanding of the eighteenth-century Sicilian antiquarians' attitudes towards the classical past and the issues of Sicilian identity. In order to address these questions the most useful text is an article published in 1764: 'Idea of a "treasury" to contain a general collection of all antiquities of Sicily, proposed by Gabriele Lancillotto Castello Principe di Torremuzza from Palermo to the Sicilian *letterati*, lovers of ancient memories of the homeland' (Torremuzza 1764: 181).

The project outlined by Torremuzza is a celebration of antiquarianism as the science of monuments in contrast to erudition as the collection of written sources. If ancient history is valued, he writes, monuments, which help to clarify it even better, should be valued even more. In the last two centuries, he continues, Sicilian writers have worked to give its ancient history a systematic order, but they, 'as if satisfied with collecting all the passages scattered here and there in the works of the ancient Greek and Latin historians, took no consideration of the monuments which then existed, as if history could not gain any advantage from them' (Torremuzza 1764: 183–4). Torremuzza wants not a history but a collection – *raccolta* – of the ancient Sicilian monuments dating from before the Arab conquest, organised with proper method and ordered in various classes. This *archeographia* is classified in eight classes: 1. *Architectographia*: plans of towns and buildings, including temples, baths, theatres, naumachias, arches, pyramids, aqueducts, tombs. 2. *Iconographia*: drawings of statues, in marble or metal, Greek or Roman, found in Sicily; ones originally from Sicily but taken abroad are also included. 3. *Toreumatographia*: drawings of sculpted marbles or bronzes, reliefs, sarcophagi, urns, stone or metal vases. 4. *Inscriptions*: including those which are now abroad. 5. *Numismatics*. 6. *Glyptographia*: gems, cameos and stones which are in museums or in the collections of aristocratic families. 7. *Painted pottery*: Torremuzza explains that there are three different kinds of this. Some pieces resemble Egyptian workmanship and are attributed to the Phoenicians or the Carthaginians; others are of Greek taste, falsely thought to be Etruscan, and must be attributed to the Greeks; finally the others, unrefined and rough, are attributed to the Romans. 8. *Drawings of all other pieces of antiquity*: domestic implements, arms, sacrificial instruments, weights, measures.

In support of this project Torremuzza advocates the authority of similar works, such as that of Caylus. He quotes also the Academy of Herculaneum, engaged in the illustration of the treasures from the Herculaneum excavation. He concludes that 'it is necessary to form a society, to have the king as patron in order to provide the means which private individuals cannot meet. He is the same king who wants the treasure of Herculaneum illustrated!' (Torremuzza 1764: 196).

The 'treasury' envisaged by Torremuzza was never realised, apart from classes 4 and 5 which materialised in his works on inscriptions and coins. But a comparison of Torremuzza's idea with that of Caylus, which is echoed in the title *raccolta*, is appropriate. One main difference is the extension of the area of provenance envisaged by the two works. Caylus includes Egyptian, Greek, Roman and Gaelic antiquities; Torremuzza limits his collection solely to objects from Sicily. This difference goes beyond parochial interests. It introduces a concept of provenance and context which is absent from Caylus. Moreover, it introduces issues of ownership of the past which are still relevant today and which are specifically interesting for questions of identity. Schnapp (1996: 240) has underlined as novel in Caylus the clear expression of the primacy of knowledge over the desire to possess: 'my taste for the arts has not led to any desire for possession ... Antiquities are there for the extension of knowledge' (Caylus 1752: I–II). Caylus introduces, from volume IV of his *Recueil*, antiquities from Gaul. But his main interest lies with antiquities from Mediterranean civilisations, which he buys from all over Europe to publish for the benefit of scholarship. Torremuzza is concerned with the objects found in Sicily and, moreover, with tracking down the ones that have been brought or sold abroad.

Torremuzza failed to have his project sponsored by the king of Naples. Still, the expenses of his work on coins were subsidised by the viceroy of Sicily, as he relates extensively in the autobiography (Torremuzza 1804: 43). The government realised the value of the island's past, and this realisation was enhanced by the attention paid by foreigners. In 1779 Torremuzza and Biscari were appointed superintendents for the preservation of the ancient monuments of Sicily. Torremuzza was busy cataloguing these and restoring the temples of Agrigentum and Segesta. About this appointment, Torremuzza writes that the interest of foreigners who were prepared to travel to Sicily to visit them testified to the value of the ancient ruins scattered around Sicily (Torremuzza 1804: 63–4).

The prince of Torremuzza held other public offices. He was responsible for the reorganisation of the University of Palermo as well as being deputy of trade (Torremuzza 1804: 53). Both he and the prince of Biscari moved in those Enlightenment circles responsible for the political and economic debates which pervaded Sicily at the time.[6] In the provincial land of Sicily, where the study of antiquity and of philosophy was not indigenous but derived from Paris, the opposition between antiquarian and *philosophe*, for which the Comte de Caylus was ridiculed in Paris by Diderot and D'Alembert, was exploded. The best example of this peculiar situation is the election of Torremuzza the numismatist as 'master of the mint' in 1774. In the pages of his autobiography he describes how, in order to accomplish his task, he learned about the welding of metal and the principles of economics and commerce to define the values of the coins (Torremuzza 1804: 51, 61–2, 71–2). He then wrote a history of Sicilian minting, attempting to establish values for coins from ancient to modern times (Torremuzza 1773).

A contextualisation of Torremuzza's work allows a reformulation of Momigliano's judgement on the antiquarians' attitude to the past. There is more to it than 'suggestions, rivalries and revisions provoked by foreign interests' (Momigliano 1978: 128). The interaction operates at a deeper level, and at stake are central issues of identity and approaches to the past.

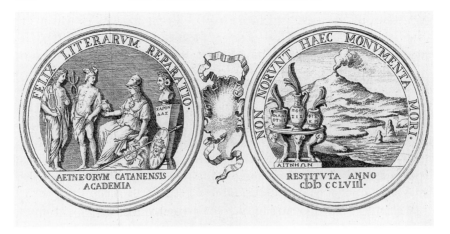

*Fig. 13.1* Outline drawing of the medallion commissioned by Biscari from
Padre Paciaudi to celebrate the foundation of the Accademia degli Etnei
(Biscari 1787: 54)

In the figure and works of Biscari these questions are revealed even more
explicitly.

The prince of Biscari is most famous for the museum that he set up
in 1752 in Catania (see Manganaro 1968). The prince succeeded in
competing with the major museums of the age; Riedesel wrote: 'the
museum is one of the most complete and beautiful in Italy, and perhaps
(without exaggeration) in the world' (Riedesel 1772: 96). It displayed
antiquities discovered and excavated in the area of Catania and others
acquired by the prince elsewhere. The prince spent maybe too much of the
family money travelling around Italy visiting museums and buying pieces
in Rome, Florence and Naples. The core of the collection was classical
antiquities, but the museum included two rooms on medieval objects,
and an entire section was devoted to the natural sciences. In this way the
museum encapsulates aspects of the Enlightenment culture to which the
prince belonged.

The same conception of knowledge bringing together sciences and arts
governed the Accademia degli Etnei, founded by the prince in 1744. The
medallion of the academy displays an iconography put together explicitly
to express the aim and nature of the enterprise (see fig. 13.1). A detailed
explanation of this iconography is in the guide to the museum written by
Biscari in 1787 (Biscari 1787: 40–53). On the recto there are three figures.
Athena, symbolising knowledge and wisdom, is seated on a rock on which
the Trinacrian symbol of Sicily is depicted. Behind Athena is a bust of the
Catanian hero, the legislator Charondas. Standing in front of Athena are
Hermes, patron of the natural sciences, and Apollo, patron of the arts:
the two fields in which the Academy is interested. On the verso in the

foreground three vases stand on a tripod. The inspiration comes from the prize vases in ancient Greek competitions: from the vases spring the palms of victory; on them the names of the three areas of competition of the academy – ΠΑΛΑΙΟΤΗ (antiquities), ΠΟΙΗΣΙΣ (poetry), and ΦΥΣΙΚΗ (physics) – are inscribed. The model for this image, including Mount Etna in the background, is from a coin of Caracalla. The legend is a hemistich from Martial spelling out the immortality of the academy: *non norunt haec monumenta mori*. The legend on the recto is a variation on a late imperial one: *felix literarum reparatio* instead of *felix temporum reparatio*. In the medallion, through the use of classical iconography, antiquity itself is promoted to the status of a *techne* such as physics or poetry: it is the formation of the study of antiquity conceived as a specific methodology.[7]

The prince of Biscari was a man of large means and of energetic initiative. He founded the academy and the museum, and also constructed a new bridge and an artificial lake on the lava beach of Catania. In the wake of the enthusiasm for the excavation of Pompeii and Herculaneum, he sought and obtained permission from the senate of Catania to excavate in the town at his own expense. Some identified this as the origin of 'scientific archaeology' in Sicily (Pace 1935: 28). This expression is ambiguous and not self-evident in its meaning. In any account it would be difficult to justify its use given the methodology applied by Biscari: the prince had no interest in stratigraphy whatsoever and just emptied the soil to reveal the monuments. Still, the impact of the emergence from the soil of some features of the ancient monuments of Catania was extremely significant for the time. Moreover, they brought frictions in the interaction of the prince with the travellers, revealing the operation of deeper tensions.

Biscari excavated the theatre, the amphitheatre, the baths and the Odeon. He did not publish these excavations, but he writes of them in other works. During the excavations at the amphitheatre he found a torso and an inscription that he published in 1771 (Biscari 1771). This publication is the occasion for a critique of D'Orville's account of Catania's monuments and the local antiquarians. The prince opens with an invocation, wishing that D'Orville had travelled in these days when so many new material discoveries would have dissuaded him of his doubts about local scholarship. D'Orville accused the local antiquarians – who in the seventeenth and early eighteenth centuries described Catania and wrote of its baths, theatre and amphitheatre as if they could see them – of credulity, parochial interest and lack of specialised scholarship. 'Moreover they show some ruins almost completely vanished, as if they were a theatre or an amphitheatre: but they report this most uncertainly and no one reinforced the argument that there was in Catania a theatre or an amphitheatre with the proof of a single piece of evidence' (D'Orville 1764: 216). D'Orville does not question the ancient presence in Catania of a theatre or amphitheatre but ridicules the attitude of the local antiquarians, who point to meaningless rocks scattered around and do not know their classics, while he is able to prove the presence of the remains through ancient written sources. Biscari is happy to prove D'Orville wrong with his excavations, which reveal the structures of the theatre and other buildings, and which can now be shown to the travellers who come to Catania.

In 1781 Biscari published *Viaggio per tutte le antichità di Sicilia*. Just as the travellers wrote up their journals in the form of travel guides, Biscari provided one written by a native. It was very successful: Goethe travelled with Biscari and Riedesel as guide books. Riedesel was one of the travellers whom Biscari had shown round his excavations in Catania. Describing the baths in Catania for his readers, Biscari remembers the visit he paid with Riedesel and what he read about it in the latter's travel book:

> correctly Riedesel doubts in his description of the travel in Sicily that this construction could really be the Baths; it seemed to him too big for a private one and too small for a public one; if he had told me at the time I could have shown him how this structure which I discovered was only a portion of the ancient one.

> (Biscari 1781: 33)

Biscari himself was a character in Riedesel, who, apart from expressing doubts on Biscari's excavations, also devoted some pages to an idealised portrait of him, highlighting his virtues as a host.

This unusual kind of intertextuality, in which the authors are also characters in each other's writings, embodies the approach I want to take to the antiquarians' attitude to the past: the two sides must be read in relation one to the other as a dialogue. What Momigliano sees as the Sicilians' lukewarm attitude to the Greek past is a reaction to the travellers' search for the Greeks, conducted partially at the Sicilians' expense. Certainly the travellers appreciated Sicilian Greekness. About the Sicilians Riedesel writes:

> Now and then you meet with some similar strokes in the characters of the modern inhabitants of Sicily, to that of its ancient natives ...: there are many Greek lineaments in persons of both sexes, and you find many beauties. The great affection of the natives to strangers, and their hospitality, is another remnant of the Greek manners. Like the Greek cities of old, each town in Sicily cherishes a desire of being more ancient, greater or more famous then the rest.

> (Riedesel 1772: 146–7)

But he qualifies this statement, noting that 'the many revolutions in the form of government and the change of masters have almost obliterated the resemblance' (Riedesel 1772: 146). This distinction between ancient and modern is made clear when he climbs Etna; once on top, he writes:

> Here I had the opportunity of pitying the wretched situation of modern Sicily, in comparison with what it was in former ages; many towns and different nations are destroyed, immense riches are dissipated; many spacious ports are without any ships for want of trade, and many people want bread, whilst the nobility and the monks are in possession of all the lands!
>
> (Riedesel 1772: 177)[8]

In Riedesel's writings the interest lies exclusively with the Greek past of the island. He shows a profound disdain for the baroque architecture of the time, the same architectural style in which the city of Catania, completely destroyed by the eruption of 1669 and the earthquake of 1693, was being reconstructed at the time.

In the context of a larger picture, the antiquarians' attitude to the Greek classical past appears in a new light. The claim to standards of scholarship put forward by Torremuzza, his mentioning of the Sicilian monuments taken abroad, and Biscari's notion of a better acquaintance with the monuments he excavated himself are all signs of an attempt to claim a past which is otherwise appropriated by the travellers. Against the discourse of identification with the Sicilian Greekness developed by the travellers, Sicilian antiquarians opposed an idea of ownership of the classical past. In order to be entitled to their own past they grounded this idea of ownership in the display of a more accurate knowledge of the remains, and pursued it by claiming a confident command of the new scholarship on antiquity. At the end of the eighteenth century, therefore, it was not the lingering presence of the supposed model of Fazello which prevented the identification of the Sicilians with the Greeks. Just as Fazello's history was being critically discussed in contemporary political debates, the antiquarians were busy confronting the travellers' interpretation of Sicilian identity as a fossil from which to retrieve the traces of the great Greek past.

The attitude to Sicilian Greekness displayed by Riedesel was part of a larger European picture in which the perception of Greek antiquity was changing dramatically. His travel book is written in the form of letters to Winckelmann. This sets him at the forefront of the origin of philhellenism. In his history of Greek art Winckelmann took stylistic analysis a step further than Caylus. Winckelmann did more than explain a culture by its material objects: stylistic analysis was not only a technical device to him, but became the 'key to the understanding of an aesthetic', and his interpretation of Greek art became the 'bible of Neo-classicism' (Schnapp

1996: 258). According to Winckelmann the Greeks had attained perfection in art: its natural simplicity expressed its sublime quality. This view offered the ground for the rise of philhellenism as the phenomenon of idealisation of the Greeks. Winckelmann's work provided the basis for a perception of ancient Greece as a 'metahistorical concept, with the Hellenes themselves less and less subject to normal canons of analysis' (Morris 1994: 18). In Riedesel's recognition of Greek traits amongst the Sicilians is captured one of the lines of the idealisation of the Greeks as the ancestors of European culture. Winckelman's contribution was to see ancient Greece as the 'childhood of Europe': through the appreciation of Greek art one could return to original, natural simplicity, and the Greeks became the source from which all European culture had originated (Morris 1994: 17).

Sicily played a major role in the rediscovery of the Greeks: people travelled to Sicily and illustrated its monuments before travelling to Greece. But by the time the process of idealisation of the Greeks was completed, Sicily found itself marginalised. This outcome is a result of the shape the process of idealisation itself was to take. In an age of nationalism the Greeks became the 'ideal nation'. The major works of ancient Greek history of the nineteenth century must be understood in this light. The history of the Greeks became the one on which the models of history as narrative of peoples and nations were experimented with most. Ancient Greek history was interpreted in terms of nationality: the primary model for interpretation was that of a people striving for unification (Walbank 1951). Moreover, as national traditions of scholarship were established each European nation found its own way back to the Greeks (Ampolo 1997: 77). The Greeks of the colonies, such as Sicily, did not fit well this national paradigm and were soon approached in terms of provincial history and culture. This is above all clear in the approaches to material remains, as can be seen in the interpretation of their artistic developments.

The Vitruvian canon for classical architecture was challenged on the basis of the Greek temples of Sicily and south Italy. Winckelmann identified the essence of Greekness – its sublime simplicity – in front of the temples of Paestum. It was on the basis of this aesthetic judgement that he refuted the Vitruvian canon and gave birth to a history of art which put the monuments before the text. But in his history of Greek art a new canon was formed: Attic classical architecture was taken as the measure of all Greek architecture. The temples of Paestum and Sicily, which had been the origin of the Doric revival and had provoked the revision of Vitruvius in the first place, ended up marginalised because of their differences or divergences from this new canon: 'their peculiarities of structure seemed to be guided by such unprecedented liberties, in the sense of deviations

from the canon', as to position them out of the main road of development
of Greek art (Settis 1990: 141).

Over the course of the nineteenth century the temples of Sicily shifted
further and further towards the periphery of the Greek world.[9] This
passage from a standard early twentieth-century textbook is an example:

> as we proceed westwards among the colonies we find even more emphasis
> on the tendency towards ostentation, accompanied however by a certain
> amount of provincialism or 'cultural lag' and also, by barbaric distortions
> resulting from the intermixture not only of colonists of various origins but
> also of native taste.

> (Dinsmoor 1927: 75)

But Fazello offered the possibility of a response to such approaches
to Sicilian classical antiquity. The history of successive invasions was
reappropriated to find an identity for the Sicilian people: this identity was
defined by the absence of identification with any of the invasions – it was
primordial, inherently native.

This process of identification culminates in the works of the Sicilian
archaeologist Biagio Pace in the early twentieth century. He resents
deeply the view of Sicilian art as a pure reflection of one Greek school or
the other, be it Doric, Peloponnesian or Attic. He argues instead for the
autonomy of Sicilian developments: to explain the character of Greek art
in Sicily it must be first severed from mainland Greece. In doing this he
argues for a continuity of Sicilian histories and peculiarities and so for an
ever reaffirmed Sicilianity. The Sicilian artistic tradition is characterised,
according to him, by an 'undeniable fundamental unity': this is the
'intimate genius of the basic stock which reappears indestructible above
the levelling of the various civilisations that came about' (Pace 1935: x,
94). This is the reappropriation of the Fazellian model, reconstituted in
terms of the nineteenth-century view of history of peoples and ethnicities.

I have argued that the continuity model of Sicilian historiography has
itself had a discontinous history. The issue is not a denial of aspects of
continuity in Sicilian material culture, but a historicisation and problematisation of the processes by which, on the basis of Sicilian monuments
and history, Sicilian identities have been constructed. The processes vary
through time according to different conceptions of identity in different
historical contexts, responding to different interests, following different
methodologies (Leighton 1996a: 11).

Sicilian material culture displays traits of continuity which strike the
archaeologist despite all the invasions of antiquity: 'the veneration of the
dead, the perpetuation of the simple Sicilian house, and most characteristic of all, sitting on the floor or on a low bench to eat from a
conveniently elevated pedestal bowl' (Holloway 1998: 627). But it is for
the archaeologists and the historians to explore the construction of an

identity for the Sicilian peoples, and there are various ways into it, as I have shown.

Tomasi di Lampedusa provides a further illustration of what I mean by the tension between a notion of continuity in Sicilian history, despite the various invasions, and its usage in the construction of an identity of the Sicilian people. In a crucial passage of *The Leopard*, the prince of Salina declines the offer of the envoy of the new Italian kingdom of Savoy to pursue a political career in the Senate, now that 'Sicily is no longer a conquered land, but a free part of a free State' (Tomasi di Lampedusa 1986a: 142). The passage is striking because of the *topos* of Sicilian 'indolence'. As the prince says: 'in Sicily it does not matter about doing things well or badly; the sin which we Sicilians never forgive is that of "doing" at all'. The Sicilians are worn out, the prince continues:

> for over twenty-five centuries we've been bearing the weight of superb and heterogeneous civilisations, all from outside, none made by ourselves, none that we could call our own. We're as white as you are, Chevalley, and as the queen of England; and yet for two thousands five hundred years we've been a colony.
>
> (Tomasi di Lampedusa 1986a: 142)

In this literary representation the process of construction of a historical identity clearly surfaces: it works by conflating the endless series of centuries and the very specific language of modern colonialism and imperialism.

Having argued against an interpretation of Fazello's model in terms of the 'identity of peoples', I would like to conclude by attempting an explanation for its powerful influence. The charm of the Siren, the appeal of the continuity model itself, poses the question: how could/can so persistent an idea of national identity be read in the Sicilian past and in works like that of Fazello? The beginnings of an answer can be found again in Anderson's interpretation of nationalism. The dynastic realm is defined not only in terms of divine legitimacy and subjects in the place of citizens:

> in the older imagining, where states were defined by centres, borders were porous and indistinct, and hence sovereignties faded imperceptibly into one another. Hence paradoxically enough, the ease with which pre-modern empires and kingdoms were able to sustain their rule over immensely heterogeneous, and often not even contiguous, populations for long periods of time.
>
> (Anderson 1991: 19)

This heterogeneity was particularly marked at the time of Fazello: Philip II, to whom he dedicates his history, was king not just of Sicily but of so many other countries that the sun was said never to set on his empire.

But in another way Sicily presents an exception. Its boundaries are not porous or indistinct at all; on the contrary, they are as sharp as they can be. They embody the perfect natural boundaries sought after by modern nation-states in the age of nationalism. Moses Finley started his book on the history of Sicily with a simple prosaic statement: 'Sicily is an island' (Finley 1968: 3). Here perhaps lies also the explanation of why Fazello's work was read as a national history – and the secret of the model's longevity.

# NOTES

## 3 INDIGENOUS SOCIETY BETWEEN THE NINTH AND SIXTH CENTURIES BC

My thanks to all the conference participants for useful discussions and to Rosa Maria Albanese Procelli, Tamar Hodos, Thomas Harrison and the editors for comments on this chapter.

1. The term 'protoarcaico' is sometimes used by Italian archaeologists for the early colonial period in Sicily, prior to 600 BC, although this is not used in Greece, where the equivalent would be Late Geometric/Orientalising.

2. This question obviously merits more detailed discussion than has yet been forthcoming, and further debate may be anticipated (e.g. Leighton 2000).

3. It is increasingly clear that northeastern Sicily and Calabria shared similar cultural patterns in most prehistoric periods and, therefore, the close similarities between these regions in the late Bronze Age no longer represent an entirely new phenomenon, as was once assumed.

4. For example: in glass-working (although not unknown locally in the Italian late Bronze Age); possibly a slightly greater use of iron (although it was already certainly produced in Italy); the finesse of some painted pottery; and some aspects of jewellery manufacture (gold and silver), which seem more advanced in the Aegean world.

5. Thucydides (6.1–4) is the main source, with additional information from various other authors, such as Polyaenus (5.5), discussed in most general works on Greek colonisation since Dunbabin (1948).

6. The Fusco burials require study afresh with this question in mind. Several authors have noted non-Greek (and non-Corinthian) practices and artefacts in certain tombs, such as those with multiple depositions and bronze ornaments (not only fibulae) of indigenous type (e.g. Albanese Procelli 1997b: 518–20; Leighton 1999: 234–6). Despite the difficulty of identifying local people (women?) in colonial burial grounds with confidence (Hodos 1999 is too dismissive; but Shepherd 1999 is more circumspect), the contrasts with homeland practices are significant and could even suggest a degree of acculturation in reverse (Greek colonists 'going native'). Not surprisingly, later Greek historians are of no help on the subject: barbarian women would hardly merit attention in the mind of Thucydides. And yet the homeland snobberies which surface in the speech of Alcibiades to the Athenians in support of the Sicilian expedition, when he contemptuously predicts a lack of cohesive opposition from Sicilian colonies due in part to the heterogeneous composition of their inhabitants, is perhaps revealing (*ochlois te gar xumeiktois poluandrousin*; Thuc. 6.17.2–3).

7. Another coastal site with Mycenaean pottery and possibly analogous structures is coming to light at Cannatello (Fiorentini 1993–4).

8. The term '*magazzino*' or storage-house may not be appropriate for the former. The hearth, spindle-whorls, millstones and good-quality local pottery, as well as imports (Greek amphorae) and storage-jars, are not so different from the spectrum of finds and

activities represented in early Iron Age houses, for example at Morgantina, which can contain considerable quantities of pottery. This is perhaps evidence of a general improvement in the standard of living in the early Iron Age. As regards the long apsidal structure, Spigo (1986: 11) notes some generic parallels in Iron Age Greece and early colonial contexts in the western Mediterranean, and suggests a conscious adoption of a Greek model. However, the simplicity of the design casts doubt on the significance of these analogies, which could reflect no more than rather diffuse convergences. In fact, late Bronze-early Iron Age rectangular and apsidal structures in Sicily provide a more direct local model for the San Mauro structure; a possibility acknowledged by Spigo (1986: 13). The idea of discontinuity at Monte San Mauro can therefore be challenged.

9. The only comment in the description of the Ortygia dwellings with which I would disagree is that they are 'ambienti spaziosi' (Pelagatti 1982: 122).

10. In a recent survey, Mertens (1996: 315) notices the analogies: 'It is fascinating to observe the extent to which the incoming colonists adopted techniques already in use by the indigenous population.'

11. From a vast bibliography, see for example de Miro (1980) and Domínguez (1989) with further references.

## 4 WINE WARES IN PROTOHISTORIC EASTERN SICILY

I would like to thank the editors for their kind invitation to participate in the conference. I am grateful to John Graham, Anthony Snodgrass, Christopher Smith, and especially Robert Leighton for their comments on previous drafts of this chapter.

1. D.S. 11.76.3, 78.5, 88.6, 90.1, 12.8.1–4 and 29.1. Some, on the other hand, have suggested that his behaviour is more Greek in character, modelled after those tyrants to whom he was opposed (Adamesteanu 1962a; Domínguez 1989: 563–9).

2. The nature of the colonial–Sikel relationship has been complicated by the notion held by some that the Sikels were enslaved by the colonising Greeks (Finley 1968: 20 or Ross Holloway 1991: 50, for instance), but there is no indication that the colonial policy was one of enslavement. Thucydides' colonial foundation history suggests that the Sikels were free, for the colonists needed to enlist their support in their squabbles against one another. In one instance, the historian even explains that the Sikels in the interior had always been politically independent (6.88). It is only in the middle of the fifth century that historians record the enslavement of Sikels (D.S. 12.29.2). Herodotus is the first to utilise a term interpreted as slaves, *kyllyrioi* (7.155), in his account of Gelon's acquisition of Syracuse. Other analogies, however, have likened the *kyllyrioi* to conquered races tilling the soil, rather than personal slaves (Dunbabin 1948: 111 and n. 1 for additional references), while some have suggested that the *kyllyrioi* be defined by their place of residence, in the Syracusan *chora*, and by their economic activity of agriculture rather than by their ethnicity or status (Domínguez 1989: 194). While there is no positive identification of the Sikels as the *kyllyrioi*, 'in no other way could the presence of a large body of slaves, more numerous than the citizens, be explained' (Dunbabin 1948: 111). But there is no significant archaeological evidence of slavery in Sicily during the Archaic period, although such a social class is difficult to identify (Himmelmann-Wildschütz 1971; Allen 1976–7: 494). Meanwhile, those contemporary sites which are identified as Sikel display a wealth of material objects unexpected in a subject people.

3. Elements of other cultures, such as those identified as belonging to the Ausonian culture, are distinct from Sikel remains; for the ethnogenesis of native peoples in Sicily, see Cusumano (1994: 141–58).

4. For overviews of approaches to acculturation as a result of the Greek colonisation of Italy and Sicily, see Pontrandolfo (1989).

5. Albanese Procelli (1996a). These are perhaps amongst the most common means of studying acculturation; see Bartel (1989).
6. See Hall (1997), Morgan (1991) for Greece; Bradley (1997) for Italy.
7. Native sites around a Euboean colony utilised Euboean motifs, while those neighbouring a Corinthian settlement took on Corinthian schemes.
8. The Thapsos *skyphoi* from Finocchito, for instance, contain mica, which is not present in other examples of Thapsos ware. As the clay is not similar to any local Sicilian fabrics (although mica is found in the Naxos region, the clay fires to different tones), it is probable that they are Greek imitations of the Thapsos class. This is not a unique possibility, for a Thapsos-type *skyphos* from T. 104 at Naxos is also thought to be an imported Greek imitation (Pelagatti 1980–1: 699). For a full discussion, see Hodos (1997: appendix 1).
9. Modica: Pelagatti (1983: 118); Villasmundo: Pelagatti (1983: 118; Pelagatti and Voza 1973, no. 191, pl. 16); Ossini: T29 (Lagona 1971); Cocolonazzo di Mola: T.10 (Orsi 1919: 364; although it is lacking the central panel portion. Pelagatti 1983: 118 notes that its profile is similar to the Modica example; see also Pelagatti 1978).
10. Pelagatti (1978), although Voza (1978: 108) says that one of the chevron *skyphoi* is an imitation; another chevron *skyphos* from Cozzo della Tignusa is also considered an imitation (d'Agostino 1974: 77). The early date of these is significant for arguments in favour of pre-colonial contact (see also Albanese Procelli 1995: 45).
11. Finocchito: N T.30, NW T.1, S T.38, from periods IIA, IIA and IIB respectively (see Steures 1980 and Frasca 1981); Ossini S7–9 (Lagona 1971; S8 is also illustrated in Villard and Vallet 1956: pl. 2.1); Morgantina (Lyons 1996: 38); for the remainder: Villard and Vallet (1956: 13–14), including Greek drinking cup fragments and a pseudo-*kantharos* from Belvedere, near Syracuse.
12. Castelluccio: from tomb 4 (Orsi 1898; Coldstream 1968: 192); La Rocca (Pelagatti and Voza 1973: no. 445 and Pelagatti 1983: 124; *BTCGI*, 10: 172; see also Pelagatti 1978).
13. Vallet and Villard (1964: 146, Bb); as for the Ossini example, Orsi, who did not describe it or illustrate it, declared it Greek, while Lagona's fabric description is vague – the fabric matches others listed as Greek, colonial and indigenous. It is impossible to determine the origin of the vessel.
14. For a description of the methodology, see Hodos (1997: 109–31).
15. Class distinctions during this period cannot be made from the funerary remains, however. Literature attests local rulers, but the evidence from graves has not allowed us to identify class distinctions within a single site, particularly signs of an elite during the Finocchito period. At Finocchito itself, for instance, those graves which contain Greek or colonial vessels do not display any greater quantity of ceramics or metal goods, and there are tombs without foreign items which are equally 'rich' in other objects (see Frasca 1981: 93–4).
16. Rathje (1983, 1994); Dentzer (1982: 143–53); see also Tuck (1994), who argues for a Villanovan origin of banqueting.
17. Such structures are not recorded in the west (largely) until the sixth century. It has been suggested that the four-room building at Morgantina, which dates only to the sixth century, may have served a banqueting function (Antonaccio 1997). Even in Etruria, only cautious suggestion is made for possible banqueting structures beginning during the sixth century at Murlo, Acqua Rossa, Castelnuovo Berardenga and Satricum (see Rathje 1990: 285), although a banqueting structure at San Giovenale dates to the seventh century (Karlsson 1996).
18. Scholars have sought an indigenous history from Pantalica South examples (Orsi 1912: pls 9.60 and 9.64; see also Leighton 1985: 420; La Rosa 1978; Frasca 1978: 117; Fouilland et al. 1995: 542); Leighton's chronological revisions (1993c), however, beg for a substantial reconsideration of the evidence for indigenous development. If Leighton is correct to suggest Greek influence, the preference for this shape on the part of the Sikels perhaps could represent an interest in a variant of the

traditional round-neck form. *Skyphoi*, on the other hand, do represent a new shape for the Sikel corpus, with a new technique of thin-walled vessels.

19. As has recently been pointed out, the symposium must have existed in Greek culture in the eighth century. Furthermore, the distribution of pendent semi-circle drinking cups of the kind found at Villasmundo reflects the function of pottery as attestation of the diffusion of a social custom of wine drinking (Murray 1994: 51, 54).

20. Written remains of the Sikel language have been found dating largely to the sixth and fifth century and are a mixture of public inscriptions and minor graffiti (see the summary in Agostiniani 1988–9; see also Zamboni 1978; Antonaccio and Neils 1995; Fouilland et al. 1995: 559–60; Albanese Procelli 1996a: 173); La Rosa refers to an additional twelve incised graffiti inscriptions in the Sikel language on Attic drinking cups of the first half of the fifth century from chamber-tomb 31 of the east necropolis at Montagna di Marzo (La Rosa 1996: 525). See Renfrew (1993) for various theoretical models of language development as symptomatic of changing environments and political patterns as a result of shifting populations; see Bradley (1997) for a comparative development in Umbria.

21. This is a separate issue to the use of language as a means of identifying ethnicities, as raised by Whitehouse and Wilkins (1985); for a further discussion, and with specific regard to the case of Sicily, see Antonaccio and Neils (1995).

22. His actions can be interpreted as the second of Glenn's reactions to foreign contact, whereby cultural contact destroyed the steady Sikel state through the introduction of cultural information which could not be handled by the existing conceptual system and social contacts which could not be handled by the existing system of reciprocity (see Glenn 1981: 139–40).

# 5 GREEKS BEARING GIFTS

I was unfortunately not able to attend the 'Sicily from Aeneas to Augustus' conference in St Andrews and so would like to thank Christopher Smith for reading my paper there as well as for his helpful editorial comments. Thanks are due also to the other participants at the conference, Anthony Snodgrass and Ken Dowden for their valuable suggestions and to Harry Buglass for illustrative work. All translations are taken from the Loeb editions.

1. The most important discussion of the subject is Graham (1971), but see also, for example, Jeffery (1978: 56); Salmon (1984: 387); Malkin (1987: 203).

2. For fuller discussion of these incidents see Graham (1971: 142–53); Shepherd (1993: 151–5); Humphreys (1966: 918–20); Salmon (1984: 390).

3. As, for example, in the episode recorded by Thucydides (1.24–6) concerning Epidamnos' plea for aid in settling internal difficulties and foreign wars. The Epidamnians went first to their mother-city Corcyra, where they were met with a complete lack of interest and obtained no help at all; they then turned to the grandmother-city Corinth, on the grounds that the oikist of Epidamnos, Phallios, had come from Corinth. Here they met with some success, but, as Thucydides records it, this was as much to do with Corinth's desire for retaliation against Corcyra as with its view that Corinth and Epidamnos were related. The resulting inroad made into Corinth's resources was lessened with the use of soldiers from its dependent colonies, Ambracia and Leukas. The oikist tradition gave Epidamnos not one but two options for recourse in time of need and the Epidamnians had the additional advantage of being able to play one city off against the other.

4. See Malkin (1987: pt 2) for discussion of oikist cults.

5. 'oute gar en panegyresi tais koinais didontes gera ta nomizomena oute Korinthio andri prokatarxomenoi ton ieron' (Thuc. 1.25.4).

6. Graham (1971: 162–3), with references. A piece of evidence for a colonial dedication at a mother-city which relates to the west is Pausanias' mention of a statue of Athena dedicated at Sparta by the colonists of Taras (3.2.5). The value of this evidence is

unclear: Pausanias' words may mean that the statue was thought to have been dedicated by departing colonists, in which case it does not have any implications for the relationship between the colony and mother-city subsequent to the departure of the colonists. Graham, however, argues that if such a tradition was correct Pausanias would have given such an ancient statue more attention. He suggests that either Pausanias is describing the Tarentines at a later date or the attribution of the statue to Taras was incorrect (Graham 1971: 162). If the statue was a later dedication from Taras to the mother-city, then the motives for its dedication may have been similar to those suggested here for dedications at Rhodes.

7. See, for example, Dunbabin (1948: 113); Graham (1964: 160–1).

8. For discussion of the fictitious aspects of the *Lindian Chronicle* see Blinkenberg (1941: 159) and Richards (1980: vii, x–xi).

9. Graham (1971: 20, n. 4); Blinkenberg (1941: 191); Humphreys (1966: 914–15).

10. Blinkenberg (1931); for a summary of major dedications listed in the *Lindian Chronicle*, see Richards (1980: x–xii). International dedications recorded in the *Lindian Chronicle* include two more from Sicily: one possibly from Pollis (*LC* XXXI; but cf. Dunbabin 1948: 93–4) and Hieron II of Syracuse (*LC* XLI).

11. Amasis also made dedications at Delphi, Cyrene and Samos (Hdt. 2. 180, 182). For a discussion of Amasis' foreign policy and motivations for making dedications at Greek sanctuaries like Lindos, see Francis and Vickers (1984).

12. A standing version exists also and there is variation in the *fibulae* and number of necklaces. See Dewailly (1992).

13. Orlandini (1968: 25–9). This is in the context of Orlandini's argument that the cult at Gela was that of Athena Lindia specifically, an issue which was under debate.

14. See Dewailly (1992: 135–7, fig. 97) for a catalogue of 'Athena Lindia' figurines found in Sicily and a distribution map. The figurines appear to have been made in Akragas and Gela and are concentrated around those areas as a result, but nevertheless have a wide distribution over Sicily.

15. Orsi (1918: 576); Snodgrass (1964: 129); Herrmann (1983: 285); Kilian-Dirlmeier (1985: 231).

16. See Pausanias Books 5 and 6 for an account of the numerous western Greek dedications at Olympia.

17. See Pace (1945, 3: 725–30) for a summary of Sicilian dedications at Delphi.

# 6  COIN TYPES AND IDENTITY

A version of this chapter was given at the Center for Old World Archaeology and Art at Brown University, RI, and I am grateful for the stimulus provided by that occasion for further work on the material and ideas presented in it. I should also like to thank my colleague Gordon Howie for his advice and encouragement..

1. On bronze hemilitrae, as *SNG* ANS, 1097–1102, dating *c*.410.

2. The phrase is used by Hugh Lloyd-Jones in a comment following the paper of Georges Vallet (Vallet 1996: 205); Vallet's paper was originally published in *Entretiens Hardt*, XXXI (Vandoeuvres–Geneva, 1984), pp. 285–319.

3. Literary references to the importance of rivers to a colonising people could be multiplied: for example, when Aeneas arrived in Latium he offered up prayers to 'the Genius of the place, and to the nymphs and rivers not yet known' (Virgil, *Aen*.7.135–8). Emma Dench has pointed out to me too the constant importance of rivers in ancient geographical texts, as a primary way of 'mapping' new lands.

4. For the dating of the nymph series of Himera, see Arnold-Biucchi (1988).

5. For discussion of the date of the ode and its historical context, see Barrett (1973).

6. As mentioned above, the chief type of Himera before the introduction of the nymph type had been a cock. It is intriguing to find that image worked into the description of Ergoteles' achievement: if *stasis* had not driven him from Crete, he would only have

been 'cock of the walk' on his home patch (l. 14). Cf. Gildersleeve's comment (1907: 225): 'Himera and Ergoteles are paralleled. The city and the victor mirror each other. The fortune of Himera is the fortune of Ergoteles.'

7. *IGCH*, 1874 (Taranto 1911), 2065 (Messina 1875), 2066 (Gela 1956), 2071 (Monte Bubbonia 1910).

8. H. Cahn, *LIMC*, II. 1 Arethousa: 582–4.

9. See last note. The oracle *ap*. Pausanias 5.7.3 (no. 2 Parke-Wormell = Q27 Fontenrose), allegedly given to Archias, may or may not be earlier than Pindar; before him the only certain reference to the Alpheus crossing over to Sicily is Ibycus, *PMG*, 323. For later references to the story, see esp. Pausanias 5.7.2, 6.22.8; Ovid, *Met*. 5.577.

10. As defined in Westermark and Jenkins (1980).

11. For the refounding by Gela in that year, see Diodorus Siculus (11.76.5).

12. 460 or 456?: Snell-Maehler; the composition of two odes celebrating the same victory is not unique in Pindar: cf. *Ol*. 2 and 3, 10 and 11; *Pyth*. 4 and 5.

13. The fullest recent treatment is Mader (1990); Bowra (1964) devotes to it appendix III: 414–20.

14. The importance of the cult of Athena at Camarina is further attested in the Pindaric scholia to *Ol*. 5.10, and also in a number of coins with obverse head of Athena dating later in the century: e.g. a gold diobol (as *SNG* ANS, 1209), and bronzes (as *SNG* ANS, 1228–32).

15. The pursuit of coin types in Pindar's poetry need not be confined to Sicily. I think of *Olympian* 7 and the island of Rhodes, the 'bride of the sun' (14) and gifted to him especially (54–76); *Olympian* 13 and Corinth, where Bellerophon tamed Pegasus (63–92); and *Olympian* 10 and Locri Epizephyrii, where the emphasis on Zeus and his thunderbolts is striking (79–83): these images formed a major element in the coin types of Locri, though coinage there did not begin for more than a century after Pindar wrote the ode.

16. On the importance of a sense of place for the definition of group identity, see Isaacs (1975: 44): 'The physical element in basic group identity has to do … with place, the land, the soil to which the group is attached, literally, historically, mythically.' In Greek coinage of the archaic and classical periods, this 'physical element' is expressed more commonly and strongly in Sicily than it is elsewhere.

## 7 SICILY IN THE ATHENIAN IMAGINATION

This chapter expands upon arguments presented more tangentially in the course of a larger study of Aeschylus' *Persians* (Duckworth, forthcoming). My thanks to Tim Rood for kindly lending me a copy of his paper (Rood 1999) in advance of publication, and to the St Andrews audience for their stimulating questions. References in the form '7.77.7' are, unless otherwise specified, to Thucydides. Translations of the *Persians* are, with some small modifications, those of Edith Hall (1996); longer translations of Thucydides are taken from the *Everyman* edition of Richard Crawley.

1. See e.g. Cornford (1907: 201–43), Kitto (1950: 45), Connor (1984, references below), and now the excellent article of Rood (1999).

2. For this expansionist Persia, see Verdin (1982); for the discontinuity between Xerxes and earlier kings presented in A. *Pers*., though not in Herodotus, see Said (1981). For Athens as adventurous and enterprising, see also the parallels cited by Hornblower (1991–6) on 1.70.8; Athens' 'continuity of aggression' is noted by Rood (1998: 200).

3. Cf. Darius' clinching argument in the debate on the constitutions: that they should not abandon the laws by which they had, through Cyrus, won their freedom (3.82.5); see also the parallels listed by Hornblower (1991–6) on 1.71.3.

4. A point subsequently made explicit, in the case of Darius' Scythian expedition, by Artabanus (Hdt. 7.10α–γ).

5. See also Rood (1999) on the parallel between 7.56.3 and 1.73.4.

6. See Macleod (1975: 51–3) for the irony that the Athenian forces were more mixed than their Sicilian opponents.

7. See esp. Fornara (1971a); see also now, on parallels between the Ionian and Samian revolts, Stadter (1992).

8. Cf. Connor (1984: 199, n. 37), seeing 7.69.2 as 'based on' A. *Pers.* 402–5 (cf. Rood 1998: 195 and n. 59); for two other echoes of the vocabulary of the *Persians,* see Hornblower (1987: 148, n. 50).

9. For the Persian wars as central even to new cult foundations, see Parker (1996: 187).

10. Contrast, however, the opinion of Pericles (1.142.6–9).

11. For the parallel rise in Athenian daring and enterprise, see Avery (1973: 6–8); see also here Macleod (1983: 143).

12. Cf. A. *Pers.* 260, 278–9, 282–3, 433–4, 516, 548–9, 595–7, 670, 677–8, 714, 718, 729, 730, 925–7, 1016.

13. Contrast Vickers (1995), attempting to tie the 'digression' into the surrounding narrative through a number of (more or less) weak allusions to Alcibiades; see, more convincingly, Connor (1984: 176–80), Rood (1998: 180–2).

14. See the comments of Connor (1984: 195–6), emphasising the dissolution of old ties between cities implicit in the alignment of cities, in fulfilment of the Corcyraean revolution.

15. See Rood (1999), adding also the analogy of Xerxes' viewing of Salamis, Hdt. 8.88, 90.

16. See Cornford (1907: 201–20), Connor (1984: 167), Harrison (forthcoming: ch. 9); for Athens as a tyranny, see esp. Connor (1977).

17. Contrast, however, Thucydides' greater emphasis on the psychological aspect of size, e.g. the observations of Lamachus, 6.49.2.

18. Cf. Nicias' remark, 6.38.3, that they were fighting for a country that was not theirs; cf. Cyrus' campaign against the Massagetai, Hdt. 1.201–14, or Cambyses' against the Ethiopians, Hdt. 3.17–25.

19. Connor (1984: 175, 202); for other echoes, esp. of an Orphic vision of the underworld, see Connor (1984: 204, n. 51).

20. A point Thuc. (1.74.1) makes about Salamis, 1.74.1, as noted by Hornblower (1991–6: ii.128). Contrast here Rood (1999), Pelling (1997: 7–8).

21. For the motif of fighting a land battle on sea, see now Flory (1993), using it, however, as evidence that Thucydides gave up on his work on the grounds that the theme would have been inappropriate after the recovery of Athens' naval strength. For the reversal of Pylos, 'a truly tragic, not merely a casual, irony', see Macleod (1983: 142–3).

22. For the analogy of Hermocrates and Themistocles (and Pericles), see Hunter (1977: 287–90), Connor (1984: 197–8); for, more broadly, Syracuse as an 'analogue' for Athens, see Connor (1984: 168–76).

23. See here the comments of Rood (1998: 141, 1999).

24. Cf. 6.37.2. Contrast Avery (1973: 8–13), envisaging the analogy with a 'colonizing effort' as emphasising the size of the expedition. Connor (1984: 176, n. 46), notes that Athens was reduced to a *phrourion* (read 7.28.1 for 7.29.1), while the expedition was identified with the city.

25. Contrast Connor (1984: 202–3): 'nothing could be more trite'. The parallel between this passage and Hdt. 8.61.2 is noted e.g. by Rood (1998: 196, n. 63).

26. Cf. Meiggs and Lewis (1984: 26): the island of Ajax holds the Corinthians; see also comparable passages referred to, n. 12 above.

27. Stressed e.g. by Avery (1964: 173–9), Said (1988: 330), Hall (1996: 24–5).

28. Marinatos Kopff and Rawlings (1978), modified sensibly by Connor (1984: 208–9).

29. Macleod (1983: 141), Hornblower (1987: 148–50); contrast, however, Connor (1984: 210) for book 8 as 'another example of a familiar pattern in the *Histories,* reopening after apparent closure' – an extreme and difficult example.

30. Cf. the comments of Cornford (1907: vii), Macleod (1983: 141) ('Thucydides' account … cannot be reduced to a trite moral or a literary effect').

31. For a compelling argument that Thucydides' 'attitude to Athens' defeat in Sicily is complex, but consistent', see Rood (1998: 159–82).
32. See e.g. Fornara (1971b), Sansone (1985), Hartog (1988: 275).
33. For the hypothesis that Thucydides read certain sections of his work in the course of symposia, see Hornblower (1991–6: ii.26–7); see now, however, Johnson (1995) for a disquieting analysis of modern assumptions concerning Herodotus' oral delivery (distinguishing this question from elements of oral style).
34. See also Rood (1998: 4); contrast Hornblower (1983: 141, 1987: 148), Tzifopoulos (1995).
35. Contrast Hornblower (1987: 148): 'it is because Thucydides' whole approach to the Sicilian disaster is essentially literary and tragic that he has exaggerated its actual importance for effect'.
36. To invert the – in my view, profoundly mistaken – formulation of Kenneth Waters (in the context of Herodotus' presentation of grievances) (1966: 170–1).
37. Such patterns of reversal are particularly well observed by Rood (1998), e.g. (in the context of the Sicilian expedition) at p. 199.
38. See also the excellent article of Redfield (1985); for geographical polarities, Romm (1989).
39. Cf. Asheri (1988: 780).
40. See esp. Boedeker (1988), Dewald (1997).
41. Fornara (1971b), with the comments of Derow (1995: esp. 36). Even a late date of 414 would not preclude Thucydidean echoes of Herodotus, given the possibility or likelihood of substantial pre-publication. See the excellent comments of Hornblower (1991–6: ii.24–38, 122–45) (establishing as firmly as is possible Thucydides' knowledge, and – often oblique – use, of Herodotus).

# 8 THE TYRANT'S MYTH

1. D.H. *Lysias* 29; Lysias 33 (*Olympic Oration*); D.S. 15.74.
2. Daughters: Plut. *Dion*. 3, 6; marriages: D.S. 14.44; see further below.
3. Plb. 1.7–11 and Fest. p.154L; Scullard (1989: 541, n. 51) suggests that the story of the *ver sacrum* may go back to the original colonists.
4. Himera was of course destroyed by the Carthaginians in 409; Valerius Maximus' account must refer to Thermae Himerese, founded by the scattered Himeraeans, which came into Dionysius' orbit in 396.
5. Sordi (1984: 534–9); see also Vattuone (1981: 139–45).
6. Hdt 6.131; Apollod. 3.12.5; Pi. fr. of Paean 8; see Lewis (1976).
7. Philist. *FGH* 556 fr. 58 (= Gel. 12.46); also Cic. *Div*. 1.73. The bees may also serve to link Dionysius with his divine namesake Dionysus: see A.R. 4.1129–37.
8. Hdt 5.92 and Roux (1963: 277–89); Melissa: Hdt 3.48; see Cook (1895: 1–24); Davies and Kathivithamby (1986: 66–9, 70–2); Steiner (1986: 109, 132–3).
9. D. Chr. 37.21ff; see Stroheker (1958: 160).
10. I have been unable to find any similar examples to elucidate the meaning of this offer.
11. The sinking of weights in the sea formed part of the ceremony when the Phocaeans left Phocaea for Alalia, swearing never to return (Hdt. 1.165), as well as the familiar occasion of the forming of the Delian League (Arist. *Ath*. 23.5).
12. Philip: D.S. 16.35.6; legendary drownings: Romulus and Remus: Liv. 1.4.3; Tennes: D.S. 4.33; Battus: Hdt. 4.154; Telephus: D.S. 5.83.4; cf. Perseus also; Procles of Epidauros: Plut. *Mor*. 403d. Other similar historical episodes occur at Demosthenes, *Against Aristocrates*,169 (the Cardians drown Miltocythes and his son in 358), and Hdt. 3.30 (the Persian king Cambyses has his brother drowned in the Red Sea).

# 10 GARRISONS AND GRAIN

I am grateful to Dr C. E. P. Adams, Dr F. de Angelis, Dr M. M. Austin, Prof. J. D. Harries, Dr M. D. Humphries, Ms K. Konstakipoulou, Dr C. J. Smith, Prof. R. J. A. Wilson and Prof. G. Woolf for their useful suggestions. All errors remain my own.

1. Coins from this period show Gelon with a diadem; Head (1911: 184).
2. Bell (1988: 316, 321–4); Sjöqvist (1960b: 130–1); for the borders of Hieron's kingdom see Karlsson (1993: 41–5).
3. Berve (1959: 40–1, 57); Holleaux (1921: 49, n. 2); for coins see Head (1911: 184–5); Holloway (1962: 17–19), *contra* Walbank (1957: I, 57, 1967: II, 33), who argues that the monarchy of Hieron was in the 'democratic Syracusan tradition … [and] … owed little to Hellenistic ideals'. For the Roman treaty with Hieron, dating from 248, see Zonar. 8. 16.
4. For the relationship of the Attalids to Pergamon see *OGIS* 267 (*RC* 23), with Allen (1983: 166–7).
5. Archimel. *ap.* Ath. 5.209e; Eutrop. 3.1; Val. Max. 8.13 ext. 1. For Hieron heading a *symmachia* of Sicilian cities see Karlsson (1993: 36).
6. *Act. Tr.* Degrassi, 74–5, 547–8; App. *Sic.* 2.2; Liv. 22.37.10; Plut. *Marc.* 8.6; Zonar. 8.10. See also *MRR* 1: 204. That the Carthaginians felt their treaty in 264 was directly with Hieron is reflected in D.S. 22.13.9.
7. For epigraphic evidence of this see *SIG³* I: 427.
8. Liv. 24.22.6. Here, Livy uses the term *senatus* to describe the Syracusan government; Sicily had never known anything like the Roman senate and therefore it is best to refer to the government by the more common Greek term of *boule* or council.
9. Gelzer (1969: 87); Manganaro (1965: 174); Robert and Robert (1953: 282); Sjöqvist (1960a: 54–5); Walbank (1986: 210).
10. Two examples of his kingdom's wealth can be seen in the Morgantina silver hoard and the three Syracusan ears of grain made from gold. Morgantina silver: Slayman (1998: 40–1); golden ear of grain: Wilson (1990a: 19, 1997: 2).
11. In Liv. 22.37.10, the senate pays him several compliments; see also Auct. *De Vir. Ill.* 37.5; Cic. *Verr.* 2.3.15; Liv. 23.21.5, 25.28.8, 29.7, 26.30.1, 32.4; Mosch. *ap.* Ath. 5.206d; Plb. 1.16.10; Sil. Ital. 14.83–4. On Hieron and client kingship in general see Braund (1984: 63, 146, 190, n. 7). On the legitimacy of Hieron's loyalty see Eckstein (1980: 200).
12. As is argued by Dahlheim (1968: 135, n. 28) and Roussel (1970: 130), *contra* Eckstein (1980: 193).
13. For other references to the treaty see App. *Sic.* 2; Auct. *De Vir. Ill.* 41.1; Nep. *Han.* 1.5; Eutrop. 2.27; Liv. *Per.* 19, 21.18.8–10, 19.2, 30.22.4, 44.1; Naev. *Poen.* 7.fr. 46–7Bl; Oros. 4.11.1; Plb. 3.21.2–3, 29.2, 30.3; Sil. Ital. 13.729–31.
14. Cic. *Verr.* 2.3.16, 5.49–51. Cic. (*Verr.* 2.3.15, 5.49–51, 56, 133) also states that Netum and Tauromenium held the same status, but it is known from D.S. 23.4.1 that these two places remained part of the Syracusan kingdom until the defection of the latter in 214, and therefore did not form part of the Roman province at this time. App. *Sic.* 5 tells us that Tauromenium was accorded special rights by Marcellus for surrendering to Rome quickly; the case of Netum is presumably similar.
15. The meaning of Cicero's words is in dispute. The standard view has been that these cities were free from Roman control and immune from taxes, but Ferrary (1988: 5–7) believes that both 'free' and 'immune' refer to taxation. So the cities were not free from Roman control, but merely free and immune from taxes. Regardless, whether they were free cities or not is of no consequence here, as the fact that they did have special status under the Romans remains unchanged.
16. Halaisa and Halicyai: D.S. 23.4.1–5 (Segesta also surrendered here); Centuripe and Segesta: Cic. *Verr.* 2.4.72, 5.83; Robert and Robert (1965: 499). Cic. (*Verr.* 2.3.13) also includes Panormos in this list, but this place was taken only with difficulty by Rome in 254, and so it is logical to assume that this status was conferred upon the city

sometime between the Second Punic War and Cicero's day. See also Lintott (1993: 71, 94); Pritchard (1975: 41–2); Scramuzza (1938: 235).

17. Richardson (1976: 151, and in general 147–51). Richardson's work has chronicled this process in Spain. He has convincingly demonstrated the lack of provincial structure in the Roman world well into the second century. See also Lintott (1993: 72–6); Richardson (1986: *passim*, esp. 1–10, 57–8, 75–94, 109–23, 1989: 580–9, 593–8).

18. See Badian's entry under '*provincia*/province' in *OCD*[3] 1265. On the appointment of provincial praetors and *imperium*, see Richardson (1991: 5).

19. Daube (1951: 66–70), *contra* Richardson (1990: 150–1); Serrao (1954: 7–13, 16–22); both of whom argue that the function of the *praetor peregrinus* was strictly judicial.

20. Asc. *Div.* 2; Cic. *Planc.* 65; *Verr.* 2.2.22. Pareti (1953: 185) and Thiel (1954: 33, n. 90), believe that a *quaestor classicus* was stationed at Lilybaeum. Harris (1976: 102) has correctly pointed out that this is speculation.

21. Harris (1976: 104). It should be noted that Harris favours 227 for the installation of the quaestor at Lilybaeum.

22. See Caven (1980: 190); Hallward (1954: 114); Lintott (1993: 3); Rickman (1980: 37).

23. See Carcopino (1914: 1–44); Lintott (1993: 70–1, 75–6); Pritchard (1970: 352–68); Rickman (1980: 36–42); Scramuzza (1938: 231–40).

24. Tauromenian alliance with Rome: App. *Sic.* 5. Treaty with grain clause: Cic. *Verr.* 2.5.56. There is no evidence for a any changes to the treaty between the Second Punic War and Cicero's time.

25. See Lintott (1993: 75, n. 29); Pritchard (1970: 365–8); Walbank (1986: 107, 209); and Bowman (1996: 71–113) for the Egyptian tithe.

26. Witness the wealthy Syracusan landholders who took refuge in the camp of Marcellus from 214 until 211 (Liv. 25.31.8). After the city fell, the Romans appropriated land from private holders (Liv. 26.21.11), and restored some of it in the following year (Liv. 26.32.6).

27. *AE* 1960: 39. See also Verbrugghe (1976: 11–16). Wiseman (1987: 144, n. 150) suggests that the road was constructed during Cotta's second consulship of 248, but in that year he operated only in western Sicily, the interior having been secured by then. Regardless of the exact date, the First Punic War context is secure.

28. See Erdkamp (1998: 71), who argues that the primary function of all Roman roads was military.

29. The navy of Hieron was certainly used to police the eastern shores of Sicily. See Liv. 21.49.3.

30. For the archaeology of the eastern city of Adranon see Wilson (1990a: 146–7).

31. De Miro and Fiorentini (1976–7: 455, pl. 49). De Miro dates the coin to the destruction layer, claiming this confirms the high date of Plin. *Nat.* 33.42–6 for the introduction of the *denarius*. However, Loomis (1996: 338–55) has convincingly argued that the *denarius* could not have been introduced before 215.

32. Evidence for Punic garrisons exists at several sites in the western half of Sicily; any number of these could have been taken over by Rome at the end of the First Punic War. These places, like Monte Adranone, contained ready-made barrack blocks and defensive fortifications. Since the Carthaginians used these forts to control the surrounding countryside, it would not be far-fetched to conjecture that the Romans employed them in a similar manner. Other Punic garrisons may have been stationed at Montagna dei Cavalli, Portelle Imbriaci and Monte Pellegrino, which may have been ancient Heirkte. For the last site see Bonanno (1973: 55–62); Falsone (1995: 683); Gandolfo (1997b: 22–4); Garofano (1997: 11–22). For the first two see Castiglione (1997: 307–14); Falsone (1995: 684); Gandolfo (1997a: 315–36); Giordano (1997: 337–48); Vassallo (1991: 114–36, 1997: 275–306).

33. Cic. *Verr.* 2.5.43, 51, 60, 88, 99. See also Brunt (1971: 65); Lintott (1993: 94); Scramuzza (1938: 288). On *socii navales* see Badian (1958: 28–30); Brunt (1971: 666–70); Thiel (1954: 77).

34. Cic. *Verr*. 2.2.92, 3.55, 61 (arrests); 4.104 (confiscation); 3.65 (bodyguards); 2.92–3 (collecting temple tax); 3.105, 4.32 (carrying out orders).

## 11 CICERONIAN SICILY

1. On Hortensius' speech, Alexander (1976); on the importance of the trial in Cicero's career, cf. especially Mitchell (1979, 1986: 6–12).
2. Cf. Mitchell (1986: 1–5); Alexander (1990: 88–90). Holm in the nineteenth century even compared it, blow for blow, with the trial of Warren Hastings, governor general at Calcutta, which lasted between 1788 and 1795: Holm (1901: 348–55).
3. Among an extensive bibliography, cf. especially Rauber (1914); Scramuzza (1938); Calderone (1964–5); Pritchard (1969, 1971, 1972); Verbrugghe (1972); Manganaro (1979); Clemente (1980–1, 1988); Mazza (1980, 1981); Coarelli (1981); Scuderi (1996).
4. Tithe according to the *lex Hieronica*: *Verr*. 2.3.6.14–8.19. See also ch. 10, n. 15, this volume. City status: Cicero, *Verr*. 2.3.6.13 and 2.5.51.133; Calderone (1964–5: 87–98); Pinzone (1978).
5. Sacks (1990) (*c*.60–30 BC), but there may have been some later revisions (cf. Wilson 1990a: 357, n. 11).
6. *Verr*. 2.3.1.120. The same passage contains the alleged figures of the drop in the number of farmers between Verres' first year and third year as governor in other districts too: Lentini (84 to 32), Modica (187 to 86) and Herbita (252 to 120).
7. For figures and references, cf. most conveniently Scramuzza (1959: 259–60, n. 2).
8. For a start showing a different approach, but dealing with Greek rather than Roman Sicily, see Muggia (1997) and De Angelis (forthcoming).
9. Camarina: *BTCGI* IV: 286–314; Mattioli (1995: 259–70). Soluntum: see below, n. 19. Acrae: Wilson (1990a: 153–4), with references, since when extensive excavations have uncovered the hellenistic agora (where there was apparently little Roman imperial activity); there were, however, late Roman structures (which ignore the earlier street pattern) further west, near the crown of the hill (unpublished excavations by G. Voza; for a summary plan, see Bietti Sestieri et al. 1996: 291).
10. *Verr*. 2.5.25.63 (Cicero calls it Megaris, 'a place not far from Syracuse'). For the archaeology of Megara Hyblaea, see Vallet et al. (1981: esp. 174–5); *BTCGI* IX: 511–34; and works cited by Wilson (1990a: 357, n. 15).
11. *Pace* Manni (1981: 204–5, 207); he in any case did not accept the identification, held by everyone else, that Morgantina has been corrrectly placed at Serra Orlando (Wilson 1985b: 298).
12. *Verr*. 2.3.18.47: the others are Herbita, Enna, Assoro (Assones), Imachara and Agira (Agyrium).
13. For a convenient summary, Tsakirgis (1995: esp. 139–43).
14. Tsakirgis (1990: 432–4) floors; (1995: 140–2) frescoes.
15. For example, that in room 1 of the House of the Ganymede. Tsarkirgis (1989: 397), takes the central portion of the floor, inside the meander border, to have consisted of plain white tesserae, but the whole of the central panel inside the frame has clearly been deliberately removed (apart from a tiny fragment of white tesserae), and the contrast between the missing centre and the excellent state of preservation of the rest of the floor is too marked to be due to the casual fate of survival.
16. *Verr*. 2.2.50.125, 3.43.103, 5.33.86, 5.46.123, 5.49.129. On Eraclea Minoa, see especially *BTCGI* VII: 234–77; De Miro (1965) with earlier bibliography.
17. De Miro (1965: 15–17).
18. Campagna (1996: esp. 117–19).
19. See most conveniently Cutroni Tusa et al. (1994); other bibliography in Wilson (1990a: 156–7, with references on 380, nn. 55–6).
20. Isler (1991); *BTCGI* X: 368–75; but both these have been rendered out of date by

more recent work, which can be followed annually in reports in *Sicilia Archeologica* and *Antike Kunst*. The definitive excavation reports are appearing in a series called *Studia Ietina* (Zurich), of which eight volumes have been published at the time of writing.

21. Nenci (1995); Camerata Scovazzo (1996); Molinari (1997). There is also much of importance on Segesta in Nenci (1997).

22. Bernabò Brea and Cavalier (1965).

23. Scibona (1971); Wilson (1990a: 46–8); Prestianni Giallombardo (1998). The 1998 excavations are unpublished.

24. Soluntum/Solus: *Verr* 2.2.42.102, 3.43.103. Iaitas/Ietas: *Verr.* 2.3.43.103. Segesta: *Verr.* 2.2.65.156, 2.69.166, 4.33.72, etc. Tindari: *Verr.* 2.2.65.156, 2.66.160, 3.43.103, 4.39.84, etc. Halaesa: *Verr.* 2.2.49.122, 2.65.156, 2.69.166, 3.73.170, etc.

25. For the location and archaeological remains of archaic Soloeis, see most recently Greco (1993–4, 1997a, 1997c).

26. Unpublished in detail, but cf. L. Natoli in Adriani et al. (1971: 107–9); Cutroni Tusa et al. (1994: 70–3). For a discussion of Sicilian *agorai* in the context of the recent work at Segesta, see Michelini (1997); for the Segesta *agora* itself, Vaggioli (1997).

27. On Sicilian *bouleuteria*, see especially the discussion by De Miro in his publication of the Agrigento *bouleuterion*: De Miro (1985–6). More recent is the survey by Iannello (1994). The fragmentary *bouleuterion* at Segesta, if correctly identified, has not yet been published in detail, but is mentioned in Nenci (1995: 692, 1997: 215 and Tav. XXVII, no. 14).

28. Lauter (1986: 173) erroneously interprets these buildings as *odeia*, following the original misinterpretation of the Solunto building. I do not accept either his contention that the Sicilian buildings provided the inspiration for the shape of the Roman *odeum* (cf. Wilson 1990b: 72 with 87, n. 17).

29. D'Andria (1997); Campagna (1997). The latest theatre in Sicily to be discovered (in the summer of 1999), that at Montagna di Marzo (possibly the ancient Herbessus), is said by its excavator, on the basis of preliminary results, to be 'databile tra il III e il I secolo a.C.' (Corradini 1999).

30. Coarelli (1981); cf. in the same vein, Clemente (1980–1, 1988); Mazza (1980, 1981); Manganaro (1980).

31. Cf. in more detail, Wilson (1990a: 20–8). For a general discussion of Diodorus' Sicilian passages against the background of the archaeological evidence, see Bejor (1991).

32. Crawford (1985: 115, 1987: 47–8); but he follows Clemente and Coarelli (see n. 30) in believing in a depressed Sicily at this time.

33. Cf. Wilson (1990a: 151, fig. 129.7 on 147, with earlier bibliography; cf. also 170–1 with n. 78 on 382 for comparative city sizes). At 28 ha Centuripae is comparable with Tauromenium (29 ha), Tyndaris (27 ha) and Segesta within the inner defences (32 ha), but is much smaller than Thermae Himeraeae (52 ha), Panormus (48 ha), Lilybaeum (77 ha) and Messina, Catania and Syracuse, which cover 100 ha or more.

34. Wilson (1990a: 355 with n. 81) for a full bibliography.

35. Some were even equestrian: cf. *Verr.* 2.2.63.154: 'in the market place at Syracuse … stands the naked figure of his son and he himself on horseback, surveying the province he has stripped bare. His statues are everywhere, as if to demonstrate that he has set up almost as many statues as he has carried off from the province'; cf. 2.2.66–7.160 for the overthrow of statues of Verres at Tauromenium, Tyndaris, Lentini and Syracuse (presumably in 71 BC, at the end of his governorship).

36. Scibona (1971: 5–14). The other inscriptions found in the *stoa* date from the imperal period.

37. Tusa (1963), but letter forms suggest a rather later date than the third-century BC one there suggested.

38. Scibona (1971: 15–16). For basilical *stoai* in the Greek east, see Coulton (1976: 183) with references; Ward-Perkins (1981: 287–8); Gros (1996: 246–8).

39. E.g. *Verr.* 2.2.63.154, 2.66.160, 3. 23.57, 4.53.119, etc.
40. *Verr.* 2.3.43.103. For bibliography on Monte Iato, see n. 20 above.
41. Cf. most conveniently Isler (1997a: 1020–1 with tav. CXCIV and references to earlier excavation reports).
42. Isler (1992: 13–18, 1997a: 1021 with tav. CXCV).
43. Cf. most conveniently Isler (1991: 42–52); more recent work is summarised in Isler (1997a: 1019–20), with other references. The sculptural decoration of the stage front is believed to belong to the first phase of the theatre, dated by Isler to the late fourth century BC (Isler-Kerényi 1976; cf. most recently Pugliese Carratelli (1996: 424 and 748, catalogue no. 376 ('320–300 BC')).
44. Isler (1996). For the full publication of this house, see Dalcher (1994), and for other hellenistic peristyle houses now under excavation at Monte Iato, see Isler (1997c).
45. Sicilian Ionic: Villa (1988: 26–35). Sicilian Corinthian: Lauter-Bufe (1987). Cf. also the discussion in Wilson (1990b: 72–3, with distribution maps on 74).
46. Wilson (1990b: 75–6 with n. 24); cf. also von Sydow (1984: 313–14 and 350, no. 20 ('um 180 v. Chr.'); Lauter-Bufe (1987: 26, no. 39). A high dating for the mosaics in this house (soon after 300 BC) was recently reiterated in a conference paper by Isler (1997b), but was questioned in the debate afterwards (Carra Bonacasa and Guidobaldi 1997: 1027–8).
47. *Verr.* 2.5.43.111, 5.45.120. For the house, Bechtold (1997a, with Tav. VI for the tables in the form of a prow) (cf. also Pugliese Carratelli 1996: 636, cat. no. 2); and for other house-types at Segesta, cf. in general Bechtold (1997b).
48. A notorious recent case is the splendid silver hoard acquired by the Metropolitan Museum in New York in 1981 and 1982, said to be 'from Taranto', which has now been shown conclusively, on the basis of a controlled excavation at the site of the looting, to have come from Morgantina in Sicily: see *Archaeology,* May–June 1998: 40–1. The deposition of the hoard can be dated precisely to the year 211 BC, the year of the destruction of Morgantina by the Romans, and so is of course nearly a century and a half earlier than the time of Verres.
49. E.g. Dio of Halesa: 'Verres had his stables stripped of mares and his house stripped of all the silver and tapestry that it contained' (*Verr.* 2.1.10.27); cf. *Verr.* 2.2.19.46 ('one thing was promptly seen to – the conveyance to Verres of all the family engraved silver plate and Corinthian vases and tapestries'), *Verr.* 2.2.72.176 ('I insist that you took away from Syracuse a great weight of gold, silver, ivory and purple fabrics, a good deal of Maltese cloth and tapestries'), 2.4.22.48–9 ('There is a man of Tyndaris … Philo, who … put on the table a dish with relief figures of exceptional merit. The moment that Verres saw it he without hesitation removed it from his host's table … He behaved the same way to Eumolpus of Calacte … Most of the silver put on the table was plain, but there were two cups of no great size but with figured work').
50. On this see Giumlia-Mair and Craddock (1993: esp. 3–4 (literary sources) and 27–9 with Abb. 11–19 (objects of Roman date)).
51. Cutroni Tusa et al. (1994: 98–100 with Tav. 36); for its pavement, Wilson (1990a: 120, fig. 108); also Greco (1997b: 57, fig. 5, with a discussion of floor-types in general at Solunto). Cutroni Tusa et al. (1994) publishes the plans of many Solunto houses for the first time, a most valuable resource for late hellenistic housing in Sicily.
52. Solunto fresco: references in Wilson (1990a: 356, n. 99). Tindari: von Boeselager (1983: 39–46 with Taf. VII). Palermo: see most recently Di Stefano (1997b, with full earlier bibliography).
53. See n. 15 above. For the practice in general, see Dunbabin (1999: 51–2, 65–8).
54. Cf. references elsewhere in the *Verrines* too: e.g. *Verr.* 2.2.34.85–35.87 (bronze statue of Himera, the female personification of that city, and a statue of Stesichorus, both at Thermae Himeraeae), 2.2.47.115 (a cupid in silver at Eryx), etc.
55. There is no adequate general account of sculpture in Sicily which tries to distinguish chronologically between 'hellenistic' production in general (i.e. from the later fourth century BC onwards) and that which falls firmly within the period of Roman control,

and many pieces remain inadequately studied and published; but see especially Coarelli (1980); Bonacasa and Joly (1985); Bonacasa (1999).

56. Tindari: Zanker (1965); Segesta: Nenci (1995: Tav. CVIII.1 and CXI – the latter = Nenci 1997: Tav. LXIII.2); Zeus: references in Wilson (1990a: 354, n. 77).

57. On the topography of Enna, cf. the works cited in Wilson (1990a: 408, n. 64) with additions in Wilson (1995–6: 84).

58. Rural farms occupied around the time of Verres include those of Piano Croce, Lupinedda, Canne Masche and Scodoni (references in Wilson 1990a: 354, n. 66), Runzi (*BTCGI* XIII: 569–70), Montevago (Castellana 1988–9: 536–40 with fig. 9) and Pagliuzza (Mantegna Pancucci et al. 1993). Refence to other sites, mostly known from surface evidence, can be found in Bejor (1986) and in Lagona (1996). None of these has, however, produced a plan sufficiently coherent to merit inclusion in fig. 11.17.

59. Wilson (1990a: 197–8 – Avola: later first century BC? – and 199–203 – Castroreale San Biagio, originally 'probably built in the late second or early first century BC').

60. Verbrugghe (1972: 545–55); Wilson (1990a: 21–3).

61. Discussion with references in Wilson (1990a: 221–3 with figs. 178–9); cf. also Belvedere (1995, 1997).

62. Johns (1992); cf. also Wilson (1995–6: 113, with fig. 46 and other references). Other surveys conducted around Morgantina and also around Entella (in progress) are so far unpublished.

## 12 BETWEEN GREECE AND ITALY

1. For Syracusan domination of this region, cf D.S. 14. 44–45, 101–108, Strab. 6.1.8 and 10, D.H. 20.7.2–3

2. For regional differences between Greek and Punic areas of Sicily, see Bejor (1983); Wilson (1990a: 316–17, 327–9).

3. Hall (1997: 17–19). For further discussion, although using different terminology, cf. Smith (1991: 20–1); Ardener (1989: 69–71).

4. An extreme example of this is the way in which Cicero manipulates identity to give moral stature to the Sicilian victims of Verres and to undermine the communities which supported him. The Sicilians are characterised exclusively in terms of a very qualified Greekness, emphasising their modest and abstemious habits, as compared to other Greeks (Cic. *Verr.* 2.2.7; on definitions of Greekness more generally, see Petrochilos 1974; Vasaly 1993). The sole exception is the city of Messana, the only community to support Verres; this is characterised entirely in terms of its Campanian culture (Cic. *Verr.* 2.2.13), which had significantly lower status in Roman eyes.

5. For the use of this methodology in Italy, see Lomas (1993: 161–86).

6. Cf. in particular Laurence (1995); Lomas (1997: 21–41); Patterson (1994: 227–38); Wallace-Hadrill (1994: 39–62). For a recent discussion of elite private housing in Roman Sicily, see Hollegaard Olsen (1995: 209–62).

7. For a similar case – the Bay of Naples – see Lomas (1993: 174–87). Despite the major problems posed by urban archaeology, it is possible to recover enough evidence of public structures to give an insight into the cultural history of the area.

8. But cf. Wilson, this volume, for recent evidence for public building in the second and first centuries BC.

9. Wilson (1990a: 48–9); Isler (1984); De Miro (1985–6); Scibona (1971: 3–20). Wilson makes a strong case for regarding the centres of some cities – for instance Monte Iato, where the *bouleuterion* was closed in the late republic – as decayed and no longer functioning administratively by the end of the first century BC.

10. Examples of imperial building of this type from Italy include the restoration of the walls at Saepinum by Tiberius and Drusus (*CIL* IX.2443), the aqueducts at Venafrum (*CIL* X.4842–3), Cingulum (*CIL* IX.5681) and Scolacium (*CIL* X.103), paid for by

Augustus (Venafrum) and Hadrian (Cingulum, Scolacium), and the harbours at Lupiae, built by Hadrian (Paus. 6.19.9), and at Ancona (*CIL* IX.5894) built by Trajan.

11. Tac. *Ann*. 4.43; Suet. *Claud*. 25.5. For the importance of the sanctuary at Eryx, cf. D.S. 4.83.4–7.

12. Wilson (1990a: 57–82); Mitens (1988); for a comparative chronology, see Jouffroy (1986: 320–32).

13. Wilson (1990: 80–7). For a chronology of amphitheatres, see Welch (1994: 59–79).

14. *CIL* X. 7295 (Panhormus); *AE* 1964: 181 (Lilybaeum); but in both cases the evidence for an amphitheatre is circumstantial, based on references to games, and to the office of *curator muneris publici*.

15. Wilson (1990a: 324–7). These were areas in which Greek was not the only (or possibly even the primary) indigenous language, and which had been under direct rule by Rome for longest. However, cf. Cic. *Caec*. 39 for the fact that Greek was spoken in western Sicily.

16. Plb. 1.7–64, 3.21–8; D.S. 23.1–24.13. Strab. 6.2.3 makes reference to the willingness of Messana to admit Romans as citizens.

17. Cic. *Verr*. 2.2.13 stresses not just Messana's support for Verres but also its Campanian identity, naming the *princeps civitatis* as G. Heius.

18. Lomas (1993: 174–87). The most vivid example of the changing emphases in cultural identity is Naples, where the unusually plentiful evidence gives an insight into the extent to which Greek and Roman features of civic life coexisted and were exploited for different audiences and different contexts.

19. Napoli (1959); Greco (1985: 132–9); Baldassare (1985: 221–32, 1984); D'Onofrio and D'Agostino (1987); Bragantini (1991).

20. E.g. *IG* XIV.277 (Lilybaeum – *M. Oualerios Chortôn*), XIV.272 (Selinus – *Markia*), XIV.21 (Syracuse – *Alphia Sôteris*), XIV.23 (Syracuse – *Aphrodisias Dionusiou*), XIV.410 (Messana – *Balerios Sôkratês*), XIV.529 (Catania – *Titos Ailis Biktôreinos*).

21. Cf. n. 20 for M. Valerius Chorton, and for Alphia Soteris. A Latin inscription from Thermae naming Antia M. F. Cleopatra (*CIL* X.7352) may also be an example.

22. There is a qualitative difference between the Greek proper names used as *cognomina* in the east, which sometimes seem to be selected for their status value, and those of Italy and the west, most of which are clearly slave names. Cf. Kajanto (1968). For high-status names in the eastern provinces see Bowie (1974: 198–201).

23. Mattingley (1976, nos 1670 and 1831). On Hadrian's philhellenic tendencies, cf. *SHA* 1.9.1; Spawforth and Walker (1985).

24. Mayer (1990) argues that onomastic and epigraphic displays of citizen status by freedmen reflect the need to demonstrate publicly a change of status.

25. Wilson (1990a: 328–9) lists both individuals and imported goods from Corinth, Crete, Syria, Athens, Alexandria and many other locations in the east.

26. Lomas (forthcoming) argues that there are major regional differences between Italy and Sicily in construction of ethnic identities and concepts of citizenship from the archaic period onwards, which are influenced by contact with non-Greek peoples.

27. Thuc. 6.17; Cic. *Verr*. 2.2.7. Both clearly have an agenda – Thucydides to stress the arguments for and against the Sicilian expedition, and Cicero to characterise the Sicilian Greeks as virtuous in opposition to the nefariousness of Verres – but nevertheless the distinction between Sicilians and other Greeks would not have had any force if it had not had some basis in either fact or cultural perception.

# 13  THE CHARM OF THE SIREN

I wish to thank Anthony Snodgrass for reading this chapter many times and for his stimulating comments. Tom Harrison has been a most challenging and encouraging reader. This chapter also benefited from conversations with Jon Hesk and comments on the final draft by Mary Beard, John Graham, Damien Browne and Guilio Lepschy. I thank them all. The translations from Italian and Latin texts are my own unless otherwise stated.

1. I owe the suggestion of an identification with Paolo Orsi to a conversation with Nigel Spivey. There have been other attempts to identify the character behind the senator; see La Rosa (1987: 702) for an identification with G. E. Rizzo, professor of Greek in Turin 1908–13.

2. For an account centred on prehistoric studies and archaeology see Leighton (1989).

3. Fazello writes that the people of Mazara should not be held responsible for having claimed that their city was the heir of Selinus; *odiosissimus* should be the man of culture who provided this wrong identification. Fazello here refers with acrimony to G. G. Adria (1485–1560), an erudite medical man, who wrote *De topographia inclytae civitatis Mazarae* in 1516. However, Fazello's preoccupation with setting apart the innocent perpetrators of the mistake from the creator of it, as well as the idea of a linear progress of knowledge, is problematised by the account of Riedesel, who writes about Mazara in 1772: 'The inhabitants insist upon it, that ancient Selinus stood here, though the ruins of three beautiful temples in Terra de Pulici, on the sea shore, prove the true situation of this town' (see Riedesel 1772: 18).

4. Now in *CIL* X.7192.

5. See Schnapp (1996: 182–5); on this see also Momigliano (1966: 10–14).

6. In the complex political scene of eighteenth-century Sicily, Biscari and Torremuzza were moderates of the anti-Spanish party. Torremuzza would discover the limits of his own reformism when faced with the loss of some of his lands to independent farmers (see Torremuzza 1804: 81). Still, his role in the reform of the University of Palermo and his support of Rosario Gregorio, the harshest critic of Fazello's model, attest to his politically progressive commitment (see Giarrizzo 1992).

7. The designer and craftsman who produced the academy's medallion was Padre Paciaudi. This man was also the main Italian correspondent of Caylus, sending to the comte in Paris the newest discoveries and 'best buys'. This coincidence of roles is suggestive of an atmosphere in which the activity of forgery could find its way into the scholarly enterprises of the time.

8. The ascent of Etna is a *topos*. Fazello had also described his ascent of Etna (see Fazello 1558: 56–63). His account is dominated by the tremendous fear provoked by the natural wonder of the volcano, which for him was a religious experience of the fear of God.

9. The different fate of Sicilian Greek art and that of classical Athens is well symbolised in the story of the metopes from Temple C at Selinus. The archaic metopes were excavated in 1823 by the British archaeologists William Harris and Samuel Angell. Through the British Consul in Naples, they asked the king for permission to bring the metopes to the British Museum, which had just received the Elgin Marbles. The permission was denied; the Sicilian government refunded the excavation expenses to the two archaeologists and offered casts of the metopes to the British Museum (see Pace 1935: 40–1).

# BIBLIOGRAPHY

Adamesteanu, D. (1955), 'Anaktora o sacelli?', *Archeologia Classica*, 7, pp. 179–86.

—— (1956), 'Le fortificazioni ad aggere nella Sicilia centro-meridionale', *Atti dell'Accademia Nazionale dei Lincei, Rendiconti*, ser. 8, 11, pp. 358–72.

—— (1962a), 'L'ellenizzazione della Sicilia e il momento di Ducetzio', in *Kokalos*, 8, pp. 167–98.

—— (1962b), 'Note su alcune vie siceliote di penetrazione', *Kokalos*, 8, pp. 199–209.

—— (1994–5), 'Butera: sede temporanea di una colonia greca arcaica?', *Atti e memorie della Società Magna Grecia*, ser. 3, pp. 109–17.

Adriani, A., Arias, P. E., Manni, E., Natoli, L. and Tusa, V. (1971), *Odeon e altri 'monumenti' archeologici*, Palermo: Banco di Sicilia.

—— (1974), 'La civiltà del ferro nell'Italia meridionale e nella Sicilia', in B. d'Agostino, P. Enrico and G. Colonna, *Popoli e civiltà dell'Italia artica*, Rome: Biblioteca di storia patria, vol. II, pp. 9–91.

Agostiniani, L. (1988–9), 'I modi del contatto linguistico tra Greci e indigeni nella Sicilia antica', *Kokalos*, 34–5, pp. 167–208.

Albanese Procelli, R. M. (1989), 'Tripodi geometrici dal rispostiglio di bronzi del Mendolito di Adrano', *MEFRA*, 101, pp. 643–77.

—— (1993), *Ripostigli di bronzi della Sicilia nel Museo Archeologico di Siracusa*, Palermo: Accademia Nazionale di Scienze, Lettere e Arti di Palermo.

—— (1995), 'Contacts and exchanges in protohistoric Sicily', in Fischer-Hansen (1995), pp. 33–49.

—— (1996a), 'Greeks and indigenous people in eastern Sicily: forms of inter-action and acculturation', in Leighton (1996a), pp. 167–76.

—— (1996b), 'Importazioni greche nei centri interni della Sicilia in età arcaica: aspetti dell'"acculturazione"', in *I vasi attici ed altre ceramiche coeve in Sicilia*, 2, Catania: C. N. R. and Centro di studio sull'archeologia greca, pp. 97–111.

—— (1997a), 'Échanges dans la Sicile archaique: amphores commerciales, intermédiaires et redistribution en milieu indigène', *RevArch*, pp. 3–25.

—— (1997b), 'Le etnie dell'età del ferro e le prime fondazioni coloniali', in S. Tusa (ed.), *Prima Sicilia: Alle origini della società siciliana*, Palermo: Ediprint, pp. 511–20.

Alexander, M. C. (1976), 'Hortensius' speech in defense of Verres', *Phoenix*, 30, pp. 46–53.

—— (1990), *Trials in the Late Roman Republic, 149–50 BC*, Toronto: University of Toronto Press.

Allen, H. L. (1976–7), 'The effect of population movements and diffusion on Iron Age Morgantina', *Kokalos,* 22–3, pp. 479–509.

Allen, R. E. (1983), *The Attalid Kingdom*, Oxford: Clarendon Press.

Alston, R. (1997), 'Changing ethnicities: from the Egyptian to the Roman city', in T. Cornell and K. Lomas (eds), *Gender and Ethnicity in Ancient Italy*, London: Accordia Research Centre, pp. 83–96.

Ampolo, C. (1997), *Storie greche: la formazione della moderna storiografia sugli antichi Greci*, Turin: Einaudi.

Anderson, B. (1991), *Imagined Communities: Reflections on the Origins and Spread of Nationalism*, London: Verso.

Andrewes, A. (1956), *The Greek Tyrants*, London: Hutchinson.

Antonaccio, C. (1997), 'Urbanism at archaic Morgantina', *Acta Hyperborea*, 7, pp. 167–93.

Antonaccio, C. and Neils, J. (1995), 'A new graffito from archaic Morgantina', *ZPE*, 101, pp. 261–77.

Ardener, E. (1989), *The Voice of Prophecy and Other Essays*, Oxford: Blackwell.

Arnold-Biucchi, C. (1988), 'La monetazione d'argento di Himera classica', *Quaderni Ticinesi di Numismatica e Antichità Classiche*, 17, pp. 85–100.

Arnold-Biucchi, C., Beer-Tobey, L. and Waggoner, N. M. (1988), 'A Greek archaic silver hoard from Selinus', *ANSMusN*, 33, pp. 1–35.

Asheri, D. (1988), 'Carthaginians and Greeks', in *CAH*², 4.2, pp. 739–80.

Avery, H. C. (1964), 'Dramatic devices in Aeschylus' *Persians*', *AJPh*, 85, pp. 173–84.

—— (1973), 'Themes in Thucydides' account of the Sicilian expedition', *Hermes*, 101, pp. 1–13.

Bacci, G. M. (1980–1), 'Ricerche a Taormina negli anni 1977–80', *Kokalos*, 26–7, pp. 348–73.

Badian, E. (1958), *Foreign Clientelae (264–70 BC)*, Oxford: Clarendon Press.

—— (1972), *Publicans and Sinners*, Oxford: Blackwell.

Baldassare, I. (1985), 'Osservazioni sull' urbanistica di Neapolis in età romana', in G. Pugliese Carratelli (ed.), *Neapolis: Atti del 25° Convegno di Studi sulla Magna Grecia*, Taranto: Instituto per la storia e l'archeologia della Magna Grecia, pp. 221–32.

Barra Bagnasco, M., De Miro, E. and Pinzone, A. (eds) (1999), *Origine e incontri di culture nell'antichità: Magna Grecia e Sicilia – stato degli studi e prospettive di ricerca* [Pelorias 4], Messina: Dipartimento di Scienze dell'Antichità della Università degli Studi di Messina.

Barrett, W. S. (1973), 'The twelfth *Olympian* and the fall of the Deinomenidai', *JHS*, 93, pp. 23–35.

Bartel, B. (1989), 'Acculturation and ethnicity in Roman Moesia Superior', in T.C. Champion (ed.), *Centre and Periphery*, London: Unwin Hyman, pp. 173–85.

Bechtold, B. (1997a), 'Una villa ellenistico-romana sull'acropoli sud di Segesta', in Nenci (1997), pp. 85–110.

—— (1997b), 'Elementi architettonici e strutturali dall'abitato ellenistico di Segesta', in Isler and Käch (1997), pp. 131–9.

Bejor, G. (1979), 'L'edificio teatrale nell'urbanizzazione Augustea', *Athenaeum*, 57, pp. 126–38.

—— (1983), 'Aspetti della romanizazzione della Sicilia', in *Modes de contacts et processus de transformation dans les sociétés anciennes* (= *Forme di contatto e processi di trasformazione nelle società antiche*), *Actes du colloque de Cortone (24–30 mai 1981)*, Pisa: Scuola Normale Superiore, pp. 345–78.

—— (1986), 'Gli insediamenti della Sicilia romana: distribuzione, tipologia e sviluppo da un primo inventario dei dati archeologici', in Giardina (1986), pp. 463–519.

—— (1991), 'Spunti diodorei e problematiche dell'archeologia siciliana', in Galvagno and Molè Ventura (1991), pp. 255–70.

Bell III, M. (1988), 'Excavations at Morgantina, 1980–1985: preliminary report XII', *AJA*, 92, pp. 313–42.

Belvedere, O. (1995), 'Land tenure and settlement in Roman Sicily', in Fischer-Hansen (1995), pp. 195–208.

—— (1997), 'Prospezione archeologica nel territorio imerese', in Isler and Käch (1997), pp. 91–6.

Berger, S. (1992), *Revolution and Society in Greek Sicily and Southern Italy*, Historia Einzelschriften 71, Stuttgart: F. Steiner Verlag.

Bergquist, B. (1990), 'Sympotic space: a functional aspect of Greek dining-rooms', in O. Murray (ed.), *Sympotica*, Oxford: Clarendon Press, pp. 37–65.

Bernabò Brea, L. (1957), *Sicily before the Greeks*, London: Thames and Hudson.

—— (1964–5), 'Due secoli di studi, scavi e restauri del teatro greco di Tindari', *RIA,* n.s. 13–14, pp. 99–144.

—— (1967), 'La necropoli di Longane', *Bullettino di Paletnologia Italiana*, 76, pp. 181–253.

—— (1990), *Pantalica: Ricerche intorno all'anaktoron*, Cahiers du Centre Jean Bérard 15, Naples: Centre Jean Bérard.

Bernabò Brea, L. and Cavalier, M. (1965), 'Tindari: area urbana. L'insula IV e le strade che la circondano', *Bollettino dell'Arte*[5], 50, pp. 205–9.

—— (1968), *Meligunìs-Lipára III: Stazioni preistoriche delle isole Panarea, Salina e Stromboli*, Palermo: Flaccovio.

—— (1980), *Meligunìs-Lipára IV: L'acropoli di Lipari nella preistoria*, Palermo: Flaccovio.

Berve, H. (1959), 'König Hieron II', *ABAW*, 47, pp. 1–99.

Bietti Sestieri, A. M., Lentini, M. C. and Voza, G. (eds) (1996), *Sicilia orientale e isole eolie*, Guide archeologiche, Preistoria e Protostoria 12, Forlì: MAC.

Biscari, I. V. (1771), *Discorso accademico sopra un'iscrizione trovata nel teatro della città di Catania*, Catania.

—— (1781), *Viaggio per tutte le antichità della Sicilia*, Naples.

—— (1787), *Descrizione del museo d'antiquaria*, Livorno.

Bitterli, L. (1989), *Cultures in Conflict: Encounters between European and Non-European Cultures, 1492–1800*, Cambridge: Polity Press.

Blinkenberg, Chr. (1917), *L'Image d'Athana Lindia: Lindiaka I*, Copenhagen: Det Kgl. Danske Videnskabernes Selskab.

—— (1931), *Lindos I: Les Petits Objets*, Berlin: Fondation Carlsberg.

—— (1941), *Lindos II: Inscriptions*, 1, Berlin: Fondation Carlsberg.

—— (1980), *The Chronicle of the Temple of Athena Lindus in Rhodes*, Chicago: Ares.

Bloesch, H. and Isler, H. P. (eds) (1976), *Studia Ietina I*, Zurich: E. Rentsch.

Boardman, J. (1980), *The Greeks Overseas*, London: Thames and Hudson.

Boedeker, D. (1988), 'Protesilaos and the end of Herodotus' Histories', *Classical Antiquity*, 7, pp. 30–48.

Bonacasa, N. (1999), 'Per una revisione della cultura figurativa ellenistica in Sicilia', in Barra Bagnasco et al. (1999), pp. 259–73.

Bonacasa, N. and Joly, E. (1985), 'L'ellenismo e la tradizione ellenistica', in Pugliese Carratelli (1985), pp. 277–358.

Bonacasa Carra, R. M. (1974), 'Le fortificazioni ad aggere della Sicilia', *Kokalos*, 20, pp. 92–118.

Bonanno, A. (1973), 'Punici e Graeci sul Monte Pellegrino', *SicArch*, 21–2, pp. 55–62.

Bowersock, G. W. (1965), *Augustus and the Greek World*, Oxford: Clarendon Press.

Bowie, E. L. (1974), 'The Greeks and their past in the Second Sophistic', in M. I. Finley (ed.), *Studies in Ancient Society*, London: Routledge, pp. 166–209.

Bowman, A. K. (1996), *Egypt After the Pharaohs 332 BC–AD 642*, 2nd edn, Oxford: Oxford University Press.

Bowra, C. M. (1964), *Pindar*, Oxford: Oxford University Press.

Bradley, G. (1997), 'Iguvines, Umbrians and Romans: ethnic identity in central Italy', in T. Cornell and K. Lomas (eds), *Gender and Ethnicity in Ancient Italy*, London: Accordia Research Centre, pp. 53–67.

Bradley, G. J. and Wilson, J. P. (forthcoming), *Parallel Studies in Greek and Roman Colonisation*, London: Duckworth and Classical Press of Wales.

Bragantini, I. (ed.) (1991), *Ricerche archeologiche a Napoli: Lo scavo di Palazzo Corigliano I*, Naples: Istituto Universitario Orientale.

Braund, D. C. (1984), *Rome and the Friendly King*, London: Croom Helm.

Brunt, P. A. (1971), *Italian Manpower*, Oxford: Clarendon Press.

Bryson, W. (1991), *Mother Tongue: The English Language*, London: Penguin.

Buckler, C. (1992), 'Two Sicilian skenai: a modified view', *Archäologischer Anzeiger*, pp. 277–93.

Burnett, A. M. (ed.) (1987), *The Coinage of the Roman World in the Late Republic*, Oxford: British Archaeological Reports.

Burnett, A. M., Amandry, M. and Ripollès, P. P. (1992), *Roman Provincial Coinage*, I, London: British Museum Press, and Paris: Bibliothèque Nationale.

Cahn, H. A. (1979), ' "Olynthus" and Syracuse', in O. Mørkholm and N. M. Waggoner (eds), *Essays in Honor of Margaret Thompson*, Wetteren: Editions NR, pp. 47–52.

Calderone, S. (1964–5), 'Problemi dell'organizzazione della provincia di Sicilia', *Kokalos*, 10–11, pp. 63–98.

Camerata Scovazzo, R. (ed.) (1996), *Segesta I: la carta archeologica*, Palermo: Sellerio.

Campagna, L. (1996), 'Una nuova abitazione ad Eraclea Minoa: primi dati', in D'Andrea and Mannino (1996), pp. 111–22.

—— (1997), 'Note sulla decorazione architettonica della scena del teatro di Segesta', in Nenci (1997), pp. 227–49.

Carcopino, J. (1914), *La Loi de Hiéron et les Romains*, Paris: de Boccard.

Carey, C. (1981), *A Commentary on Five Odes of Pindar*, Salem NH: Ayer.

Carra Bonacasa, R. M. and Guidobaldi, F. (eds) (1997), *Atti del IV Colloquio dell'Associazione italiana per lo studio e la conservazione del mosaico*, Ravenna: Edizioni del Girasole.

Castellana, G. (1988–9), 'Ricerche nel territorio agrigentino', *Kokalos*, 34–5, pp. 503–40.

—— (1992), 'Nuovi dati su scavi condotti nel versante orientale del Basso Belice e nel bacino finale del Platani', *Giornate internazionali di studi sull'area elima (Gibellina 1991)*, Atti 1, pp. 191–202.

Castiglione, M. A. (1997), 'La ceramica a Vernice Nera', in C. A. Di Stefano (ed.), *Archeologia e Territorio*, Palermo: Palumbo, pp. 307–14.

Caven, B. (1980), *The Punic Wars*, London: Weidenfeld and Nicolson.

—— (1990), *Dionysius I: Warlord of Syracuse*, London: Yale University Press.

Caylus, A. C. F. de (1752), *Recueil d'Antiquités Egyptiennes, Romaines, Grecques et Gauloises*, 1–7, Paris: Desaint and Saillaut.

Clark, E. D. (1994), 'Roman legionary forces in Sicily during the Second Punic War: the number of legions stationed on the island from 214 to 210', *AHB*, 4. 4 (Trent University: World Wide Web Page, <www.trentu.ca/ahb>).

Clemente, G. (1980–1), 'Considerazioni sulla Sicilia nell'impero romano (III sec. a.C.–V sec. d.C.)', *Kokalos*, 26–7, pp. 192–219.

—— (1988), 'Sicily and Rome: the impact of empire on a Roman province', in Yuge and Doi (1988), pp. 105–20.

Coarelli, F. (1980), 'La cultura figurativa in Sicilia nei secoli IV–III a.C.', in Gabba and Vallet (1980), pp. 157–82.

—— (1981), 'La Sicilia tra la fine della guerra annibalica e Cicerone', in Giardina e Schiavone (1981), pp. 1–18.

Coldstream, J. N. (1968), *Greek Geometric Pottery*, London: Methuen.

Coleman, K. M. (forthcoming), 'Augustus and the spectacles of the arena', in T. J. Cornell and K. Lomas (eds), *Bread and Circuses: Patronage and Euergetism in Roman Italy*, London: Routledge.

Colley, L. (1992), *Britons: Forging the Nation 1707–1837*, New York: Yale University Press.

Connor, W. R. (1977), 'Tyrannis polis', in J. H. D'Arms and J. W. Eadie (eds), *Ancient and Modern: Essays in Honour of Gerald F. Else,* Ann Arbor: Centre for Coordination of Ancient and Modern Studies, pp. 95–109.

—— (1984), *Thucydides*, Princeton NJ: Princeton University Press.

Cook, A. B. (1895), 'The bee in Greek mythology', *JHS*, 15, pp. 1–24.

Cooper, F. and Morris, S. (1990), 'Dining in round buildings', in O. Murray (ed.), *Sympotica*, Oxford: Clarendon Press, pp. 66–85.

Cordsen, A. (1995), 'The Pastas House in archaic Greek Sicily', in Fischer–Hansen (1995), pp. 103–21.

Cornell, T. (1996), 'Hannibal's legacy: the effects of the Hannabalic war on Italy', in T. Cornell, B. Rankov and P. Sabin (eds), *The Second Punic War: A Reappraisal*, London: Institute of Classical Studies, University of London, pp. 97–117.

Cornford, F. M. (1907), *Thucydides Mythistoricus*, London: Arnold.

Corradini, A. M. (1999), 'Erbesso, dalle rovine il teatro: un' altra avventura archeologica', Giornale di Sicilia 11/8/99, 42.

Costabile, F. (1978), *Municipium Locrensium*, Naples: Conte.

Costantini, L., Piperno, M. and Tusa, S. (1987), 'La néolithisation de la Sicile occidentale d'après les résultats des fouilles à la grotte de l'Uzzo (Trapani)', in J. Guileine (ed.), *Premières communautés paysannes en méditerranée occidentale: Actes du colloque international du C. N. R. S.*, Paris: Editions du Centre National de la Recherche Scientifique, pp. 400–20.

Coulton, J. J. (1976), *The Architectural Development of the Greek Stoa*, Oxford: Clarendon Press.

Crawford, M. (1985), *Coinage and Money under the Roman Republic: Italy and the Mediterranean Economy*, London: Methuen.

—— (1987), 'Sicily', in Burnett (1987), pp. 43–51.

Cristofani, M. (1987), 'Il banchetto in Etruria', in *L'alimentazione nel mondo antico*, Rome: Istituto poligrafico e Zecca dello Stato, pp. 123–32.

Curti, E., Dench, E. and Patterson, J. (1996), 'The archaeology of central and southern Roman Italy: recent trends and approaches', *JRS*, 86, pp. 170–89.

Cusumano, N. (1994), *Una terra splendida e facile da possedere*, Rome: G. Bretschneider.

Cutroni Tusa, A., Italia, A., Lima, D. and Tusa, V. (1994), *Solunto*, Itinerari XV, Rome: Libreria dello Stato.

Daehn, H.-St (1991), *Studia Ietina III: Die Gebaüde an der West seite der Agora von Iaitas*, Zurich: E. Rentsch.

D'Agostino, B. (1987), 'L'immagine, la pittura e la tomba nell'Etruria arcaica', in *Images et société en Grèce ancienne*, in Cahiers d'Archéologie Romande, 36, Lausanne: Institut d'archéologie et d'histoire ancienne, Université de Lausanne, pp. 215–19.

—— (1989), 'Image and society in archaic Etruria', *JRS,* 79, pp. 1–10.

Dahlheim, W. (1968), *Struktur und Entwicklung des römischen Völkerrechts*, Munich: Beck.

Dalcher, K. (1994), *Studia Ietina VI: Das Peristylhaus 1*, Zurich: E. Rentsch.

D'Andrea, F. (1997), 'Ricerche archeologiche sul teatro di Segesta', in Nenci (1997), pp. 429–50.

D'Andrea, F. and Mannino, K. (eds) (1996), *Ricerche sulla casa in Magna Grecia e in Sicilia,* Atti del Colloquio – Lecce, 23–4 June 1992, Galatina: Congedo Editore.

Daube, D. (1951), 'The peregrine praetor', *JRS*, 41, pp. 66–70.

Davies, J. K. (1993), *Democracy and Classical Greece*, 2nd edn, London: Fontana.

Davies, M. and Kathivithamby, J. (1986), *Greek Insects*, London: Duckworth.

De Angelis, F. (1998), 'Ancient past, imperial present: the British Empire in T. J. Dunbabin's *The Western Greeks*', *Antiquity*, 72, pp. 539–49.

—— (forthcoming), 'Subsistence and surplus: the agricultural basis of Greek Sicily', *PBSR*, 68.

De Miro, E. (1965), *L'antiquarium e la zona archeologica di Eraclea Minoa*, Itinerari dei Musei, Gallerie e monumenti d'Italia 110, Rome: Libreria dello Stato.

—— (1980), 'La casa greca in Sicilia: testimonianze nella Sicilia centrale dal VI al III sec.a.C.', in M. José Fontana, M. R. Paraino and F. P. Rizzo (eds), Φιλίας χάριν: *Miscellanea di studi classici in onore di E. Manni*, Rome: G. Bretschneider, pp. 709–37.

—— (1985–6), 'Il bouleuterion di Agrigento: aspetti topografici, archeologici e storici', *QuadMess*, 1, pp. 7–12.

—— (1988), 'Polizzello, centro della Sicania', *Quad Mess*, 3, pp. 25–41.

—— (1988–9), 'Gli "indigeni" della Sicilia centro-meridionale', *Kokalos*, 34–5, pp. 19–46.

De Miro, E. and Fiorentini, G. (1976–7), 'Relazione sull'attività della Soprintendenza alle antichità di Agrigento (1972–1976)', *Kokalos*, 22–3, pp. 423–55.

Dench, E. (1995), *From Barbarians to New Men: Greek, Roman and Modern Perceptions of Peoples of the Central Apennines*, Oxford: Clarendon Press.

Dentzer, J. M. (1982), *Le motif du banquet couché dans le proche-Orient et le monde grec du VIIe du IVe siècle avant J.-C.*, Rome: École française de Rome.

De Polignac, F. (1991), *La nascità della città greca: culti, spazio e società nei secoli VIII e VII a.C.*, Milan: Jaca.

De Rosalia, A. (1992), 'Il De rebus Siculis di Tommaso Fazello', in Fazello (1992), pp. 17–38.

Derow, P. S. (1995), 'Herodotus readings', *Classics Ireland*, 2, pp. 229–51.

Dewailly, M. (1992), *Les statuettes aux parures du sanctuaire de la Malaphoros à Selinonte*, Naples: Cahiers du Centre Jean Bérard.

Dewald, C. (1997), 'Wanton kings, pickled heroes and gnomic founding fathers: strategies of meaning at the end of Herodotus' *Histories*', in D. H. Roberts, F. M. Dunn and D. Fowler (eds), *Classical Closure*, Princeton NJ: Princeton University Press, pp. 62–82.

Dietler, M. (1989), 'Greeks, Etruscans and thirsty barbarians: early Iron Age interaction in the Rhône basin of France', in T. C. Champion (ed.), *Centre and Periphery*, London: Unwin Hyman, pp. 127–41.

Dinsmoor, W. (1927 repr. with revisions 1950), *The Architecture of Ancient Greece*, London: Batsford.

Di Stefano, C. A. (ed.) (1993), *Di terra in terra: nuove scoperte archeologiche nella provincia di Palermo*, Palermo: Regione Siciliana and Soprintendenza per i beni culturali ambientali e P. I.

—— (1997a), 'Ricerche archeologiche su Monte Pellegrino', in C. A. Di Stefano (ed.), *Archeologia e Territorio*, Palermo: Palumbo, pp. 3–11.

—— (1997b), 'Nuove ricerche nell'edificio B di Piazza della Vittoria a Palermo e interventi di restauro del mosaico della caccia', in Carra Bonacasa and Guidobaldi (1977), pp. 7–18.

Di Stefano, G. (1987), 'Il territorio di Camarina in età arcaica', *Kokalos*, 33, pp. 129–207.

Domínguez, A. J. (1989), *La Colonización Griega en Sicilia. Griegos, Indígenas y Púnicos en la Sicilia arcaica: Interacción y Acculteración*, Oxford: British Archaeological Reports.

D'Onofrio, A. M. and D'Agostino, B. (eds) (1987), *Ricerche archeologiche a Napoli: lo scavo in Largo S. Aniello (1982–83)*, Naples: Istituto Universitario Orientale.

D'Orville, J. P. (1764), *Sicula quibus Siciliae veteris rudera illustrantur*, Amsterdam.

Dunbabin, K. M. D. (1999), *Mosaics of the Greek and Roman World*, Cambridge: Cambridge University Press.

Dunbabin, T. J. (1948), *The Western Greeks*, Oxford: Clarendon Press.

—— (ed.), (1962), *Perachora II*, Oxford: Clarendon Press.

Eckstein, A. M. (1980), '*Unicum subsidium populi Romani*: Hiero II and Rome, 263 BC–215 BC', *Chiron*, 10, pp. 183–203.

Erdkamp, P. (1998), *Hunger and the Sword*, Amsterdam: Gieben.

Falsone, G. (1995), 'Sicile', in V. Krings (ed.), *La Civilisation Phénicienne et Punique*, Leiden: Brill, pp. 674–97.

Fazello, T. (1558), *De rebus Siculis decades duae*, Palermo.

—— (1753), *De rebus Siculis decades duae: auctarium ad res Sicules ab anno 1556 ad 1750*, Catania.

—— (1992), *Storia di Sicilia*, Palermo: Regione Siciliana, Assessorato dei beni Culturali e Ambientali e della Pubblica Instruzione.

Feldherr, A. (1995), 'Ships of state: *Aeneid* 5 and Augustan circus spectacle', *Classical Antiquity,* 14, pp. 245–65.

Fentress, E., Kennet, D. and Valenti, I. (1986), 'A Sicilian villa and its landscape (contrada Mirabile, Mazara del Vallo, 1988)', *Opus*, 5 [publ. 1990], pp. 75–87.

Ferrary, J.-L. (1988), *Philhellénisme et Impérialisme. Aspects idéologiques de la Conquête Romaine du Monde Hellénistique*, Rome: École française de Rome.

Filippi, A. (1996), *Antichi insediamenti nel territorio di Alcamo*, Alcamo: Carrubba Editore.

Finley, M. I. (1968 2nd edn, 1979), *Ancient Sicily*, London: Chatto and Windus.

Fiorentini, G. (1988–9), 'Sovrintendenza ai Beni Culturali e Ambientali per le provincie di Agrigento, di Caltanisetta e di Enna. Sezione Beni Archeologici, Attività della Sezione Beni Archeologici (1987–1989)', *Beni culturali e ambientali Sicilia*, ix–x.3, 11–35.

—— (1993–4), 'Attività di indagini archeologiche della soprintendenza beni culturali e ambientali di Agrigento', *Kokalos*, 39–40, pp. 717–33.

—— (1995), *Monte Adranone*, Rome: Libreria dello Stato.

Fischer-Hansen, T. (ed.) (1995), *Ancient Sicily*, Acta Hyperborea 6, Copenhagen: Museum Tusculanum Press.

Flory, S. (1993), 'The death of Thucydides and the motif of "land on sea"', in R. M. Rosen and J. Farrell (eds), *Nomodeiktes: Greek Studies in Honor of Martin Ostwald*, Ann Arbor: University of Michigan Press, pp. 113–23.

Fornara, C. W. (1971a), *Herodotus: An Interpretative Essay*, Oxford: Oxford University Press.

—— (1971b), 'Evidence for the date of Herodotus' publication', *JHS*, 91, pp. 25–34.

Fouilland, F., Frasca, M. and Pelagatti, P. (1995), 'Monte Casasia', *NSc*, ser. 9, 5–6, pp. 323–583.

Foxhall, L. (1998), 'Cargoes of the heart's desire: the character of trade in the archaic Mediterranean world', in N. Fisher and H. van Wees (eds), *Archaic Greece: New Approaches and New Evidence*, London: Duckworth and Classical Press of Wales, pp. 295–309.

Francis, E. D. and Vickers, M. (1984), 'Amasis and Lindos', *BICS*, 31, pp. 119–30.

Frank, T. (ed.) (1938), *Economic Survey of Ancient Rome. Volume III: Britain, Spain, Sicily, Gaul*, Baltimore: Johns Hopkins University Press.

Frasca, M. (1978), 'Interventi', *Cronache di Archeologia e di Storia dell'Arte*, 17, pp. 116–18.

—— (1981), 'La necropoli di M. Finocchito', *Cronache di Archeologia e di Storia dell'Arte*, 20, pp. 13–102.

—— (1983), 'Una nuova capanna "sicula" a Siracusa, in Ortigia: tipologia dei materiali', *MEFRA*, 95, pp. 565–98.

Freeman, E. A. (1891–4), *The History of Sicily from the Earliest Times*, Oxford: Clarendon Press.

Frézouls, E. (1983), 'Le théâtre romain et la culture urbain', in *La città come fatta di cultura*, Como: Newpress, pp. 105–30.

Fusaro, D. (1982), 'Note di architettura domestica greca nel periodo tardo-geometrico e arcaico', *Dd'A*, 1.4, pp. 5–30.

Gabba, E. and Vallet, G. (eds) (1980), *La Sicilia antica*, vol. 2, Naples: Società editrice storia di Napoli e della Sicilia.

Galinsky, G. K. (1969), *Aeneas, Sicily, and Rome*, Princeton NJ: Princeton University Press.

—— (1977), *Augustan Culture: An Interpretive Introduction*, Princeton NJ: Princeton University Press.

Gallini, C. (1973), 'Che cosa intendere per ellenizzazione? Problemi di metodo', *Dd'A*, 7, pp. 175–91.

Galvagno, E. and Molè Ventura, C. (eds) (1991), *Mito, storia, tradizione: Diodoro Siculo e la storiografia classica*, Atti del Convegno Internazionale, Catania-Agira, 7–8 December 1984, Catania: Edizioni del Prisma.

Ganci, M. (1992), *Presentazione*, in Fazello (1992), pp. 5–14.

Gandolfo, L. (1997a), 'Rinvenimenti monetari', in C. A. Di Stefano (ed.), *Archeologia e Territorio*, Palermo: Palumbo, pp. 315–36.

—— (1997b), 'Le monete', in C. A. Di Stefano (ed.), *Archeologia e Territorio*, Palermo: Palumbo, pp. 22–4.

Gardner, P. (1876), 'Segesta', in R. S. Poole (ed.), *A Catalogue of Greek Coins in the British Museum: Sicily*, London: British Museum, pp. 130–7.

Garofano, I. (1997), 'Il materiale ceramico', in C. A. Di Stefano (ed.), *Archeologia e Territorio*, Palermo: Palumbo, pp. 11–22.

Gelzer, M. (1969), *The Roman Nobility*, Oxford: Blackwell.

Genière, J. de la (1995), 'Les Grecs et les autres: quelques aspects de leurs relations en Italie du Sud à l'époque archaïque', in *Les Grecs et l'Occident: Actes de Colloque de la Villa 'Kerylos' (1991)*, Rome: École française de Rome, pp. 29–39.

Gernet, L. (1968), 'Mariages de tyrans', in L. Gernet, *Anthropologie de la Grèce Antique*, Paris: Maspero, pp. 344–59.

Giardina, A. (ed.) (1986), *Società romana e impero tardoantico: le merci, gli insediamenti*, Rome and Bari: Laterza.

Giardina, A. and Schiavone, A. (eds) (1981), *Società romana e produzione schiavistica. L'Italia: insediamenti e forme economiche*, Rome and Bari: Laterza.

Giardino, C. (1995), *Il Mediterraneo Occidentale fra XIV e VIII secolo a.C: cerchie minerarie e metallurgiche. The West Mediterranean between the 14th and 8th Centuries BC: Mining and Metallurgical Spheres*, Oxford: British Archaeological Reports.

—— (1996), 'Miniere e tecniche metallurgiche nella Sicilia protostorica', in Leighton (1996a), pp. 129–38.

Giarrizzo, G. and Aymard, M. (eds) (1987), *Storia d'Italia. Le regioni dall'unità a oggi: la Sicilia*, Turin: Einaudi.

—— (1992), *Cultura e Economia nella Sicilia del '700*, Rome: Salvatore Sciascia.

Gildersleeve, B. L. (1907), *Pindar, the Olympian and Pythian Odes*, London: Macmillan.

Giordano, P. (1997), 'Ricognizioni nel territorio', in C. A. Di Stefano (ed.), *Archeologia e Territorio*, Palermo: Palumbo, pp. 337–48.

Giumlia-Mair, A. R. and Craddock, P. T. (1993), *Corinthium aes: das schwarze Gold der Alchimisten*, Sondernummer 1993 *Antike Welt*, Mainz: P. von Zabern.

Glenn, E. S. (1981), *Man and Mankind: Conflict and Communication between Cultures*, Norwood NJ: Ablex.

Goldhill, S. D. (1988), 'Battle narrative and politics in Aeschylus' *Persae*', *JHS*, 108, pp. 189–93.

Graham, A. J. (1971), *Colony and Mother City in Ancient Greece*, 2nd edn, Manchester: Manchester University Press.

Gras, M. (1983), 'Vin et société à Rome et dans le Latium à l'époque archaique', in *Modes du contacts et processus de transformation dans les sociétés anciennes*, Actes du Colloque de Cortone 1981, Pisa: Scuola normale superiore, pp. 1067–75.

Greco, C. (1993–4), 'Note di topografia soluntina: saggi di scavo sul promontorio di Sòlanto', *Kokalos*, 39–40, pp. 1165–76.

—— (1997a), 'Solunto: scavi e ricerche nel biennio 1992–93', in Nenci (1997), pp. 889–908.

—— (1997b), 'Pavimenti in *opus signinum* e tessellati geometrici da Solunto:

una messa a punto', in Carra Bonacasa and Guidobaldi (1997), pp. 39–62.

—— (1997c), 'Nuovi elementi per l'identificazione di Solunto arcaica', in Isler and Käch (1997), pp. 97–111.

Greco, E. (1985), 'Problemi urbanistici', in L. Macchiaroli (ed.), *Napoli Antica*, Naples: Museo Archeologico Nazionale di Napoli, pp. 132–9.

Greco, E. and Theodorescu, D. (1983), *Poseidonia–Paestum II: L'Agora*, Rome: L'Erma di Bretschneider.

—— (1987), *Poseidonia–Paestum III: Forum Nord*, Rome: L'Erma di Bretschneider.

Greco, G. and Pontrandolfo, A. (eds) (1990), *Fratte: un insediamento etrusco-campano*, Modena: F. C. Panini.

Gros, P. (1994), 'Les théâtres en Italie au Ier siècle de notre ère: situation et fonctions dans l'urbanisme impérial', in *L'Italie d'Auguste à Dioclétien: actes du colloque internationale de l'École française de Rome*, CEFAR, 94, Rome: École française de Rome, pp. 285–307.

—— (1996), *L'architecture romaine du début du III<sup>e</sup> siècle av. J.-C. à la fin du Haut-Empire. I: les monuments publics*, Paris: Picard.

Gruen, E. S. (1992), *Culture and National Identity in Republican Rome*, Ithaca NY: Cornell University Press.

Guzzone, C. (1985–6), 'Sulla necropoli protostorica di Butera: i recinti funerari 138 e 139', *Archivio storico per la Sicilia Orientale*, 81–2, pp. 7–41.

Hall, E. (1996), *Aeschylus: Persians*, Warminster: Aris and Phillips.

Hall, J. M. (1997), *Ethnic Identity in Greek Antiquity*, Cambridge: Cambridge University Press.

Hallward, B. L. (1954), 'Scipio and victory', in S. A. Cook, F. E. Adcock and M. P. Charlesworth (eds), *CAH*, 8, Cambridge: Cambridge University Press, pp. 83–115.

Harris, W. V. (1976), 'The development of the quaestorship, 267–81 BC', *CQ*, n.s. 26, pp. 92–106.

Harrison, T. (2000), *Divinity and History: The Religion of Herodotus*, Oxford: Oxford University Press.

Hartog, F. (1988), *The Mirror of Herodotus*, tr. J. Lloyd, Berkeley CA: University of California Press.

Head, B. V. (1911), *Historia Numorum*, 2nd edn, Oxford: Clarendon Press.

Henig, M. (ed.) (1990), *Architecture and Architectural Sculpture in the Roman Empire*, Oxford: Oxford University Committee for Archaeology.

Herring, E. (1991), 'Power relations in Iron Age southeast Italy', in E. Herring, R. Whitehouse and J. Wilkins (eds), *The Archaeology of Power,* papers of the fourth conference of Italian archaeology, 2.2, London: Accordia Research Centre, Queen Mary and Westfield College, University of London, pp. 117–33.

Herrmann, H. V. (1983), 'Altitalisches und Etruskisches in Olympia', *Annuario della Scuola Archeologica di Atene*, 61, pp. 271–94.

Herskovits, M. J. (1948), *Man and his Works: The Science of Cultural Anthropology*, New York: Alfred A. Knopf.

Hill, G. F. (1903), *Coins of Ancient Sicily*, Westminster: Constable.

Himmelmann-Wildschütz, N. (1971), *Archäologisches zum Problem der griechischen Sklaverei*, Mainz: Verlag der Akademie der Wissenschaften und der Literatur Wiesbaden.

Hodos, T. (1997), 'Craft relations in South-eastern Sicily during the period of Greek colonisation', Oxford: unpublished DPhil dissertation.

—— (1999), 'Intermarriage in the western Greek colonies', *OJA*, 18.1, pp. 61–78.

Hoepfner, W. and Brands, G. (eds) (1996), *Basileia: die Paläste der hellenistischen Könige*, Internationales Symposion in Berlin vom 16.12.1992 bis 20.12.1992, Mainz: P. von Zabern.

Holleaux, M. (1921), *Rome, la Grèce et les monarchies hellénistiques au IIIe siècle avant J.-C. (273–205)*, Paris: de Boccard.

Hollegaard Olsen, C. (1995), 'The Roman *domus* of the early empire. A case study: Sicily', in Fischer-Hansen (1995), pp. 209–62.

Holloway, R. R. (1962), 'Eagle and fulmen on the coins of Syracuse', *RBN*, 108, pp. 5–27.

—— (1990), 'The geography of the southern Sicels', in J. P. Descoeudres (ed.), ΕΥΜΟΥΣΙΑ: *Ceramic and Iconographic Studies in Honour of Alexander Cambitoglou*, Mediterranean Archaeology Supplement, 1, pp. 147–53.

—— (1991), *The Archaeology of Ancient Sicily*, London: Routledge.

—— (1998), Review of Leighton (1996a), *AJA*, 102, pp. 626–7.

Holloway, R. R. and Lukesh, S. S. (1997), 'Ustica, località Faraglioni: perché castello?', in C. A. Di Stefano (ed.), *Archeologia e Territorio*, Palermo: Palumbo, pp. 455–60.

Holm, A. (1901), *Storia della Sicilia nell'antichità*, III, Turin: C. Clausen.

Hornblower, S. (1983), *The Greek World 479–323 BC*, London: Methuen.

—— (1987), *Thucydides*, London: Duckworth.

—— (1991–6), *A Commentary on Thucydides*, 1–2, Oxford: Oxford University Press.

Humphreys, S. C. (1966), 'Colonie e madre patria nella Grecia antica', *Rivista Storica Italiana*, 78, pp. 912–21.

Hunter, V. (1973), *Thucydides the Artful Reporter*, Toronto: Hakkert.

—— (1977), 'The composition of Thucydides', *History*: a new answer to the problem', *Historia*, 26, pp. 269–94.

Iannello, A. (1994), 'I *bouleuteria* in Sicilia: fonti e monumenti', *QuadMess*, 9, pp. 63–98.

Isaacs, H. R. (1975), 'Basic group identity: the idols of the tribe', in N. Glazer and D. P. Moyhihan (eds), *Ethnicity: Theory and Experience*, Cambridge MA: Harvard University Press.

Isler, H. P. (1991), *Monte Iato: guida archeologica*, Palermo: Sellerio.

—— (1984), *Studia ietina II*, Zurich: Eugen Rentsch.

—— (1992), 'Monte Iato: la ventunesima campagna di scavo', *Sicilia archeologica,* 25.78–9, pp. 7–43.

—— (1996), 'Einflüsse der makedonischen Palastarchitektur in Sizilien?', in Hoepfner and Brands (1996), pp. 252–7.

—— (1997a), 'Monte Iato: scavi 1992–1994', in Nenci (1997), pp. 1019–28.

—— (1997b), 'Monte Iato: mosaici e pavimenti', in Carra Bonacasa and Guidobaldi (1997), pp. 19–32.

—— (1997c), 'Monte Iato – L'abitato di epoca ellenistica', in Isler and Käch (1997), pp. 29–35.

Isler, H. P. and Käch, D. (eds) (1997), *Wohnbauforschung in Zentral- und Westsizilien: Akten/Sicilia occidentale e centro-meridionale: ricerche archeologiche nell'abitato. Atti*, Zurich: Archäologisches Institut der Universität Zürich.

Isler-Kerényi, C. (1976), 'Die Stützfiguren des griechischen Theaters von Iaitas: Teil II', in Bloesch and Isler (1976), pp. 30–48.

Jeffery, L. H. (1978), *Archaic Greece*, London: Methuen.

Jenkins, G. K. (1990), *Ancient Greek Coins*, 2nd revised edn, London: Seaby.

Johns, J. (1992), 'Monreale survey: l'insediamento umano nell'alto Belice dall'età paleolitica al 1250 d.C.', in Nenci (1992), pp. 407–20.

Johnson, W. A. (1995), 'Oral performance and the composition of Herodotus' *Histories*', *Greek, Roman and Byzantine Studies*, 36, pp. 229–54.

Jones, R. E. and Vagnetti, L. (1991), 'Traders and craftsmen in the central Mediterranean: archaeological evidence and archaeometric research', in N. H. Gale (ed.), *Bronze Age Trade in the Mediterranean*, Jonsered: Åström, pp. 127–47.

Jones, S. (1996), 'Discourses of identity in the interpretation of the past', in P. Graves-Brown (ed.), *Cultural Identity and Archaeology*, London: Routledge, pp. 62–80.

Jouffroy, H. (1986), *La construction publique en Italie et dans L'Afrique Romaine*, Strasbourg: AECR.

Kajanto, I. (1968), 'The significance of non-Latin *cognomina*', *Latomus*, 27, pp. 517–34.

Karlsson, L. (1993), 'Did the Romans allow the Sicilian Greeks to fortify their cities in the third century BC?', *Acta Hyperborea*, 5, pp. 31–51.

—— (1996), 'A "dining-room" on the acropolis of San Giovenale? Preliminary notes on House 1', *Opuscula Romana*, 20, pp. 265–9.

Keppie, L. (1983), *Colonisation and Veteran Settlement in Italy 47–14 BC*, London: British School at Rome.

Kilian-Dirlmeier, I. (1985), 'Fremde Weihungen in griechischen Heiligtümern vom 8. bis zum Beginn des 7. Jahrhunderts v. Chr.', *Jahrbuch des Römisch-Germanischen Zentralmuseums*, 32, pp. 215–54.

Kitto, H. D. F. (1950), *Greek Tragedy. A Literary Study*, 2nd edn, London: Methuen.

Kurke, L. (1991), *The Traffic in Praise*, Ithaca NY: Cornell University Press.

Lagona, S. (1971), 'La necropoli di Ossini – S. Lio', *Cronache di Archeologia e di Storia dell'Arte*, 10, pp. 16–40.

—— (ed.) (1996), *Atti delle Giornate di Studio sugli insediamenti rurali nella Sicilia antica* (Caltagirone 29/30 June 1992) = Aitna. Quaderni di Topografia Antica 2, Catania: Edizioni Greco.

Lampela, A. (1998), *Rome and the Ptolemies of Egypt*, Helsinki: Societas Scientiarum Fennica.

La Rosa, V. (1978), 'Per il problema della ceramica di produzione siceliota', *Cronache di Archeologia e di Storia dell'Arte*, 17, pp. 64–7.

—— (1987), 'Archaiologhia e storiografia: quale Sicilia?', in Giarrizzo and Aymard (1987), pp. 700–31.

—— (1991), 'Un anaktoron alla Serra del Palco di Milena? Relazione preliminare sullo scavo del 1992', in *Quaderni dell'Istituto di Archeologia della Facoltà di Lettere e Filosofia dell'Università di Messina*, 6, pp. 5–16.

—— (1996), 'The impact of the Greek colonies on the non-Hellenic inhabitants of Sicily', in Pugliese Carratelli (1996), pp. 523–32.

Laurence, R. M. (1995), *Roman Pompeii: Space and Society*, London: Routledge.

Lauter, H. (1986), *Die Architektur des Hellenismus*, Darmstadt: Wissenschaftliche Buchgesellschaft.

Lauter-Bufe, H. (1987), *Die Geschichte des sikeliotisch-korinthischen Kapitells: der sogennante italisch-republikanische Typus*, Mainz: P. von Zabern.

Lazenby, J. F. (1996), *The First Punic War*, London: University College London Press.

Leighton, R. (1989), 'Antiquarianism and prehistory in West Mediterranean islands', *Antiquaries Journal*, 69.2, pp. 183–204.

—— (1985), 'Evidence, extent and effects of Mycenaean contacts with southeast Sicily during the late Bronze Age', in Malone and Stoddart (1985), IV.iii, pp. 399–412.

—— (1993a), *Morgantina IV: The Protohistoric Settlement on the Cittadella*, Princeton NJ: Princeton University Press.

—— (1993b), 'Sicily during the centuries of darkness', *CAJ*, 3.2, pp. 271–83.

—— (ed.) (1996a), *Early Societies in Sicily: New Developments in Archaeological Research*, London: University of London.

—— (1996b), 'From chiefdom to tribe? Social organisation and change in later prehistory', in Leighton (1996a), pp. 101–16.

—— (1999), *Sicily Before History: An Archaeological Survey from the Palaeolithic to the Iron Age*, London: Duckworth.

—— (2000), 'Time versus tradition: Iron Age chronologies in Sicily and south Italy', in *Ancient Italy in its Mediterranean Setting: Studies in Honour of Ellen Macnamara*, Accordia Specialist Studies on Italy, London: University of London, pp. 33–48.

Leiwo, M. (1994), *Neapolitana: A Study of Population and Language in Graeco-Roman Naples*, Helsinki: Societas Scientiarum Fennica.

Lewis, N. (1976), *The Interpretation of Dreams and Portents*, Toronto: Stevens.

Lintott, A. (1981), 'What was the "Imperium Romanum"?', *Greece and Rome*, n.s. 28, pp. 53–67.

—— (1993), *Imperium Romanum*, London: Routledge.

Lomas, K. (1993), *Rome and the Western Greeks: Conquest and Acculturation in Southern Italy*, London: Routledge.

—— (1997), 'The idea of a city: elite ideology and the evolution of urban form in Italy, 200 BC–AD 100', in H. M. Parkins (ed.), *Roman Urbanism: Beyond the Consumer City*, London: Routledge, pp. 21–41.

—— (forthcoming), 'The *polis* in Italy: ethnicity, colonisation and citizenship in the western Mediterranean', in R. Brock and S. Hodkinson (eds), *Alternatives to Athens: Varieties of Political Experience and Community in Ancient Greece*, Oxford: Oxford University Press.

Loomis, W. T. (1996), 'The introduction of the denarius', in R. W. Wallace and E. M. Harris (eds), *Transitions to Empire: Essays in Greco-Roman History, 360–146 BC, in Honor of E. Badian*, Norman OK: University of Oklahoma Press, pp. 338–55.

Lyons, C. L. (1996a), *Morgantina V: The Archaic Cemeteries*, Princeton NJ: Princeton University Press.

—— (1996b), 'Sikel burials at Morgantina: defining social and ethnic identities', in Leighton (1996a), pp. 177–89.

Macleod, C. (1975), 'Rhetoric and history (Thuc. VI, 16–18)', *Quaderna di Storia*, 1, pp. 39–65.

—— (1983), 'Thucydides and tragedy', in *Collected Essays*, Oxford: Clarendon Press, pp. 140–58.

Mader, W. (1990), *Die Psaumis-Oden Pindars (O.4 und O.5)*, Innsbruck: Universitätsverlag Wagner.

Maddoli, G. (1982), 'Il concetto di Magna Grecia: gennesi di un realtà storico-politiche', in G. Pugliese Carratelli (ed.), *Megale Hellas: Nome e immagine. Atti di 21° Convegno di studi sulla Magna Grecia*, Taranto: Istituto per la storia e l'archeologia della Magna Grecia, pp. 9–30.

Malkin, I. (1987), *Religion and Colonization in Ancient Greece*, Leiden: Brill.

—— (1994), 'Inside and outside: colonization and the formation of the mother city', in B. d'Agostino and D. Ridgway (eds), *APOIKIA: Scritti in onore di Giorgio Buchner*, Naples: Scuola Normale, pp. 1–10.

Malone, C. and Stoddart, S. (eds) (1985), *Papers in Italian Archaeology IV.i–iv*, Oxford: British Archaeological Reports International Series.

Manganaro, G. (1965), 'Per la storia dei culti in Sicilia', *Parola del Passato*, 20, pp. 163–78.

—— (1968), 'Biscari', *Dizionario Biografico degli Italiani*, 10, pp. 658–60.

—— (1979), 'La provincia romana', in Gabba and Vallet (1980), pp. 415–61.

Manni, E. (1981), *Geografia fisica e politica della Sicilia antica*, Rome: G. Bretschneider.

Mantegna Pancucci, E., Pancucci, D. and Vassallo, S. (1993), 'Il ripostiglio monetale e l'insediamento rurale in località Pagliuzza', in Di Stefano (1993), pp. 141–6.

Marchetti, P. (1972), 'La deuxième guerre punique en Sicile: les années 215–214 et le récit de Tite-Live', *Bulletin de l'Institut historique belge de Rome*, 42, pp. 5–26.

Marinatos Kopff, N. and Rawlings, H. R. (1978), '*Panolethria* and divine punishment', *Parola del Passato*, 33, pp. 331–7.

Martin, T. R. (1995), 'Coins, mints and the *polis*', in M. H. Hansen (ed.), *Sources for the Ancient Greek City State*, Copenhagen: Royal Danish Academy of Sciences and Letters, pp. 257–91.

Mattingly, H. (1976), *Coins of the Roman Empire in the British Museum*, London: British Museum.

Mattioli, M. (1995), 'Camarina in età ellenistico-romana', *Kokalos*, 41, pp. 229–70.

Mayer, E. A. (1990), 'Explaining the epigraphic habit in the Roman Empire: the evidence of epitaphs', *JRS*, 80, pp. 74–96.

Mazarakis Ainian, A. (1997), *From Rulers' Dwellings to Temples. Architecture, Religion and Society in Early Iron Age Greece (1100–700 BC)*. Studies in Mediterranean Archaeology, 121, Lund: Aström.

Mazza, M. (1980), 'Recenti prospettive sull'economia agraria siciliana in età ciceroniana', *Ciceroniana*, n.s. 4, pp. 222–38.

—— (1981), 'Terra e lavoratori nella Sicilia tardorepubblicana', in Giardina and Schiavone (1981), pp. 19–49.

McGlew, J. F. (1993), *Tyranny and Political Culture in Ancient Greece*, Ithaca NY: Cornell University Press.

Meiggs, R. and Lewis, D. M. (1984), *A Selection of Greek Historical Inscriptions to the End of the Fifth Century*, Oxford: Clarendon Press.

Mello, M. (1974), *Paestum Romana*, Rome: Istituto Italiana per la storia antica.

Meritt, B. (1957), 'Greek inscriptions', *Hesperia*, 26, pp. 198–211.

Mertens, D. (1996), 'Greek architecture in the West', in Pugliese Carratelli (1996), pp. 315–416.

Messina, A. (1993), 'Tre edifici del medioevo siciliano', *Sicilia Archeologica*, 82, pp. 61–5.

Michelini, C. (1997), 'Le *agorai* di ambiente coloniale e il caso di Segesta', in Nenci (1997), pp. 1139–58.

Millar, F. (1986), 'Italy and the Roman Empire: Augustus to Constantine', *Phoenix*, 40, pp. 295–318.

Millett, M. (1990), *The Romanization of Britain: An Essay in Archaeological Interpretation*, Cambridge: Cambridge University Press.

Miranda, E. (1990), *Iscrizione grechi di Napoli*, Rome: Quasar.

Mitchell, T. N. (1979), *Cicero: The Ascending Years*, New Haven CT: Yale University Press.

—— (1986), *Cicero: Verrines II.1. Translation and Commentary*, Warminster: Aris and Phillips.

Mitens, K. (1988), *Teatri greci e teatri ispirati all'architettura greca in Sicilia e nell'Italia meridionale c.350–50 a.C.: un catalogo*, Rome: L'Erma di Bretschneider.

Molinari, A. (1997), *Segesta II: Il castello e la moschea (scavi 1989–1995)*, Palermo: Soprintendenza per i Beni Culturali e Ambientali di Trapani.

Momigliano, A. (1966), *Studies in Historiography*, London: Weidenfeld and Nicolson.

—— (1978), 'La riscoperta della Sicilia antica da T. Fazello a P. Orsi', *Studi Urbinati*, 52, pp. 5–23; reprinted in A. Momigliano (1984), *Settimo Contributo alla Storia degli Studi Classici e del Mondo Antico*, Rome: Edizioni di storia e letteratura, pp. 114–32.

—— (1979), 'The rediscovery of Greek history: the case of Sicily', *Studies in XVIIIth Century Culture*, 9, pp. 167–87; reprinted in A. Momigliano (1984), *Settimo Contributo alla Storia degli Studi Classici e del Mondo Antico*, Rome:

Edizioni di storia e di letteratura, pp. 135–53.

Morgan, C. (1991), 'Ethnicity and early Greek states: historical and material perspectives', *PCPS*, 37, pp. 131–63.

Morris, I. (1994), 'Archaeologies of Greece', in I. Morris (ed.), *Classical Greece: Ancient Histories and Modern Archaeologies*, Cambridge: Cambridge University Press, pp. 8–47.

Mossé, C. (1989), *La Tyrannie dans la Grèce Antique*, 2nd edn, Paris: Presses Universitaires de France.

Muggia, A. (1997), *L'area di rispetto nelle colonie magne-greche e siceliote*, Palermo: Sellerio Editore.

Murray, O. (1983), 'The symposion as social organisation', in R. Hägg (ed.), *The Greek Renaissance of the Eighth Century BC: Tradition and Innovation*, Stockholm: Svenska Institutet i Athen, pp. 195–9.

—— (1988), 'Death and the symposion', *AION ArchStAnt*, 10, pp. 239–57.

—— (1990), 'Sympotic history', in O. Murray (ed.), *Sympotica*, Oxford: Clarendon Press, pp. 3–13.

—— (1994), 'Nestor's cup and the origin of the Greek *Symposion*', *Apoikia: Annali dell'Istituto Universitario Orientale di Napoli, Dipartimento di Studi del Mondo Classico e del Mediterraneo Antico, Sezione Archeologica e Storia Antica*, n.s. 1, pp. 47–54.

Napoli, M. (1959), *Napoli Greco-Romana*, Naples: Fiorentino.

Neeft, C. W. (1987), *Protocorinthian Subgeometric Aryballoi*, Amsterdam: Allard Pierson Museum.

Nenci, G. (ed.) (1992), *Giornate internazionali di studi sull'area elima: Atti*, Pisa and Gibellina: CESDAE.

—— (ed.) (1995), 'Parco archeologico e relazioni preliminari delle campagne di scavo 1990–1993', *ASNP*[3], 25, pp. 537–1295.

—— (ed.) (1997), *Seconde giornate internazionali di studi sull'area elima: Atti*, Pisa and Gibellina: CESDAE.

Nenci, G. and Vallet, G. (eds) (1977–), *BTCGI*, Pisa: Scuola normale superiore.

Ogden, D. (1996), *The Crooked Kings of Ancient Greece*, London: Duckworth.

Oost, S. I. (1976), 'The tyrant kings of Syracuse', *Classical Philology*, 71, pp. 224–36.

Orlandini, P. (1962), 'L'espansione di Gela nella Sicilia centro-meridionale', *Kokalos*, 8, pp. 69–121.

—— (1968), 'Gela – topografia dei santuari e documentazione archeologia dei culti', *RIA*, 15, pp. 20–66.

Orsi, P. (1895), 'Siracusa – Gli scavi nella necropoli del Fusco a Siracusa nel giugno, novembre e dicembre del 1893', *NSc*, pp. 109–92.

—— (1897), 'Nuove esplorazioni nella necropoli sicula di Monte Finocchito presso Noto', *BPI*, 23, pp. 157–97.

—— (1898), 'Le necropoli di Licodia Eubea', *MDAI(R)*, 13, pp. 305–66.

—— (1900), 'Gela – Frammenti archeologici', *NSc*, pp. 272–84.

—— (1902), 'Licodia Eubea – sepolcri siculi dell'ultimo periodo', *NSc*, pp. 219–33.

—— (1909), 'Sepolcri di transizione dalla civiltà sicula all greca II: necropoli di

Ossini fra Lentini e Militello', *MDAI(R)*, 23, pp. 73–84.

—— (1911), 'Di un'anonima città sicula-greca a Monte S. Mauro presso Caltagirone', *Monumenti Antichi dei Lincei*, 20, pp. 729–850.

—— (1912), 'Le necropoli di Pantalica e M. Dessiren', *Monumenti Antichi dei Lincei*, 21, 301-408.

—— (1918), 'Gli scavi intorno all'Athenaion di Siracusa negli anni 1912–1917', *Monumenti Antichi dei Lincei*, 27, pp. 353–754.

—— (1919), 'Taormina – necropoli sicula al Cocolonazzo di Mola', *NSc*, pp. 360–9.

Ortolani di Bordonaro, G. (1941), 'G. L. Torremuzza e gli studi di antiquaria siciliana nel secolo XVIII', *Archivio Storico per la Sicilia*, 7, pp. 223–50.

Osborne, R. (1998), 'Early Greek colonisation? The nature of Greek settlement in the West', in N. Fisher and H. van Wees (eds), *Archaic Greece: New Approaches and New Evidence,* London: Duckworth and Classical Press of Wales, pp. 251–69.

Pace, B. (1935), *Arte e Civiltà della Sicilia Antica*, 1, Milan: Società Anonima Editrice Dante Alighieri.

Paduano, G. (1978), *Sui Persiani di Eschilo: problemi di focalizzazione drammatica*, Rome: Edizioni dell' Ateneo e Bizzarri.

Panvini, R. (1997), 'Osservazioni sulle dinamiche formative socio-culturali a Dessueri', in S. Tusa (ed.), *Prima Sicilia: alle origini della società siciliana*, Palermo: Ediprint, pp. 493–501.

Pareti, L. (1953), *Storia di Roma e del mondo Romano*, 2, Turin: Unione Tipografico-Editrice Torinese.

Parker, R. (1996), *Athenian Religion: A History*, Oxford: Oxford University Press.

Parlangèli, G. (1964–5), 'Il sostrato linguistico in Sicilia', *Kokalos*, 10–11, pp. 211–58.

Patterson, J. R. (1994), 'The *collegia* and the transformation of the towns of Italy in the 2nd century AD', *L'Italie d'Auguste à Dioclétien: actes du colloque internationale de l'École française de Rome*, Rome: École française de Rome, pp. 227–38.

Payne, H. (1940), *Perachora I*, Oxford: Clarendon Press.

Pearson, L. (1987), *The Greek Historians of the West: Timaeus and his Predecessors*, Atlanta: Scholars Press.

Pelagatti, P. (1970), 'Akrai. Ricerche nel territorio. Contrada Aguglia 1960–1962: la fattoria tardo-ellenistica', *NSc*, pp. 447–99.

—— (1978), 'Materiali tardo geometrici dal retroterra di Siracusa', *Cronache di Archeologia e di Storia dell'Arte*, 17, pp. 111–12.

—— (1980–1), 'L'attività della soprintendenza alla antichità della Sicilia orientale', *Kokalos*, 26–7, pp. 694–730.

—— (1982), 'Siracusa: le ultime ricerche in Ortigia', *Atti del Convegno Internazionale, Grecia, Italia e Sicilia nell'VIII e VII secolo a.C: annuario della Scuola Archeologica di Atene e delle Missioni Italiane in Oriente*, 60, pp. 117–63.

—— (1983), 'I più antichi materiali di importazione a Siracusa, a Naxos e in altri siti della Sicilia orientale', in *La céramique grecque ou de tradition grecque au VIIIe siècle en Italie centrale et méridionale*, Naples: Centre Jean Bérard, pp. 113–80.

Pelagatti, P. and Voza, G. (1973), *Archeologia nella Sicilia Sud-Orientale*, Naples: Centre Jean Bérard.

Pelling, C. (1997), 'Aeschylus' *Persae* and history', in C. Pelling (ed.), *Greek Tragedy and the Historian*, Oxford: Oxford University Press, pp. 1–19.

Pinzone, A. (1978), 'Sulle *civitates foederatae* di Sicilia: problemi di storia e cronologia', *Archivio Storico Messinese*[3], 29, pp. 353–79.

Podlecki, A. J. (1966), *The Political Background to Aeschylean Tragedy*, Ann Arbor: University of Michigan Press.

Pontrandolfo, A. (1989), 'Greci e indigeni', in *Un secolo di ricerche in Magna Grecia: atti del XXIV convengo di studi sulla Magna Grecia*, Taranto: Istituto per la storia e l'archeologia della Magna Grecia, pp. 329–50.

—— (1992), 'Le necropoli dalla città greca alla colonia latina', in *Poseidonia–Paestum: atti del XXVII convegno di studi sulla Magna Grecia*, Taranto: Istituto per la storia e l'archeologia della Magna Grecia, pp. 225–65.

—— (1995), 'Simposio e élites sociali nel mondo etrusco e italico', in O. Murray and M. Tecusan (eds), *In Vino Veritas*, London: British School at Rome, pp. 176–95.

Pottino, G. (1994), 'Accampamenti della Prima Guerra Punica a sud di Punta Raisi', *Archivio storico Siciliano*, 20, pp. 5–16.

Prestianni Giallombardo, A. M. (ed.) (1998), *Colloquio Alesino*, Atti del Colloquio held 7 May 1995 in S. Maria delle Palate (Tusa), Catania: Edizione del Prisma.

Pritchard, R. T. (1969), 'Land tenure in Sicily in the first century BC', *Historia*, 18, pp. 545–56.

—— (1970), 'Cicero and the *Lex Hieronica*', *Historia*, 19, pp. 352–68.

—— (1971), 'Gaius Verres and the Sicilian farmers', *Historia*, 20, pp. 224–38.

—— (1972), 'Some aspects of first-century Sicilian agriculture', *Historia,* 21, pp. 646–60.

—— (1975), '*Perpaucae Siciliae civitates*: notes on *Verr*. 2, 3, 6, 13', *Historia*, 24, pp. 33–47.

Procelli, E. (1989), 'Aspetti e problemi dell'ellenizzazione calcidese nella Sicilia orientale', *MEFRA*, 101.2, pp. 679–89.

Procelli, E. and Albanese, R. M., (1992), 'Ramacca (Catania): saggi di scavo nelle contrade Castellito e Montagna negli anni 1978, 1981 e 1982', *NSc*, ser. 8, 42–3 (1988–9), pp. 7–159.

Prosdocimi, A. L. and Agostiniani, L. (1976–7), 'Lingue e dialetti della Sicilia antica', *Kokalos*, 22–3, pp. 215–53.

Pugliese Carratelli, G. (ed.) (1985), *Sikanie*, Milan: Istituto Veneto di arti Grafiche.

—— (ed.) (1996), *The Western Greeks: Classical Civilization in the Western Mediterranean*, London: Thames and Hudson.

Rathje, A. (1983), 'A banquet service from the Latin city of Ficana', *Analecta Romana*, 12, pp. 7–29.

—— (1988), 'Manners and customs in central Italy in the Orientalising period: influence from the Near East', *Acta Hyperborea*, 1, pp. 81–90.

—— (1990), 'The adoption of the Homeric banquet in central Italy in the Orientalizing period', in O. Murray (ed.), *Sympotica*, Oxford: Clarendon Press, pp. 279–88.

—— (1994), 'Banquet and ideology: some new considerations about banqueting at Poggio Civitate (Murlo)', in R. de Puma and J. P. Small (eds), *Murlo and the Etruscans*, Wisconsin: University of Wisconsin Press, pp. 95–9.

—— (1995), 'Il banchetto in Italia centrale: quale stile di vita?', in O. Murray and M. Tecusan (eds), *In Vino Veritas*, London: British School at Rome, pp. 167–75.

Rauber, H. (1914), 'Die agrarischen Verhältnisse Siziliens im Altertum besonders zur Zeit Ciceros', PhD dissertation, Erlangen.

Rawson, E. D. (1987), '*Discrimina Ordinum*: the *Lex Julia Theatralis*', *PBSR*, 55, pp. 83–114.

Redfield, J. (1985), 'Herodotus the tourist', *CPh*, 80, pp. 97–118.

Renfrew, C. (1993), *The Roots of Ethnicity: Archaeology, Genetics and the Origins of Europe*, Rome: Unione internazionale degli istituti di archeologia, storia e storia dell' arte in Roma.

Rich, J. W. (1976), *Declaring War in the Roman Republic in the Period of Transmarine Expansion*, Brussels: Latomus.

Richards, G. C. (1980), 'Introduction', in Blinkenberg (1980), pp. vi–xii.

Richardson, J.S. (1986), *Hispaniae*, Cambridge: Cambridge University Press.

—— (1976), 'The Spanish mines and the development of provincial taxation in the second century BC', *JRS*, 66, pp. 139–52.

—— (1989), 'The administration of the empire', *CAH*[2], 9, Cambridge: Cambridge University Press, pp. 564–98.

—— (1990), 'Les *peregrini* et l'idée d'"empire" sous la République romaine', *Revue Historique de Droit Français et Étranger*, 68, pp. 147–55.

—— (1991), '*Imperium Romanum*: empire and the language of power', *JRS*, 81, pp. 1–9.

Rickman, G. (1980), *The Corn Supply of Ancient Rome*, Oxford: Clarendon Press.

Ridgway, D. (1992a), 'Demaratus and his predecessors', in G. Kopcke and I. Tokumaru (eds), *Greece between East and West: 10th–8th centuries BC*, Mainz: P. von Zabern, pp. 85–92.

—— (1992b), *The First Western Greeks*, Cambridge: Cambridge University Press.

Riedesel, J. H. von (1772), *Travels through Sicily and that Part of Italy Formerly called Magna Graecia: And a Tour though Egypt, with an Accurate Description of its Cities, and the Modern State of the Country*, London: Dilly.

Rizza, G. (1962), 'Siculi e greci sui colli di Leontini', *Cronache di Archeologia e di Storia dell'Arte*, 1, pp. 3–27.

Robert, J. and Robert, L. (1953), 'Bulletin épigraphique', *REG*, 66, p. 282.

—— (1965), 'Bulletin épigraphique', *REG*, 78, p. 499.

Romm, J. (1989), 'Herodotus and mythic geography: the case of the Hyperboreans', *TAPhA*, 119, pp. 97–113.

Rood, T. (1998), *Thucydides: Narrative and Explanation*, Oxford: Oxford University Press.

—— (1999), 'Thucydides' Persian wars', in C. S. Kraus (ed.), *The Limits of Historiography: Genre and Narrative in Ancient Historical Texts*, Leiden: E. J. Brill.

Rosenbloom, D. (1993), 'Shouting "fire" in a crowded theater: Phrynichus' *Capture of Miletus* and the politics of fear in early Attic theater', *Philologus*, 137, pp. 159–96.

Roussel, D. (1970), *Les Siciliens entre les Romains et les Carthaginois à l'époque de la première guerre Punique*, Paris: Belles Lettres.

Roux, G. (1963), 'Kupselé: où avait-on caché le petit Kypselos?', *REA*, 65, pp. 277–89.

Rutter, N. K. (1998a), *Greek Coinages of Southern Italy and Sicily*, London: Spink.

—— (1998b), 'The coinage of Syracuse in the early fifth century BC', in R. Ashton and S. Hurter (eds), *Studies in Greek Numismatics in Memory of Martin Jessop Price*, London: Spink, pp. 307–15.

Sacks, K. (1990), *Diodorus Siculus and the First Century*, Princeton NJ: Princeton University Press.

Said, S. (1981), 'Darius et Xerxes dans les *Perses* d'Eschyle', *Ktema*, 6, pp. 17–38.

—— (1988), 'Tragédie et renversement: l'exemple des *Perses*', *Metis*, 3, pp. 321–41.

Salmon, J. B. (1984), *Wealthy Corinth*, Oxford: Clarendon Press.

Sanders, L. J. (1987), *Dionysius I and Greek Tyranny*, London: Croom Helm.

Sansone, D. (1981), 'The date of Herodotus' publication', *BICS*, 10, pp. 1–9.

Sartori, F. (1957), 'Le dodici tribù di Lilibeo', *Kokalos*, 3, pp. 38–60.

Schmitt, H. H. (1988), 'Forme della vita interstatale nell'antichità', *Critica Storica*, 25, pp. 529–46.

Schnapp, A. (1996), *The Discovery of the Past: The Origins of Archaeology*, London: British Museum Press.

Scibona, G. (1971), 'Epigraphica Halaesina I (Schede 1970)', *Kokalos*, 17, pp. 3–20.

Scramuzza, V. M. (1938), 'Roman Sicily', in Frank 1938, pp. 225–377.

Scuderi, R. (1996), 'La raffigurazione ciceroniana della Sicilia e dei suoi abitanti: un fattore ambientale per la condanna di Verere', in Stella and Valvo (1996), pp. 409–30.

Scullard, H. H. (1989), 'Carthage and Rome', in *CAH*², 7. 2, Cambridge: Cambridge University Press, pp. 486–569.

Serrao, F. (1954), *La 'iurisdictio' del pretore peregrino*, Milan: Giuffre.

Settis, S. (1990), 'Idea dell'arte greca d'occidente fra otto e novecento: Germania e Italia', in *Un secolo di ricerche in Magna Grecia: atti del XXVIII convegno di studi sulla Magna Grecia*, Taranto: Istituto per la storia e l'archeologia della Magna Grecia, pp. 135–76.

Shepherd, G. B. (1993), 'Death and religion in archaic Greek Sicily: a study in colonial relationships', Cambridge, unpublished PhD thesis.

—— (1995), 'The pride of most colonials: burial and religion in the Sicilian colonies', in Fischer-Hansen (1995), pp. 51–82.

—— (1999), 'Fibulae and females: intermarriage in the western Greek colonies and the evidence from the cemeteries', in Tsetskhladze (ed.), *Ancient Greeks West and East*, Leiden: Brill, pp. 267–300.

Sjöqvist, E. (1960a), 'Numismatic notes from Morgantina: the ΣΙΚΕΛΙΩΤΑΝ coinage', *ANSMusN*, 9, pp. 53–63.

—— (1960b), 'Excavations at Morgantina (Serra Orlando), 1959: preliminary report IV', *AJA*, 64, pp. 125–35.

Slayman, A. L. (1998), 'The Morgantina hoard', *Archaeology*, 51.3, pp. 40–1.

Small, J. P. (1994), 'Eat, drink, and be merry', in R. de Puma and J. P. Small (eds), *Murlo and the Etruscans*, Wisconsin: University of Wisconsin Press, pp. 85–94.

Smith, A. D. (1991), *National Identity*, Harmondsworth: Penguin.

Snodgrass, A. M. (1964), *Early Greek Armour and Weapons*, Edinburgh: Edinburgh University Press.

Sordi, M. (1984), 'Il fr.29 Jacoby di Timeo e la lettura augustea di un passo di Filisto', *Latomus*, 43, pp. 534–9.

Spawforth, A. J. S. and Walker, S. (1985), 'The world of the Panhellenion I: Athens and Eleusis', *JRS*, 75, pp. 78–104.

Spigo, U. (1979), 'Monte San Mauro di Caltagirone, scavi 1978: aspetti di un centro greco della Sicilia interna', *Bollettino d'Arte⁶*, 4, pp. 21–42.

—— (1980–1), 'Ricerche a Monte S. Mauro, Francavilla di Sicilia, Acireale, Adrano, Lentini, Solarino', *Kokalos*, 26–7, pp. 771–95.

—— (1986), 'L'anonimo centro greco di Monte S. Mauro di Caltagirone nel quadro dell'arcaismo siceliota: prospettive di ricerca', in *Decima miscellanea greca e romana*, Rome: Istituto Italiano per la Storia Antica, pp. 1–32.

Sposito, A. (ed.) (1995), *Morgantina: architettura e città ellenistiche*, Palermo: Alloro.

Stadter, P. (1992), 'Herodotus and the Athenian *Arche*', *ASNP³*, 22.3–4, pp. 781–809.

Steiner, D. (1986), *The Crown of Song: Metaphor in Pindar*, London: Duckworth.

Stella, C. and Valvo, A. (eds) (1996), *Studi in onore di Albino Garzetti*, Brescia: Ateneo di Brescia.

Steures, D. C. (1980), *Monte Finocchito Revisited, Part 1: The Evidence*, Amsterdam: Allard Pierson Museum.

Stewart, R. (1998), *Public Office in Early Rome*, Ann Arbor: University of Michigan Press.

Stoddart, S. (1989), 'Divergent trajectories in central Italy 1200–500 BC', in T. C. Champion (ed.), *Centre and Periphery*, London: Unwin Hyman, pp. 88–101.

Stroheker, K. F. (1958), *Dionysius I: Gestalt und Geschichte des Tyrannen von Syrakus*, Wiesbaden: F. Steiner Verlag.

Swain, S. (1996), *Hellenism and Empire: Language, Classicism and Power in the Greek World, AD 50–250*, Oxford: Clarendon Press.

Tagliente, M. (1985), 'Elementi del banchetto in un centro arcaico della Basilicata (Chiaromonte)', *MEFRA*, 97, pp. 159–91.

Thiel, J. H. (1954), *A History of Roman Sea-Power Before the Second Punic War*, Amsterdam: North-Holland.

Tilly, C. (1990), *Coercion, Capital, and European States*, AD *990–1990*, Oxford: Blackwell.

Tomasi di Lampedusa, G. (1986a), *The Leopard: With a Memory and Two Short Stories*, trans. A. Colquhoun, London: Collins Havril.

—— (1986b), 'The Professor and the Siren', in Tomasi di Lampedusa (1986a), pp. 261–86.

Torremuzza, G. L. (1745), *Dissertazione sopra una statua di marmo scoverta nelle rovine dell'antica città d'Alesa in Sicilia*, Palermo.

—— (1753), *Storia di Alesa, antica città di Sicilia*.

—— (1762), *Le antiche iscrizioni di Palermo*.

—— (1764), 'Idea di un tesoro che contenga una generale raccolta di tutte le antichità di Sicilia', *Opuscoli di Autori Siciliani*, 8, pp. 181–97.

—— (1769), *Siciliae et objacentium insularum veterum inscriptionum nova collectio prolegomena et notis illustrata*, Palermo.

—— (1773), 'Memorie delle zecche di Sicilia, e delle monete in esse in vari tempi coniate', *Opuscoli di Autori Siciliani*, 16, pp. 261–400.

—— (1784), *Siciliae et objacentium insularum veterum nummorum nova collectio*, Palermo.

—— (1790), *Alla Sicilia numismatica*.

—— (1804), *Memorie della vita letteraria di Gabriele Lancillotto Castello Principe di Torremuzza scritte da lui stesso: con annotazioni di Giovanni D'Angelo*, Palermo.

Tozzi, C. (1968), 'Relazione preliminare sulla prima e seconda campagna di scavi effettuata a Pantelleria', *Rivista di Scienze Preistoriche*, 23, pp. 315–88.

Tsakirgis, B. (1989), 'The decorated pavements of Morgantina I: the mosaics', *AJA*, 89, pp. 395–416.

—— (1990), 'The decorated pavements of Morgantina II: the *opus signinum*', *AJA*, 90, pp. 425–43.

—— (1995), 'Morgantina: a Greek town in central Sicily', in Fischer-Hansen (1995), pp. 123–47.

Tuck, A. S. (1994), 'The Etruscan seated banquet: Villanovan ritual and Etruscan iconography', *AJA*, 98, pp. 617–28.

Tusa, V. (1963), 'L'*anfipolia* a Solunto', *Kokalos,* 9, pp. 185–94.

Tzifopoulos, Y. Z. (1995), 'Thucydidean rhetoric and the propaganda of the Persian wars topos', *Parola del Passato*, 50, pp. 91–115.

Vaggioli, M. A. (1997), 'Ricerche archeologiche e topografiche sull'*agora* di Segesta', in Nenci (1997), pp. 1329–54.

Vagnetti, L. (1993), 'Mycenaean pottery in Italy: fifty years of study', in C. Zerner (ed.), *Wace and Blegen: Pottery as Evidence for Trade in the Aegean Bronze Age 1939–1989*, Amsterdam: J. C. Gieben, pp. 143–54.

Vallet, G. (1962), 'La colonisation chalcidienne et l'Hellénisation de la Sicile orientale', *Kokalos*, 8, pp. 30–51.

—— (1984–5), 'L'apporto dell'urbanistica: le fait urbain en Grèce et en Sicile a l'époque archaique', *Kokalos*, 30–1, pp. 133–55.

—— (1996), 'Pindare et Sicile', in *Le monde grec colonial d'Italie du sud et de Sicile*, Rome: École française de Rome, pp. 177–202.

Vallet, G. and Villard, F. (1964), *Megara Hyblaea II: la céramique archaïque*, Paris: De Boccard.

Vallet, G., Villard, G. and Auberson, P. (1981), *Megara Hyblaea 3: guide des fouilles*, Rome: École française de Rome.

Vasaly, D. A. (1993), *Representations: Images of the World in Ciceronian Oratory*, Berkeley CA: University of California Press.

Vassallo, S. (1991), 'Montagna dei Cavalli', in Di Stefano (1993), pp. 114–36.

—— (1997), 'Scavi 1988–1991 a Montagna dei Cavalli–Hippana', in C. A. Di Stefano (ed.), *Archeologia e Territorio*, Palermo: Palumbo, pp. 275–306.

Vattuone, R. (1981), 'Su Timeo F29 Jacoby', *RSA*, 11, pp. 139–45.

Verbrugghe, G. P. (1972), 'Sicily 210–70 BC: Livy, Cicero and Diodorus', *TAPhA*, 103, pp. 535–39.

—— (1976), *Sicilia*, Bern: Kümmerly and Frey.

Verdin, H. (1982), 'Hérodote et la politique expansionniste des Achéménides: notes sur Hdt. VII.8', in J. Quaegebeur (ed.), *Studia Paulo Naster Oblata II, Orientalia Antiqua*, Louvain: Orientalia Lovaniensia analecta, 13, Departement Oriëntalistiek, Peeters, pp. 327–36.

Vickers, M. (1995), 'Thucydides 6.53.3–59: not a "digression"', *DHA*, 21, pp. 193–200.

Villa, A. (1988), *I capitelli di Solunto*, Sikelika 3, Rome: G. Bretschneider.

Villard, F. and Vallet, G. (1956), 'Géométrique grec, géométrique siciliote, géométrique sicule', *MEFRA*, 68, pp. 7–27.

Von Boeselager, D. (1983), *Antike Mosaiken in Sizilien: Hellenismus und römische Kaiserzeit, 3 Jahrhundert v. Chr.–3 Jahrhundert n. Chr.*, Rome: G. Bretschneider.

Von Reden, S. (1995), *Exchange in Ancient Greece*, London: Duckworth.

Von Sydow, W. (1979), 'Späthellenistischen Stuckgesimse in Sizilien', *MDAI(R)*, 86, pp. 181–231.

—— (1984), 'Die hellenistischen Gebälke in Sizilien', *MDAI(R)*, 91, pp. 239–358.

Voza, G. (1973), 'Thapsos: resoconto sulle campagne di scavo del 1970–71,' in *Atti della XV Riunione Scientifica dell'Istituto Italiano di Preistoria e Protostoria*, Florence: Istituto Italiano di Preistoria e Protostoria, pp. 133–57.

—— (1978), 'La necropoli della Valle del Marcellino presso Villasmundo', *Cronache di Archeologia e di Storia dell'Arte*, 17, pp. 104–10.

—— (1980–1), 'L'attività della soprintendenza alle antichità della Sicilia orientale', *Kokalos*, 26–7, pp. 674–93.

—— (1984–5), 'Attività nel territorio della soprintendenza alle antichità di Siracusa nel quadriennio 1980–1984', *Kokalos*, 30–1, pp. 657–77.

Walbank, F. (1951), 'The problem of Greek nationality', *Phoenix*, 5, pp. 41–60; reprinted in F. Walbank, *Selected Papers in Greek and Roman History and Historiography*, Cambridge: Cambridge University Press, pp. 1–19.

—— (1957–79), *A Historical Commentary on Polybius*, 1–3, Oxford: Clarendon Press.

—— (1986), *The Hellenistic World*, London: Fontana.

Wallace-Hadrill, A. (1994), *Houses and Society in Pompeii and Herculaneum*, Princeton NJ: Princeton University Press.

Ward-Perkins, J. B. (1981), *Roman Imperial Architecture*, Harmondsworth: Penguin.

Waters, K. (1966), 'The purpose of dramatisation in Herodotus', *Historia*, 15, pp. 155–71.

Weiss, C. (1984), *Griechische Flussgottheiten in vorhellenistischer Zeit*, Würzburg: Triltsch.

Welch, K. (1994), 'The Roman arena in late-Republican Italy: a new interpretation', *JRA*, 7, pp. 59–79.

Westermark, U. and Jenkins, G. K. (1980), *The Coinage of Camarina*, London: Royal Numismatic Society.

Whitehouse, R. D. and Wilkins, J. B. (1985), 'Magna Grecia before the Greeks: towards a reconciliation of the evidence', in Malone and Stoddart (1985), IV.iii, pp. 89–109.

—— (1989), 'Greeks and natives in southeast Sicily: approaches to the archaeological evidence', in T. C. Champion (ed.), *Centre and Periphery*, London: Unwin Hyman, pp. 102–27.

Wiegand, A. (1997), *Das Theater von Solunt: ein besonderer Skenentyp des späthellenismus auf Sizilien*, Mainz: P. von Zabern.

Wilson, R. J. A. (1985a), 'Changes in the pattern of urban settlement in Roman, Byzantine and Arab Sicily', in Malone and Stoddart (1985), IV.i, pp. 313–44.

—— (1985b), Review of Manni (1981), *JRS*, 75, pp. 296–9.

—— (1990a), *Sicily under the Roman Empire: The Archaeology of a Roman Province 36 BC–AD 535*, Warminster: Aris and Phillips.

—— (1990b) 'Roman architecture in a Greek world: the example of Sicily', in Henig (1990), pp. 67–90.

—— (1996), 'Archaeology in Sicily 1988–95', *Archaeological Reports for 1995–1996*, 42, pp. 59–123.

—— (1997), *La Sicilia Romana: tra arte e storia*, Palermo: Ariete.

—— (forthcoming), 'Rural settlement in hellenistic and Roman Sicily: excavations at Campanaio (AG), 1994–1998', *PBSR*, 68.

Winckelmann, J. J. (1968), *History of Ancient Art*, New York: Ungar.

Wiseman, T. P. (1987), *Roman Studies*, Liverpool: Cairns.

Yuge, T. and Doi, M. (eds) (1988), *Forms of Control and Subordination in Antiquity*, Tokyo and Leiden: Brill.

Zamboni, A. (1978), 'Il Siculo', in A. L. Prosdocimi (ed.), *Popoli e Civiltà dell'Italia Antica*, 6, Rome: Biblioteca di storia patria, pp. 949–1012.

Zanker, P. (1965), 'Zwei Akroterfiguren aus Tyndaris', *MDAI(R)*, 72, pp. 93–9.

—— (1988), *The Power of Images in the Age of Augustus*, Ann Arbor: University of Michigan Press.

# INDEX

## GEOGRAPHICAL NAMES

## PEOPLE

Tyndarides, 98

Verres, 113, 134–60

Xanthippos, 96
Xenagoras, 60
Xenocrates, 75
Xerxes, 84–96

## SUBJECTS

Acculturation, 41–54, 161–73
Antiquarianism, 174–93
Ausonians, 18

Biscari, Prince I. V., 185–8

Caylus, Comte A. C. F. de, 181–2
Chronology, 16–17
Coinage, 73–83

D'Orville, T. P., 187–8

Epigraphic evidence, 37, 52–3, 168–70
Ethnic identity, 17–19, 73–83, 161–73, 174–93

Fazello, T., 175–80, 191, 192–3
Fortifications, 39
Funerary evidence, 15–40, 45, 49

Garrisons, 115–33
Glass-working, 194n4
Grain, 115–33

Housing, 29–40

Jewellery, 194n4
    Fibulae, 17, 62–4, 67–9

Lex Hieronica, 112–13, 115–19, 120–6, 134, 204n4

Lex Rupilia, 112–13

Mamertines, 99–100, 110, 121–2, 168
Mycenaeans, 10, 18, 48

Orsi, P., 174–5

Pottery
    Etruscan, 15–28
    Greek imports, 15–28, 41–54
    Local, 15–40, 41–54
Private housing, 151–4
Provincial administration, 115–33
Public buildings, 134–50, 161–73

Religion
    Apollo, of Didyma, 59
    Arethusa, 79–80
    Athena, 80–1; Athena Lindia, 55–70
    Ceres, 156
    Dionysus, 74, 102
    Hera of Perachora, 67–8
    Hera of Samos, 60, 68
    Heracles, 77
    Venus Erycina, 132, 166
    Zeus, 80; Zeus Eleutherios, 101
Riedesel, J. H. von, 189–90
Romanisation, 44

Sculpture, 154–7
Settlement patterns, 15–40
Sikans, 9, 18, 162
Sikels, 9, 12, 18–40, 41–54, 162

Taxation, 115–33
Tomaso di Lampedusa, G., 174, 192
Torremuzza, Prince G. L., 182–5

Venerii, 132
Votive deposits, 15–28

Wine, 36–7, 41–54

## DATE DUE

| MAY 31 2002 | |
|---|---|
| | |
| | |
| | |
| | |
| | |
| | |
| | |
| | |
| | |
| | |
| | |
| | |
| | |
| | |
| | |
| | |

BRODART, CO.                    Cat. No. 23-221-003